BLACK LEGACY PRESS™

WWW.BLACKLEGACYPRESS.ORG

SLAVE NARRATIVES

VOLUME XI
NORTH CAROLINA NARRATIVES
PART 1

By
United States.
Work Projects Administration

ISBN: 978-1-63652-197-8

SLAVE NARRATIVES

A Folk History of Slavery in the United States.
From Interviews with Former Slaves

UNITED STATES.
WORK PROJECTS ADMINISTRATION

TYPEWRITTEN RECORDS PREPARED BY
THE FEDERAL WRITERS' PROJECT
1936-1938
ASSEMBLED BY
THE LIBRARY OF CONGRESS PROJECT
WORK PROJECTS ADMINISTRATION
FOR THE DISTRICT OF COLUMBIA
SPONSORED BY THE LIBRARY OF
CONGRESS

WASHINGTON 1941

VOLUME XI

NORTH CAROLINA NARRATIVES PART 1

Prepared by
The Federal Writers' Project of
The Works Progress Administration
For the State of North Carolina

CONTENTS

N.C. District:	No. 2
Worker:	T. Pat Matthews
No. Words:	1384
Subject:	Louisa Adams
Person Interviewed:	Louisa Adams
Editor:	Daisy Bailey Waitt
Date Stamp:	"JUL 7 1937"

LOUISA ADAMS

My name is Louisa Adams. I wuz bawned in Rockingham, Richmond County, North Carolina. I wuz eight years old when the Yankees come through. I belonged to Marster Tom A. Covington, Sir. My mother wuz named Easter, and my father wuz named Jacob. We were all Covingtons. No Sir, I don't know whur my mother and father come from. Soloman wuz brother number one, then Luke, Josh, Stephen, Asbury. My sisters were Jane, Frances, Wincy, and I wuz nex'. I 'members grandmother. She wuz named Lovie

Wall. They brought her here from same place. My aunts were named, one wuz named Nicey, and one wuz named Jane. I picked feed for the white folks. They sent many of the chillun to work at the salt mines, where we went to git salt. My brother Soloman wuz sent to the salt mines. Luke looked atter the sheep. He knocked down china berries for ‘em. Dad and mammie had their own gardens and hogs. We were compelled to walk about at night to live. We were so hongry we were bound to steal or parish. This trait seems to be handed down from slavery days. Sometimes I thinks dis might be so. Our food wuz bad. Marster worked us hard and gave us nuthin. We had to use what we made in the garden to eat. We also et our hogs. Our clothes were bad, and beds were sorry. We went barefooted in a way. What I mean by that is, that we had shoes part of the time. We got one pair o’ shoes a year. When dey wored out we went barefooted. Sometimes we tied them up with strings, and they were so ragged de tracks looked like bird tracks, where we walked in the road. We lived in log houses daubed with mud. They called ‘em the slaves houses. My old daddy partly raised his chilluns on game. He caught rabbits, coons, an’ possums. We would work all day and hunt at night. We had no holidays. They did not give us any fun as I know. I could eat anything I could git. I tell you de truth, slave time wuz slave time wid us. My brother wore his shoes out, and had none all thu winter. His feet cracked open and bled so bad you could track him by the blood. When the Yankees come through, he got shoes.

I wuz married in Rockingham. I don’t ‘member when Mr. Jimmie Covington, a preacher, a white man, married us. I married James Adams who lived on a plantation near Rockingham. I had a nice blue wedding dress. My husband wuz dressed in kinder light clothes, best I rickerlect. It's been a good long time, since deen.

I sho do 'member my Marster Tom Covington and his wife too, Emma. Da old man wuz the very Nick. He would take what we made and lowance us, dat is lowance it out to my daddy after he had made it. My father went to Steven Covington, Marster Tom's brother, and told him about it, and his brother Stephen made him gib father his meat back to us.

My missus wuz kind to me, but Mars. Tom wuz the buger. It wuz a mighty bit plantation. I don't know how many slaves wuz on it, there were a lot of dem do'. Dere were overseers two of 'em. One wuz named Bob Covington and the other Charles Covington. They were colored men. I rode with them. I rode wid 'em in the carriage sometimes. De carriage had seats dat folded up. Bob wuz overseer in de field, and Charles wuz carriage driver. All de plantation wuz fenced in, dat is all de fields, wid rails; de rails wuz ten feet long. We drawed water wid a sweep and pail. De well wuz in the yard. De mules for the slaves wuz in town, dere were none on the plantation. Dey had 'em in town; dey waked us time de chicken crowed, and we went to work just as soon as we could see how to make a lick wid a hoe.

Lawd, you better not be caught wid a book in yor han'. If you did, you were sold. Dey didn't 'low dat. I kin read a little, but I can't write. I went to school after slavery and learned to read. We didn't go to school but three or four week a year, and learned to read.

Dere wuz no church on the plantation, and we were not lowed to have prayer meetings. No parties, no candy pullings, nor dances, no sir, not a bit. I 'member goin' one time to the white folkses church, no baptizing dat I 'member. Lawd have mercy, ha! ha! No. De pateroller were on de place at night. You couldn't travel without a pas.

We got few possums. I have greased my daddy's back after he had been whupped until his back wuz cut to pieces. He had to work jis the same. When we went to our houses at night, we cooked our suppers at night, et and then went to bed. If fire wuz out or any work needed doin' around de house we had to work on Sundays. They did not gib us Christmas or any other holidays. We had corn shuckings. I herd 'em talkin' of cuttin de corn pile right square in two. One wud git on one side, another on the other side and see which out beat. They had brandy at the corn shuckin' and I herd Sam talkin' about gittin' drunk.

I 'member one 'oman dying. Her name wuz Caroline Covington. I didn't go to the grave. But you know they had a little cart used with hosses to carry her to the grave, jist a one horse wagon, jist slipped her in there.

Yes, I 'member a field song. It wuz 'Oh! come let us go where pleasure never dies. Great fountain gone over'. Dat's one uv 'em. We had a good doctor when we got sick. He come to see us. The slaves took herbs dey found in de woods. Dat's what I do now, Sir. I got some 'erbs right in my kitchen now.

When the Yankees come through I did not know anything about 'em till they got there. Jist like they were poppin up out of de ground. One of the slaves wuz at his master's house you know, and he said, 'The Yankees are in Cheraw, S. C. and the Yankees are in town'. It didn't sturb me at tall. I wuz not afraid of de Yankees. I ‘member dey went to Miss Emma’s house, and went in de smoke house and emptied every barrel of ‘lasses right in de floor and scattered de cracklings on de floor. I went dere and got some of ‘em. Miss Emma wuz my missus. Dey just killed de chickens, hogs too, and old Jeff the dog; they shot him through the thoat. I ‘member how his mouth flew open when dey shot him. One uv ‘em went into de tater bank, and we chillun wanted to go out dere. Mother wouldn’t let us. She wuz fraid uv ‘em.

Abraham Lincoln freed us by the help of the Lawd, by his help. Slavery wuz owin to who you were with. If you were with some one who wuz good and had some feelin’s for you it did tolerable well; yea, tolerable well.

We left the plantation soon as de surrender. We lef’ right off. We went to goin’ towards Fayetteville, North Carolina. We climbed over fences and were just broke down chillun, feet sore. We had a little meat, corn meal, a tray, and mammy had a tin pan. One night we came to a old house; some one had put wheat straw in it. We staid there, next mornin’, we come back home. Not to Marster’s, but to a white ‘oman named Peggy McClinton, on her plantation. We stayed there a long time. De Yankees took everything dey could, but dey didn’t give us anything to eat. Dey give some of de ‘omen shoes.

I thinks Mr. Roosevelt is a fine man and he do all he can for us.

N.C. District:	No. 3
Worker:	Travis Jordan
No. Words:	1500
Title:	Ida Adkins Ex-slave
Person Interviewed:	Ida Adkins
Editor:	Daisy Bailey Waitt
	County Home, Durham, N.C.
Date Stamp:	"JUN 1 1937"

IDA ADKINS

TR note: Numerous hand written notations and additions in the following interview (i.e. wuz to was; er to a; adding t to the contractions.) Made changes where obvious without comment. Additions and comments were left as notation only.

I wuz bawn befo' de war. I wuz about eight years ole when de Yankee mens come through.

My mammy an' pappy, Hattie an' Jim Jeffries belonged to Marse Frank Jeffries. Marse Frank come from Mississippi, but when I wuz bawn he an' Mis' Mary Jane wuz livin' down herr near Louisburg in North Carolina whare dey had er big plantation an' don' know how many niggers. Marse Frank wuz good to his niggers, 'cept he never give dem ernough to eat. He worked dem hard on half rations, but he didn' believe in all de time beatin' an' sellin' dem.

My pappy worked at de stables, he wuz er good

horseman, but my mammy worked at de big house helpin' Mis' Mary Jane. Mammy worked in de weavin' room. I can see her now settin' at de weavin' machine an' hear de pedals goin' plop, plop, as she treaded dem wid her feets. She wuz a good weaver. I stayed 'roun' de big house too, pickin' up chips, sweepin' de yard an' such as dat. Mis' Mary Jane wuz quick as er whippo'-will. She had black eyes dat snapped, an' dey seed everythin'. She could turn her head so quick dat she'd ketch you every time you tried to steal a lump of sugar. I liked Marse Frank better den I did Mis' Mary Jane. All us little chillun called him Big Pappy. Every time he went to Raleigh he brung us niggers back some candy. He went to Raleigh erbout twice er year. Raleigh wuz er far ways from de plantations—near 'bout sixty miles. It always took Marse Frank three days to make de trip. A day to go, er' day to stay in town, an' a day to come back. Den he always got home in de night. Ceptn' he rode ho'se back 'stead of de carriage, den sometimes he got home by sun down.

Marse Frank didn' go to de war. He wuz too ole. So when de Yankees come through dey foun' him at home. When Marse Frank seed de blue coats comin' down de road he run an' got his gun. De Yankees was on horses. I ain't never seed so many men. Dey was thick as hornets comin' down de road in a cloud of dus'. Dey come up to de house an' tied de horses to de palin's; 'roun' de yard . When dey seed Marse Frank standin' on de po'ch wid de gun leveled on dem, dey got mad. Time Marse Frank done shot one time a bully Yankee snatched de gun away an' tole Marse Frank to hold up his hand. Den dey tied his hands an' pushed him down on de floor 'side de house an' tole him dat if he moved dey would shoot him. Den dey went in de house.

I wuz skeered near 'bout to death, but I run in de kitchen an' got a butcher knife, an' when de Yankees wasn' lookin', I tried to cut de rope an' set Marse Frank free. But one of dem blue debils seed me an' come runnin'. He say:

'Whut you doin', you black brat! you stinkin' little alligator bait!' He snatched de knife from my hand an' told me to stick out my tongue, dat he wuz gwine to cut it off. I let out a yell an' run behin' de house.

Some of de Yankees was in de smoke house gettin' de meat, some of dem wuz at de stables gettin' de ho'ses, an' some of dem wuz in de house gettin' de silver an' things. I seed dem put de big silver pitcher an' tea pot in a bag. Den dey took de knives an' fo'ks an' all de candle sticks an' platters off de side board. Dey went in de parlor an' got de gol' clock dat wuz Mis' Mary Jane's gran'mammy's. Den dey got all de jewelry out of Mis' Mary Jane's box.

Dey went up to Mis' Mary Jane, an' while she looked at dem wid her black eyes snappin', dey took de rings off her fingers; den dey took her gol' bracelet; dey even took de ruby ear rings out of her ears an' de gol' comb out of her hair.

I done quit peepin' in de window an' wuz standin' 'side de house when de Yankees come out in de yard wid all de stuff dey wuz totin' off. Marse Frank wuz still settin' on de po'ch floor wid his han's tied an' couldn' do nothin'. 'Bout dat time I seed de bee gums in de side yard. Dey wuz a whole line of gums. Little as I wuz I had a notion. I run an' got me a long stick an' tu'ned over every one of dem gums. Den I stirred dem bees up wid dat stick 'twell dey wuz so mad I could smell de pizen. An' bees! you ain't never seed de like of bees. Dey wuz swarmin' all over de place. Dey sailed into dem Yankees like bullets, each one madder den de other. Dey lit on dem ho'ses 'twell dey looked like dey wuz live wid varmints. De ho'ses broke dey bridles an' tore down de palin's an' lit out down de road. But dey runnin' wuzn' nothin' to what dem Yankees done. Dey bust out cussin', but what did a bee keer about cuss words! Dey lit on dem blue coats an' every time dey lit dey stuck in a pizen sting. De Yankee's forgot all about de meat an' things dey done stole; dey took off down de road on er run, passin' de horses. De bees was right after dem in a long line. Dey'd zoom an' zip, an' zoom an' zip, an' every time dey'd zip a Yankee would yell.

When dey'd gone Mis' Mary Jane untied Marse Frank. Den dey took all de silver, meat an' things de Yankees lef' behin' an' buried it so if dey come back dey couldn' fin' it.

Den day called ma an' said:

'Ida Lee, if you hadn't tu'ned over dem bee gums dem Yankees would have toted off near 'bout everythin' fine we got. We want to give you somethin' you can keep so' you'll always remember dis day, an' how you run de Yankees away.'

Den Mis' Mary Jane took a plain gold ring off her finger an' put it on mine. An' I been wearin' it ever since.

N.C. District:	No. 2
Worker:	Mary A. Hicks
No. Words:	402
Subject:	Ex-Slave Story
Person Interviewed:	Martha Allen
Editor:	Daisy Bailey Waitt
Date Stamp:	"JUN 7 1937"

HW: good short sketch

MARTHA ALLEN

I wuz borned in Craven County seventy eight years ago. My pappa wuz named Andrew Bryant an' my mammy wuz named Harriet. My brothers wuz John Franklin, Alfred, an' Andrew. I ain't had no sisters. I reckon dat we is what yo' call a general mixture case I am part Injun, part white, an' part nigger.

My mammy belonged ter Tom Edward Gaskin an' she wuzn't half fed. De cook nussed de babies while she cooked, so dat de mammies could wuck in de fiel's, an' all de mammies done wuz stick de babies in at de kitchen do' on dere way ter de fiel's. I'se hyard mammy say dat dey went ter wuck widout breakfast, an' dat when she put her baby in de kitchen she'd go by de slop bucket an' drink de slops from a long handled gourd.

De slave driver wuz bad as he could be, an' de slaves got awful beatin's.

De young marster sorta wanted my mammy, but she tells him no, so he chunks a lightwood knot an' hits her on de haid wid it. Dese white mens what had babies by nigger wimmens wuz called 'Carpet Gitters'. My father's father wuz one o' dem.

Yes mam, I'se mixed plenty case my mammy's grandmaw wuz Cherokee Injun.

I doan know nothin' 'bout no war, case marster carried us ter Cedar Falls, near Durham an' dar's whar we come free.

I 'members dat de Ku Klux uster go ter de Free Issues houses, strip all de family an' whup de ole folkses. Den dey dances wid de pretty yaller gals an' goes ter bed wid dem. Dat's what de Ku Klux wuz, a bunch of mean mens tryin' ter hab a good time.

I'se wucked purty hard durin' my life an' I done my courtin' on a steer an' cart haulin' wood ter town ter sell. He wuz haulin' wood too on his wagin, an' he'd beat me ter town so's dat he could help me off'n de wagin. I reckon dat dat wuz as good a way as any.

I tries ter be a good christian but I'se got disgusted wid dese young upstart niggers what dances in de chu'ch. Dey says dat dey am truckin' an' dat de Bible ain't forbid hit, but I reckin dat I knows dancin' whar I sees hit.

N.C. District:	No. 2
Worker:	Mrs. Edith S. Hibbs
No. Words:	275
Subject:	Story of Joseph Anderson
Interviewed:	Story of Joseph Anderson
	113 Rankin St., Wilmington, N.C.
Edited:	Mrs. W. N. Harriss

JOSEPH ANDERSON

Yes'm I was born a slave. I belong to Mr. T. C. McIlhenny who had a big rice plantation "Eagles Nest" in Brunswick County. It was a big place. He had lots of slaves, an' he was a good man. My mother and father died when I was fourteen. Father died in February 1865 and my mother died of pneumonia in November 1865. My older sister took charge of me.

Interviewer: "Can you read and write?"

Joseph: "Oh yes, I can write a little. I can make my marks. I can write my name. No'm I can't read. I never went to school a day in my life. I just "picked up" what I know."

I don't remember much about slave times. I was fourteen when I was freed. After I was freed we lived between 8th and 9th on Chestnut. We rented a place from Dan O'Connor a real estate man and paid him $5 a month rent. I've been married twice. First time was married by Mr. Ed Taylor, magistrate in Southport, Brunswick County. I was married to my first wife twenty years and eight months. Then she died. I was married again when I was seventy-five years old. I was married to my second wife just a few years when she died.

I was on the police force for a year and a half. I was elected April 6, 1895. Mr. McIlhenny was an ole man then an' I used to go to see him.

I was a stevedore for Mr. Alexander Sprunt for sixty years.

Joseph is now buying his house at 1113 Rankin Street. Rents part of it for $8.50 a month to pay for it. He stays in one room.

NOTE: Joseph's health is none too good, making information sketchy and incoherent.

N.C. District:	No. 2
Worker:	T. Pat Matthews
No. Words:	1905
Subject:	MARY ANDERSON
Person Interviewed:	Mary Anderson
Editor:	G. L. Andrews
Date Stamp:	"AUG 23 1937"

MARY ANDERSON

My name is Mary Anderson. I was born on a plantation near Franklinton, Wake County, N.C. May 10, 1851. I was a slave belonging to Sam Brodie, who owned the plantation at this place. My missus' name was Evaline. My father was Alfred Brodie and my mother was Bertha Brodie.

We had good food, plenty of warm homemade clothes and comfortable houses. The slave houses were called the quarters and the house where marster lived was called the great house. Our houses had two rooms each and marster's house had twelve rooms. Both the slave and white folks buildings were located in a large grove one mile square covered with oak and hickory nut trees. Marster's house was exactly one mile from the main Louisburg Road and there was a wide avenue leading through the plantation and grove to marster's house. The house fronted the avenue east and in going down the avenue from the main road you traveled directly west.

The plantation was very large and there were about two hundred acres of cleared land that was farmed each year. A pond was located on the place and in winter ice was gathered there for summer use and stored in an ice house which was built in the grove where the other buildings were. A large hole about ten feet deep was dug in the ground; the ice was put in that hole and covered. [HW: *]

A large frame building was built over it. At the top of the earth there was an entrance door and steps leading down to the bottom of the hole. Other things besides ice were stored there. There was a still on the plantation and barrels of brandy were stored in the ice house, also pickles, preserves and cider.

Many of the things we used were made on the place. There was a grist mill, tannery, shoe shop, blacksmith shop, and looms for weaving cloth.

There were about one hundred, and sixty-two slaves on the plantation and every Sunday morning all the children had to be bathed, dressed, and their hair combed and carried down to marster's for breakfast. It was a rule that all the little colored children eat at the great house every Sunday morning in order that marster and missus could watch them eat so they could know which ones were sickly and have them doctored.

The slave children all carried a mussel shell in their hands to eat with. The food was put on large trays and the children all gathered around and ate, dipping up their food with their mussel shells which they used for spoons. Those who refused to eat or those who were ailing in any way had to come back to the great house for their meals and medicine until they were well.

Marster had a large apple orchard in the Tar River low grounds and up on higher ground and nearer the plantation house there was on one side of the road a large plum orchard and on the other side was an orchard of peaches, cherries, quinces and grapes. We picked the quinces in August and used them for preserving. Marster and missus believed in giving the slaves plenty of fruit, especially the children.

Marster had three children, one boy named Dallas, and two girls, Bettie and Carrie. He would not allow slave children to call his children marster and missus unless the slave said little marster or little missus. He had four white overseers but they were not allowed to whip a slave. If there was any whipping to be done he always said he would do it. He didn't believe in whipping so when a slave got so bad he could not manage him he sold him.

Marster didn't quarrel with anybody, missus would not speak short to a slave, but both missus and marster taught slaves to be obedient in a nice quiet way. The slaves were taught to take their hats and bonnets off before going into the house, and to bow and say, 'Good morning Marster Sam and Missus Evaline'. Some of the little negroes would go down to the great house and ask them when it wus going to rain, and when marster or missus walked in the grove the little Negroes would follow along after them like a gang of kiddies. Some of the slave children wanted to stay with them at the great house all the time. They knew no better of course and seemed to love marster and missus as much as they did their own mother and father. Marster and missus always used gentle means to get the children out of their way when they bothered them and the way the children loved and trusted them wus a beautiful sight to see.

Patterollers were not allowed on the place unless they came peacefully and I never knew of them whipping any slaves on marster's place. Slaves were carried off on two horse wagons to be sold. I have seen several loads leave. They were the unruly ones. Sometimes he would bring back slaves, once he brought back two boys and three girls from the slave market.

Sunday wus a great day on the plantation. Everybody got biscuits Sundays. The slave women went down to marsters for their Sunday allowance of flour. All the children ate breakfast at the great house and marster and missus gave out fruit to all. The slaves looked forward to Sunday as they labored through the week. It was a great day. Slaves received good treatment from marster and all his family.

We were allowed to have prayer meetings in our homes and we also went to the white folks church.

They would not teach any of us to read and write. Books and papers were forbidden. Marster's children and the slave children played together. I went around with the baby girl Carrie to other plantations visiting. She taught me how to talk low and how to act in company. My association with white folks and my training while I was a slave is why I talk like white folks.

Bettie Brodie married a Dr. Webb from Boylan, Virginia. Carrie married a Mr. Joe Green of Franklin County. He was a big southern planter.

The war was begun and there were stories of fights and freedom. The news went from plantation to plantation and while the slaves acted natural and some even more polite than usual, they prayed for freedom. Then one day I heard something that sounded like thunder and missus and marster began to walk around and act queer. The grown slaves were whispering to each other. Sometimes they gathered in little gangs in the grove. Next day I heard it again, boom, boom, boom. I went and asked missus 'is it going to rain?' She said, 'Mary go to the ice house and bring me some pickles and preserves.' I went and got them. She ate a little and gave me some. Then she said, 'You run along and play.' In a day or two everybody on the plantation seemed to be disturbed and marster and missus were crying. Marster ordered all the slaves to come to the great house at nine o'clock. Nobody was working and slaves were walking over the grove in every direction. At nine o'clock all the slaves gathered at the great house and marster and missus came out on the porch and stood side by side. You could hear a pin drap everything was so quiet. Then marster said, 'Good morning,' and missus said, 'Good morning, children'. They were both crying. Then marster said, 'Men, women and children, you are free. You are no longer my slaves. The Yankees will soon be here.'

Marster and missus then went into the house got two large arm chairs put them on the porch facing the avenue and sat down side by side and remained there watching.

In about an hour there was one of the blackest clouds coming up the avenue from the main road. It was the Yankee soldiers, they finally filled the mile long avenue reaching from marster's house to the main Louisburg road and spread out over the mile square grove. The mounted men dismounted. The footmen stacked their shining guns and began to build fires and cook. They called the slaves, saying, 'Your are free.' Slaves were whooping and laughing and acting like they were crazy. Yankee soldiers were shaking hands with the Negroes and calling them Sam, Dinah, Sarah and asking them questions. They busted the door to the smoke house and got all the hams. They went to the ice-house and got several barrels of brandy, and such a time. The Negroes and Yankees were cooking and eating together. The Yankees told them to come on and join them, they were free. Marster and missus sat on the porch and they were so humble no Yankee bothered anything in the great house. The slaves were awfully excited. The Yankees stayed there, cooked, eat, drank and played music until about night, then a bugle began to blow and you never saw such getting on horses and lining up in your life. In a few minutes they began to march, leaving the grove which was soon as silent as a grave yard. They took marster's horses and cattle with them and joined the main army and camped just across Cypress Creek one and one half miles from my marster's place on the Louisburg Road.

When they left the country, lot of the slaves went with them and soon there were none of marster's slaves left. They wandered around for a year from place to place, fed and working most of the time at some other slave owner's plantation and getting more homesick every day.

The second year after the surrender our marster and missus got on their carriage and went and looked up all the Negroes they heard of who ever belonged to them. Some who went off with the Yankees were never heard of again. When marster and missus found any of theirs they would say, 'Well, come on back home.' My father and mother, two uncles and their families moved back. Also Lorenza Brodie, and John Brodie and their families moved back. Several of the young men and women who once belonged to him came back. Some were so glad to get back they cried, 'cause fare had been mighty bad part of the time they were rambling around and they were hungry. When they got back marster would say, 'Well you have come back home have you, and the Negroes would say, 'Yes marster.' Most all spoke of them as missus and marster as they did before the surrender, and getting back home was the greatest pleasure of all.

We stayed with marster and missus and went to their church, the Maple Springs Baptist church, until they died.

Since the surrender I married James Anderson. I had four children, one boy and three girls.

I think slavery was a mighty good thing for mother, father, me and the other members of the family, and I cannot say anything but good for my old marster and missus, but I can only speak for those whose conditions I have known during slavery and since. For myself and them, I will say again, slavery was a mighty good thing.

N.C. District:	No. 2
Worker:	Mary A. Hicks
No. Words:	789
Subject:	Cornelia Andrews
Story Teller:	Cornelia Andrews
Editor:	Daisy Bailey Waitt
Date Stamp:	"JUN 7 1937"

CORNELIA ANDREWS

De fust marster dat I 'members wuz Mr. Cute Williams an' he wuz a good marster, but me an' my mammy an' some of de rest of 'em wuz sold to Doctor McKay Vaden who wuz not good ter us.

Doctor Vaden owned a good-sized plantation, but he had just eight slaves. We had plank houses, but we ain't had much food an' clothes. We wored shoes wid wooden bottom in de winter an' no shoes in de summer. We ain't had much fun, nothin' but candy pullin's 'bout onct a year. We ain't raised no cane but marster buyed one barrel of 'lasses fer candy eber year.

Yo' know dat dar wuz a big slave market in Smithfield dem days, dar wuz also a jail, an' a whippin' post. I 'members a man named Rough somethin' or other, what bought forty er fifty slaves at de time an' carried 'em ter Richmond to re-sell. He had four big black horses hooked ter a cart, an' behind dis cart he chained de slaves, an' dey had ter walk, or trot all de way ter Richmond. De little ones Mr. Rough would throw up in de cart an' off dey'd go no'th. Dey said dat der wuz one day at Smithfield dat three hundret slaves wuz sold on de block. Dey said dat peoples came from fer an' near, eben from New Orleans ter dem slave sales. Dey said dat way 'fore I wuz borned dey uster strip dem niggers start naked an' gallop' em ober de square so dat de buyers could see dat dey warn't scarred nor deformed.

While I could 'member dey'd sell de mammies 'way from de babies, an' dere wuzn't no cryin' 'bout it whar de marster would know 'bout it nother. Why? Well, dey'd git beat black an' blue, dat's why.

Wuz I eber beat bad? No mam, I wuzn't.

(Here the daughter, a graduate of Cornell University, who was in the room listening came forward. "Open your shirt, mammy, and let the lady judge for herself." The old ladies eyes flashed as she sat bolt upright. She seemed ashamed, but the daughter took the shirt off, exposing the back and shoulders which were marked as though branded with a plaited cowhide whip. There was no doubt of that at all.)

"I wuz whupped public," she said tonelessly, "for breaking dishes an' 'bein' slow. I wuz at Mis' Carrington's den, an' it wuz jist 'fore de close o' de war. I wuz in de kitchen washin' dishes an' I draps one. De missus calls Mr. Blount King, a patteroller, an' he puts de whuppin' yo' sees de marks of on me. My ole missus foun' it out an' she comed an' got me."

A friend of the interviewer who was present remarked, "That must have been horrible to say the least."

"Yo' 'doan know nothin," the old Negro blazed. "Alex Heath, a slave wuz beat ter death, hyar in Smithfield. He had stold something, dey tells me, anyhow he wuz sentenced ter be put ter death, an' de folkses dar in charge 'cided ter beat him ter death. Dey gib him a hundret lashes fer nine mornin's an' on de ninth mornin' he died."

"My uncle Daniel Sanders, wuz beat till he wuz cut inter gashes an' he wuz tu be beat ter death lak Alex wuz, but one day atter dey had beat him an' throwed him back in jail wid out a shirt he broke out an' runned away. He went doun in de riber swamp an' de blow flies blowed de gashes an' he wuz unconscious when a white man found him an' tuk him home wid him. He died two or three months atter dat but he neber could git his body straight ner walk widout a stick; he jist could drag."

"I 'specks dat I doan know who my pappy wuz, maybe de stock nigger on de plantation. My pappy an' mammy jist stepped ober de broom an' course I doan know when. Yo' knows dey ain't let no little runty nigger have no chilluns. Naw sir, dey ain't, dey operate on dem lak dey does de male hog so's dat dey can't have no little runty chilluns."

"Some of de marsters wuz good an' some of dem wuz bad. I wuz glad ter be free an' I lef' der minute I finds out dat I is free. I ain't got no kick a-comin' not none at all. Some of de white folkses wuz slaves, ter git ter de United States an' we niggers ain't no better, I reckons."

N.C. District:	No. 2	
Worker:	T. Pat Matthews	
No. Words:	22,289	
Subject:	A SLAVE STORY (Princess Quango Hennadonah Perceriah).	
Reference:	MARY ANNGADY	HW: 80 years
Editor:	George L. Andrews	
Date Stamp:	"OCT 25 1937"	

MARY ANNGADY

I was eighteen years old in 1875 but I wanted to get married so I gave my age as nineteen. I wish I could recall some of the ole days when I was with my missus in Orange County, playing with my brothers and other slave children.

I was owned by Mr. Franklin Davis and my madam was Mrs. Bettie Davis. I and my brother used to scratch her feet and rub them for her; you know how old folks like to have their feet rubbed. My brother and I used to scrap over who should scratch and rub her feet. She would laugh and tell us not to do that way that she loved us both. Sometimes she let me sleep at her feet at night. She was plenty good to all of the slaves. Her daughter Sallie taught me my A B C's in Webster's Blue Back spelling Book. When I learned to Spell B-a-k-e-r, Baker,

I thought that was something. The next word I felt proud to spell was s-h-a-d-y, shady, the next l-a-d-y, lady. I would spell them out loud as I picked up chips in the yard to build a fire with. My missus Bettie gave me a blue back spelling book.

My father was named James Mason, and he belonged to James Mason of Chapel Hill. Mother and I and my four brothers belonged to the same man and we also lived in the town. I never lived on a farm or plantation in my life. I know nothing about farming. All my people are dead and I cannot locate any of marster's family if they are living. Marster's family consisted of two boys and two girls—Willie, Frank, Lucy and Sallie. Marster was a merchant, selling general merchandise. I remember eating a lot of brown sugar and candy at his store.

My mother was a cook. They allowed us a lot of privileges and it was just one large happy family with plenty to eat and wear, good sleeping places and nothing to worry about. They were of the Presbyterian faith and we slaves attended Sunday school and services at their church. There were about twelve slaves on the lot. The houses for slaves were built just a little ways back from marster's house on the same lot. The Negro and white children played together, and there was little if any difference made in the treatment given a slave child and a white child. I have religious books they gave me. Besides the books they taught me, they drilled me in etiquette of the times and also in courtesy and respect to my superiors until it became a habit and it was perfectly natural for me to be polite.

The first I knew of the Yankees was when I was out in my marster's yard picking up chips and they came along, took my little brother and put him on a horse's back and carried him up town. I ran and told my mother about it. They rode brother over the town a while, having fun out of him, then they brought him back. Brother said he had a good ride and was pleased with the blue jackets as the Yankee soldiers were called.

We had all the silver and valuables hid and the Yankees did not find them, but they went into marster's store and took what they wanted. They gave my father a box of hardtack and a lot of meat. Father was a Christian and he quoted one of the Commandments when they gave him things they had stolen from others. 'Thou shalt not steal', quoth he, and he said he did not appreciate having stolen goods given to him.

I traveled with the white folks in both sections of the country, north and south, after the War Between the States. I kept traveling with them and also continued my education. They taught me to recite and I made money by reciting on many of the trips. Since the surrender I have traveled in the north for various Charitable Negro Societies and Institutions and people seemed very much interested in the recitation I recited called "When Malinda Sings".

The first school I attended was after the war closed. The school was located in Chapel Hill, North Carolina, and was taught by a Yankee white woman from Philadelphia. We remained in Chapel Hill only a few years after the war ended when we all moved to Raleigh, and I have made it my home ever since. I got the major part of my education in Raleigh under Dr. H. M. Tupper[1] who taught in the second Baptist Church, located on Blount Street. Miss Mary Lathrop, a colored teacher from Philadelphia, was an assistant teacher in Dr. Tupper's School. I went from there to Shaw Collegiate Institute, which is now Shaw University.

I married Aaron Stallings of Warrenton, North Carolina while at Shaw. He died and I married Rev. Matthews Anngady of Monrovia, west coast of Africa, Liberia, Pastor of First Church. I helped him in his work here, kept studying the works of different authors, and lecturing and reciting. My husband, the Rev. Matthews Anngady died, and I gave a lot of my time to the cause of Charity, and while on a lecture tour of Massachusetts in the interest of this feature of colored welfare for Richmond, Va., the most colorful incident of my eventful life happened when I met Quango Hennadonah Perceriah, an Abyssinian Prince, who was traveling and lecturing on the customs of his country and the habits of its people. Our mutual interests caused our friendship to ripen fast and when the time of parting came, when each of us had finished our work in Massachusetts, he going back to his home in New York City and I returning to Richmond, he asked me to correspond with him. I promised to do so and our friendship after a year's correspondence became love and he proposed and I accepted him. We were married in Raleigh by Rev. J. J. Worlds, pastor of the First Baptist Church, colored.

P. T. Barnum had captured my husband when he was a boy and brought him to America from Abyssinia, educated him and then sent him back to his native country. He would not stay and soon he was in America again. He was of the Catholic faith in America and they conferred the honor of priesthood upon him but after he married me this priesthood was taken away and he joined the Episcopal Church. After we were married we decided to go on an extensive lecture tour. He had been a headsman in his own country and a prince. We took the customs of his people and his experiences as the subject of our lectures. I could sing, play the guitar, violin and piano, but I did not know his native language. He began to teach me and as soon as I could sing the song How Firm A Foundation in his language which went this way:

Ngama i-bata, Njami buyek
Wema Wemeta, Negana i
bukek diol, di Njami,
i-diol de Kak
Annimix, Annimix hanci
Bata ba Satana i-bu butete
Bata ba Npjami i bunanan
Bata be satana ba laba i wa—
Bata ba Njami ba laba Munonga

We traveled and lectured in both the north and the south and our life, while we had to work hard, was one of happiness and contentment. I traveled and lectured as the Princess Quango Hennadonah Perceriah, wife of the Abyssinian Prince. I often recited the recitation written by the colored poet, Paul Lawrence Dunbar When Malinda Sings to the delight of our audiences.

The following incidents of African life were related to me by my husband Quango Hennadonah Perceriah and they were also given in his lectures on African customs while touring the United States.

The religion of the Bakuba tribe of Abyssinia was

almost wholly Pagan as the natives believed fully in witchcraft, sorcery, myths and superstitions. The witch doctor held absolute sway over the members of the tribe and when his reputation as a giver of rain, bountiful crops or success in the chase was at stake the tribes were called together and those accused by the witch doctor of being responsible for these conditions through witchery were condemned and speedily executed.

The people were called together by the beating of drums. The witch doctor, dressed in the most hellish garb imaginable with his body painted and poisonous snake bone necklaces dangling from his neck and the claws of ferocious beasts, lions, leopards and the teeth of vicious man-eating crocodiles finishing up his adornment, sat in the middle of a court surrounded by the members of the tribe. In his hand he carried a gourd which contained beads, shot, or small stones. He began his incantations by rattling the contents of the gourd, shouting and making many weird wails and peculiar contortions. After this had gone on for sometime until he was near exhaustion his face assumed the expression of one in great pain and this was the beginning of the end for some poor ignorant savage. He squirmed and turned in different directions with his eyes fixed with a set stare as if in expectancy when suddenly his gaze would be fixed on some member of the tribe and his finger pointed directly at him. The victim was at once seized and bound, the doctor's gaze never leaving him until this was done. If one victim appeased his nervous fervor the trial was over but if his wrought-up feelings desired more his screechings continued until a second victim was secured. He had these men put to death to justify himself in the eyes of the natives of his tribe for his failing to bring rain, bountiful crops and success to the tribe.

The witch doctor who sat as judge seemed to have perfect control over the savages minds and no one questioned his decisions. The persons were reconciled to their fate and were led away to execution while they moaned and bade their friends goodbye in the doleful savage style. Sometimes they were put on a boat, taken out into the middle of a river and there cut to pieces with blades of grass, their limbs being dismembered first and thrown into the river to the crocodiles. A drink containing an opiate was generally given the victim to deaden the pain but often this formality was dispensed with. The victims were often cut to pieces at the place of trial with knives and their limbs thrown out to the vultures that almost continuously hover 'round the huts and kraals of the savage tribes of Africa.

In some instances condemned persons were burned at the stake. This form of execution is meted out at some of the religious dances or festivities to some of their pagan gods to atone and drive away the evil spirits that have caused pestilences to come upon the people. The victims at these times are tortured in truly savage fashion, being burned to death by degrees while the other members of the tribe dance around and go wild with religious fervor calling to their gods while the victim screeches with pain in his slowly approaching death throes. Young girls, women, boys and men are often accused of witchcraft. One method they used of telling whether the victim accused was innocent or guilty was to give them a liquid poison made from the juice of several poisonous plants. If they could drink it and live they were innocent, if they died they were guilty. In most cases death was almost instantaneous. Some vomited the poison from their stomachs and lived.

The Bakubas sometimes resorted to cannibalism and my husband told me of a Bakuba girl who ate her own mother. Once a snake bit a man and he at once called the witch doctor. The snake was a poisonous one and the man bitten was in great pain. The witch doctor whooped and went through several chants but the man got worse instead of better. The witch doctor then told the man that his wife made the snake bite him by witchery and that she should die for the act. The natives gathered at once in response to the witch doctor's call and the woman was executed at once. The man bitten by the snake finally died but the witch doctor had shifted the responsibility of his failure to help the man to his wife who had been beheaded. The witch doctor had justified himself and the incident was closed.

The tribe ruled by a King has two or more absolute rules. The Kings word is law and he has the power to condemn any subject to death at any time without trial. If he becomes angry or offended with any of his wives a nod and a word to his bodyguard and the woman is led away to execution. Any person of the tribe is subject to the King's will with the exemption of the witch doctor. Executions of a different nature than the ones described above are common occurrences. For general crimes the culprit after being condemned to death is placed in a chair shaped very much like the electric chairs used in American prisons in taking the lives of the condemned. He is then tied firmly to the chair with thongs. A pole made of a green sapling is firmly implanted in the earth nearby. A thong is placed around the neck of the victim under the chin. The sapling is then bent over and the other end of the thong tied to the end of the sapling pole. The pole stretches the neck to its full length and holds the head erect. Drums are sometimes beaten to drown the cries of those who are to be killed. The executioner who is called a headsman then walks forward approaching the chair from the rear. When he reaches it he steps to the side of the victim and with a large, sharp, long-bladed knife lops off the head of the criminal. The bodies of men executed in this manner are buried in shallow holes dug about two feet deep to receive their bodies.

The rank and file of the savage tribes believe explicitly in the supernatural powers of the witch doctor and his decisions are not questioned. Not even the King of the tribe raises a voice against him. The witch doctor is crafty enough not to condemn any of the King's household or any one directly prominent in the King's service. After an execution everything is quiet in a few hours and the incident seems forgotten. The African Negroes attitude towards the whole affair seems to be instinctive and as long as he escapes he does not show any particular concern in his fellowman. His is of an animal instinctive nature.

The males of the African tribes of savages have very little respect for a woman but they demand a whole lot of courtesies from their wives, beating them unmercifully when they feel proper respect has not been shown them. The men hunt game and make war on other tribes and the women do all the work. A savage warrior when not engaged in hunting or war, sleeps a lot and smokes almost continuously during his waking hours. Girls are bought from their parents while mere children by the payment of so many cows, goats, etc. The King can take any woman of the tribe whether married or single he desires to be his wife. The parents of young girls taken to wife by the King of a tribe feel honored and fall on their knees and thank the King for taking her.

The prince of a tribe is born a headsman and as soon as he is able to wield a knife he is called upon to perform the duty of cutting off the heads of criminals who are condemned to death by the King for general crimes. Those condemned by the witch doctor for witchcraft are executed by dismemberment or fire as described above.

My husband was a cannibal headsman and performed this duty of cutting off persons heads when a boy and after being civilized in America this feature of his early life bore so heavily upon his mind that it was instrumental in driving him insane. By custom a prince was born a headsman and it was compulsory that he execute criminals. He died in an insane ward of the New Jersey State Hospital.

[1] **Handwritten Footnote:** *Dr. Henry M. Tupper, a Union Army chaplain, who helped to start Shaw University in 1865.*

N.C. District:	No. 2
Worker:	T. Pat Matthews
No. Words:	1051
Subject:	JANE ARRINGTON
Story Teller:	Jane Arrington
Editor:	Geo. L. Andrews
Date Stamp:	"AUG 4 1937"

JANE ARRINGTON

I ort to be able to tell sumpin cause I wus twelve years old when dey had de surrender right up here in Raleigh. If I live to see dis coming December I will be eighty five years old. I was born on the 18th of December 1852.

I belonged to Jackson May of Nash County. I wus born on de plantation near Tar River. Jackson May never married until I wus of a great big girl. He owned a lot of slaves; dere were eighty on de plantation before de surrender. He married Miss Becky Wilder, sister of Sam Wilder. De Wilders lived on a jining plantation to where I wus borned.

Jackson May had so many niggers he let Billy Williams who had a plantation nearby have part of 'em. Marster Jackson he raised my father and bought my mother. My mother wus named Louisa May, and my father wus named Louis May. My mother had six chilluns, four boys and two girls. The boys were Richard, Farro, Caeser, and Fenner. De girls Rose and Jane. Jane, dats me.

We lived in log houses with stick an' dirt chimleys. They called 'em the slave houses. We had chicken feather beds to sleep on an' de houses wus good warm comfortable log houses. We had plenty of cover an' feather pillows.

My grandmother on my mother's side told me a lot of stories 'bout haints and how people run from 'em. Dey told me 'bout slaves dat had been killed by dere marster's coming back and worryin' 'em. Ole Missus Penny Williams, before Jackson May bought mother, treated some of de slaves mighty bad. She died an' den come back an' nearly scared de slaves to death. Grandmother told all we chillun she seed her an' knowed her after she been dead an' come back.

John May a slave wus beat to death by Bill Stone an' Oliver May. Oliver May wus Junius May's son. Junius May wus Jackson May's Uncle. John May come back an' wurried both of 'em. Dey could hardly sleep arter dat. Dey said dey could hear him hollerin' an' groanin' most all de time. Dese white men would groan in dere sleep an' tell John to go away. Dey would say, 'Go way John, please go away'. De other slaves wus afraid of 'em cause de ghost of John wurried 'em so bad.

I wurked on de farm, cuttin' corn stalks and tendin' to cattle in slavery time. Sometimes I swept de yards. I never got any money for my work and we didn't have any patches. My brothers caught possums, coons and sich things an' we cooked 'em in our houses. We had no parties but we had quiltin's. We went to the white folks church, Peach Tree Church, six miles from de plantation an' Poplar Springs Church seven miles away. Both were missionary Baptist Churches.

There were no overseers on Jackson May's plantation. He wouldn't have nary one. Billy Williams didn't have none. Dey had colored slave foremen.

After wurkin' all day dere wus a task of cotton to be picked an' spun by 'em. Dis wus two onces of cotton. Some of de slaves run away from Bill Williams when Marster Jackson May let him have 'em to work. Dey run away an' come home. Aunt Chaney runned away an' mother run away. Marster Jackson May kept 'em hid cause he say dey wus not treated right. He wouldn't let 'em have 'em back no more.

I never saw a grown slave whupped or in chains and I never saw a slave sold. Jackson May would not sell a slave. He didn't think it right. He kept 'em together. He had eighty head. He would let other white people have 'em to wurk for 'em sometimes, but he would not sell none of 'em.

If dey caught a slave wid a book you knowed it meant a whuppin', but de white chillun teached slaves secretey sometimes. Ole man Jake Rice a slave who belonged to John Rice in Nash County wus teached by ole John Rice's son till he had a purty good mount of larnin'.

We did not have prayer meeting at marster's plantation or anywhur. Marster would not allow dat.

When I wus a child we played de games of three handed reels, 'Old Gray Goose', 'All Little Gal, All Little Gal, All Little Gal remember me'. We took hold of hands an' run round as we sang dis song.

We sang 'Old Dan Tucker'. Git outen de way, ole Dan Tucker, Sixteen Hosses in one stable, one jumped out an' skined his nable an' so on.

Dr. Mann and Dr. Sid Harris and Dr. Fee Mann and Dr. Mathias looked arter us when we wus sick. Mother and de other grown folks raised herbs dat dey give us too. Chillun took a lot of salts.

Jackson May wus too rich to go to de war. Billy Williams didn't go, too rich too, I reckons. I remember when dey said niggers had to be free. De papers said if dey could not be freedom by good men dere would be freedom by blood. Dey fighted an' kept on fightin' a long time. Den de Yankees come.

I heard dem beat de drum. Marster tole us we wus free but mother an' father stayed on with Marster. He promised 'em sumptin, but he give 'em nothin'. When de crop wus housed dey left.

Father and mother went to Hench Stallings plantation and stayed there one year. Then they went to Jim Webbs farm. I don't remember how long they stayed there but round two years. They moved about an' about among the white folks till they died. They never owned any property. They been dead 'bout thirty years.

I married Sidney Arrington. He has been dead six years las' September.

I am unable to do any kind of work. My arm is mighty weak.

I know slavery wus a bad thing. I don't have to think anything about it. Abraham Lincoln wus the first of us bein' free, I think he wus a man of God. I think Roosevelt is all right man. I belongs to the Pentecostal Holiness Church.

AC

N.C. District:	No. 2
Worker:	T. Pat Matthews
No. Words:	1426
Subject:	Sarah Louise Augustus
Source:	Sarah Louise Augustus
Editor:	George L. Andrews

SARAH LOUISE AUGUSTUS

I wus born on a plantation near Fayetteville, N.C., and I belonged to J. B. Smith. His wife wus named Henrietta. He owned about thirty slaves. When a slave was no good he wus put on the auction block in Fayetteville and sold.

My father wus named Romeo Harden and my mother wus named Alice Smith. The little cabin where I wus born is still standing.

There wus seven children in marster's family, four girls and two boys. The girls wus named Ellen, Ida, Mary and Elizabeth. The boys wus named Harry, Norman and Marse George. Marse George went to the war. Mother had a family of four girls. Their names wus: Mary, Kate, Hannah and myself, Sarah Louise. I am the only one living and I would not be living but I have spent most of my life in white folk's houses and they have looked after me. I respected myself and they respected me.

My first days of slavery wus hard. I slept on a pallet on the floor of the cabin and just as soon as I wus able to work any at all I wus put to milking cows.

I have seen the paterollers hunting men and have seen men they had whipped. The slave block stood in the center of the street, Fayetteville Street, where Ramsey and Gillespie Street came in near Cool Springs Street. The silk mill stood just below the slave market. I saw the silkworms that made the silk and saw them gather the cocoons and spin the silk.

They hung people in the middle of Ramsey Street. They put up a gallows and hung the men exactly at 12 o'clock.

I ran away from the plantation once to go with some white children to see a man hung.

The only boats I remember on the Cape Fear wus the Governor Worth, The Hurt, The Iser and The North State. Oh! Lord yes, I remember the stage coach. As many times as I run to carry the mail to them when they come by! They blew a horn before they got there and you had to be on time 'cause they could not wait. There wus a stage each way each day, one up and one down.

Mr. George Lander had the first Tombstone Marble yard in Fayetteville on Hay Street on the point of Flat Iron place. Lander wus from Scotland. They gave me a pot, a scarf, and his sister gave me some shells. I have all the things they gave me. My missus, Henrietta Smith, wus Mr. Lander's sister. I waited on the Landers part of the time. They were hard working white folks, honest, God fearing people. The things they gave me were brought from over the sea.

I can remember when there wus no hospital in Fayetteville. There wus a little place near the depot where there wus a board shanty where they operated on people. I stood outside once and saw the doctors take a man's leg off. Dr. McDuffy wus the man who took the leg off. He lived on Hay Street near the Silk Mill.

When one of the white folks died they sent slaves around to the homes of their friends and neighbors with a large sheet of paper with a piece of black crepe pinned to the top of it. The friends would sign or make a cross mark on it. The funerals were held at the homes and friends and neighbors stood on the porch and in the house while the services were going on. The bodies were carried to the grave after the services in a black hearse drawn by black horses. If they did not have black horses to draw the hearse they went off and borrowed them. The colored people washed and shrouded the dead bodies. My grandmother wus one who did this. Her name wus Sarah McDonald. She belonged to Capt. George McDonald. She had fifteen children and lived to be one hundred and ten years old. She died in Fayetteville of pneumonia. She wus in Raleigh nursing the Briggs family, Mrs. F. H. Briggs' family. She wus going home to Fayetteville when she wus caught in a rain storm at Sanford, while changing trains. The train for Fayetteville had left as the train for Sanford wus late so she stayed wet all night. Next day she went home, took pneumonia and died. She wus great on curing rheumatism; she did it with herbs. She grew hops and other herbs and cured many people of this disease.

She wus called black mammy because she wet nursed

so many white children. In slavery time she nursed all babies hatched on her marster's plantation and kept it up after the war as long as she had children.

Grandfather wus named Isaac Fuller. Mrs. Mary Ann Fuller, Kate Fuller, Mr. Will Fuller, who wus a lawyer in Wall Street, New York, is some of their white folks. The Fullers were born in Fayetteville. One of the slaves, Dick McAlister, worked, saved a small fortune and left it to Mr. Will Fuller. People thought the slave ought to have left it to his sister but he left it to Mr. Will. Mr. Fuller gives part of it to the ex-slaves sister each year. Mr. Will always helped the Negroes out when he could. He was good to Dick and Dick McAlister gave him all his belongings when he died.

The Yankees came through Fayetteville wearing large blue coats with capes on them. Lots of them were mounted, and there were thousands of foot soldiers. It took them several days to get through town. The Southern soldiers retreated and then in a few hours the Yankees covered the town. They busted into the smokehouse at marstar's, took the meat, meal and other provisions. Grandmother pled with the Yankees but it did no good. They took all they wanted. They said if they had to come again they would take the babies from the cradles. They told us we were all free. The Negroes begun visiting each other in the cabins and became so excited they began to shout and pray. I thought they were all crazy.

We stayed right on with marster. He had a town house and a big house on the plantation. I went to the town house to work, but mother and grandmother stayed on the plantation. My mother died there and the white folks buried her. Father stayed right on and helped run the farm until he died. My uncle, Elic Smith, and his family stayed too. Grandfather and grandmother after a few years left the plantation and went to live on a little place which Mrs. Mary Ann Fuller gave them. Grandmother and grandfather died there.

I wus thirty years old when I married. I wus married in my missus' graduating dress. I wus married in the white folks' church, to James Henry Harris. The white folks carried me there and gave me away. Miss Mary Smith gave me away. The wedding wus attended mostly by white folks.

My husband wus a fireman on the Cape Fear river boats and a white man's Negro too. We had two children, both died while little. My husband and I spent much of our time with the white folks and when he wus on his runs I slept in their homes. Often the children of the white families slept with me. We both tried to live up to the standards of decency and honesty and to be worthy of the confidence placed in us by our white folks.

My husband wus finally offered a job with a shipping concern in Deleware and we moved there. He wus fireman on the freighter Wilmington. He worked there three years, when he wus drowned. After his death I married David Augustus and immediately came back to North Carolina and my white folks, and we have been here ever since. I am a member of several Negro Lodges and am on the Committee for the North Carolina Colored State Fair.

There are only a few of the old white folks who have always been good to me living now, but I am still working with their offspring, among whom I have some mighty dear friends. I wus about eight years old when Sherman's

Army came through. Guess I am about eighty years of age now.

AC

N.C. District:	No. 2
Worker:	T. Pat Matthews
No. Words:	908
Subject:	A Slave Story
Story Teller:	Charity Austin
Editor:	Daisy Bailey Waitt
Date Stamp:	"JUN 26 1937"

CHARITY AUSTIN

I wus borned in the year 1852, July 27. I wus born in Granville County, sold to a slave speculator at ten years old and carried to Southwest, Georgia. I belonged to Samuel Howard. His daughter took me to Kinston, North Carolina and I stayed there until I wus sold. She married a man named Bill Brown, and her name wus Julia Howard Brown. My father wus named Paul Howard and my mother wus named Chollie Howard. My old missus wus named Polly Howard.

John Richard Keine from Danville, Virginia bought me and sent me to a plantation in Georgia. We only had a white overseer there. He and his wife and children lived on the plantation. We had slave quarters there. Slaves were bought up and sent there in chains. Some were chained to each other by the legs, some by the arms. They called the leg chains shackles. I have lived a hard life. I have seen mothers sold away from their babies and other children, and they cryin' when she left. I have seen husbands sold from their wives, and wives sold from their husbands.

Abraham Lincoln came through once, but none of us knew who he wus. He wus just the raggedest man you ever saw. The white children and me saw him out at the railroad. We were settin' and waitin' to see him. He said he wus huntin' his people; and dat he had lost all he had. Dey give him somethin' to eat and tobacco to chew, and he went on. Soon we heard he wus in de White House then we knew who it wus come through. We knowed den it wus Abraham Lincoln.

We children stole eggs and sold 'em durin' slavery. Some of de white men bought 'em. They were Irishmen and they would not tell on us. Their names were Mulligan, Flanagan and Dugan. They wore good clothes and were funny mens. They called guns flutes.

Boss tole us Abraham Lincoln wus dead and we were still slaves. Our boss man bought black cloth and made us wear it for mourning for Abraham Lincoln and tole us that there would not be freedom. We stayed there another year after freedom. A lot o' de niggers knowed nothin' 'cept what missus and marster tole us. What dey said wus just de same as de Lawd had spoken to us.

Just after de surrender a nigger woman who wus bad, wus choppin' cotton at out plantation in Georgie. John Woodfox wus de main overseer and his son-in-law wus a overseer. Dey had a colored man who dey called a nigger driver. De nigger driver tole de overseer de woman wus bad. De overseer came to her, snatched de hoe from her and hit her. The blow killed her. He was reported to de Freedman's Bureau. Dey came, whupped de overseer and put him in jail. Dey decided not to kill him, but made him furnish de children of de dead woman so much to live on. Dere wus a hundred or more niggers in de field when this murder happened.

We finally found out we were free and left. Dey let me stay with Miss Julia Brown. I was hired to her. She lived in Dooley County, Georgia. I next worked with Mrs. Dunbar after staying with Mrs. Brown four years. Her name wus Mrs. Winnie Dunbar and she moved to Columbia, South Carolina takin' me with her. I stayed with her about four years. This wus the end of my maiden life. I married Isaac Austin of Richmond County, Georgia. He wus a native of Warrenton County and he brought me from his home in Richmond County, Georgia to Warrenton and then from Warrenton to Raleigh. I had two brothers and thirteen sisters. I did general house work, and helped raise children during slavery, and right after de war. Then you had to depend on yourself to do for children. You had to doctor and care for them yourself. You just had to depend on yourself.

Dey had 320 acres o' cleared fields in Georgia and then de rice fields, I just don't know how many acres. I have seen jails for slaves. Dey had a basement for a jail in Georgia and a guard at de holes in it.

No, No! you better not be caught tryin' to do somethin' wid a book. Dey would teach you wid a stick or switch. De slaves had secret prayer meetin's wid pots turned down to kill de soun' o' de singin'. We sang a song, 'I am glad salvation's free.' Once dey heard us, nex' mornin' dey took us and tore our backs to pieces. Dey would say, 'Are you free? What were you singin' about freedom?' While de niggers were bein' whupped they said, 'Pray, marster, pray.'

The doctor came to see us sometimes when we were sick, but not after. People just had to do their own doctorin'. Sometimes a man would take his patient, and sit by de road where de doctor travelled, and when he come along he would see him. De doctor rode in a sully drawn by a horse. He had a route, one doctor to two territories.

When de white folks were preparing to go to de war they had big dinners and speakin'. Dey tole what dey were goin' to do to Sherman and Grant. A lot of such men as Grant and Sherman and Lincoln came through de South in rags and were at some o' dese meetings, an' et de dinners. When de white folks foun' it out, dere wus some sick folks. Sometimes we got two days Christmas and two days July. When de nigger wus freed dey didn't know where to go and what to do. It wus hard, but it has been hard since. From what de white folks, marster and missus tole us we thought Lincoln wus terrible. By what mother and father tole me I thought he wus all right. I think Roosevelt wus put in by God to do the right things.

EH

N.C. District:	No. 2
Worker:	Mary A. Hicks
No. Words:	367
Subject:	BLOUNT BAKER
Person Interviewed:	Blount Baker
Editor:	G. L. Andrews
Date Stamp:	"SEP 10 1937"

BLOUNT BAKER

Yes'um, I 'longed ter Marse Henry Allen of Wilson County an' we always raise terbacker. Marse Henry wus good ter us so we had a heap of prayer meetin's an' corn shuckin's an' such.

I 'members de big meetin's dat we'd have in de summer time an' dat good singin' we'd have when we'd be singin' de sinners through. We'd stay pretty nigh all night to make a sinner come through, an' maybe de week atter de meetin' he'd steal one of his marster's hogs. Yes'um, I'se had a bad time.

You know, missy, dar ain't no use puttin' faith in nobody, dey'd fool you ever time anyhow. I know once a patteroller tol' me dat iffen I'd give him a belt I found dat he'd let me go by ter see my gal dat night, but when he kotch me dat night he whupped me. I tol' Marse Henry on him too so Marse Henry takes de belt away from him an' gives me a possum fer hit. Dat possum shore wus good too, baked in de ashes like I done it.

I ain't never hear Marse Henry cuss but once an' dat wus de time dat some gentlemens come ter de house an' sez dat dar am a war 'twixt de north an' de south. He sez den, 'Let de damn yaller bellied Yankees come on an' we'll give 'em hell an' sen' dem a-hoppin' back ter de north in a hurry.'

We ain't seed no Yankees 'cept a few huntin' Rebs. Dey talk mean ter us an' one of dem says dat we niggers am de cause of de war. 'Sir,' I sez, 'folks what am a wantin' a war can always find a cause'. He kicks me in de seat of de pants fer dat, so I hushes.

I stayed wid Marse Henry till he died den I moved ter Wilson. I has worked everwhere, terbacker warehouses an' ever'thing. I'se gittin' of my ole age pension right away an' den de county won't have ter support me no mo', dat is if dey have been supportin' me on three dollars a month.

LE

N.C. District:	No. 2
Worker:	T. Pat Matthews
No. Words:	745
Subject:	LIZZIE BAKER
Person Interviewed:	Lizzie Baker
Editor:	Daisy Bailey Waitt

LIZZIE BAKER

I was born de las' year o' de surrender an'course I don't remember seein' any Yankee soldiers, but I knows a plenty my mother and father tole me. I have neuritis, an' have been unable to work any fer a year and fer seven years I couldn't do much.

My mother wus named Teeny McIntire and my father William McIntire. Mammy belonged to Bryant Newkirk in Duplin County. Pap belonged to someone else, I don't know who.

Dey said dey worked from light till dark, and pap said dey beat him so bad he run away a lot o' times. Dey said de paterollers come to whare dey wus havin' prayer meetin' and beat 'em.

Mammy said sometimes dey were fed well and others dey almost starved. Dey got biscuit once a week on Sunday. Dey said dey went to de white folks's church. Dey said de preachers tole 'em dey had to obey dere missus and marster. My mammy said she didn't go to no dances 'cause she wus crippled. Some o' de help, a colored woman, stole something when she wus hongry. She put it off on mother and missus made mother wear trousers for a year to punish her.

Mammy said dey gave de slaves on de plantation one day Christmas and dat New Years wus when dey sold 'em an' hired 'em out. All de slaves wus scared 'cause dey didn't know who would have to go off to be sold or to work in a strange place. Pap tole me 'bout livin' in de woods and 'bout dey ketchin' him. I 'member his owner's name den, it wus Stanley. He run away so bad dey sold him several times. Pap said one time dey caught him and nearly beat him to death, and jest as soon as he got well and got a good chance he ran away again.

Mammy said when de Yankees come through she wus 'fraid of 'em. De Yankees tole her not to be 'fraid of 'em. Dey say to her, 'Do dey treat you right', Mammy said 'Yes sir', 'cause ole missus wus standin' dere, an' she wus 'fraid not to say yes. Atter de war, de fust year atter de surrender dey moved to James Alderman's place in Duplin County and stayed dere till I wus a grown gal.

Den we moved to Goldsboro. Father wus a carpenter and he got a lot of dat work. Dat's what he done in Goldsboro. We come from Goldsboro to Raleigh and we have lived here every since. We moved here about de year o' de shake and my mother died right here in Raleigh de year o' de shake. Some of de things mother tole me 'bout slavery, has gone right out of my min'. Jes comes and goes.

I remember pap tellin' me' bout stretchin' vines

acrost roads and paths to knock de patterollers off deir horses when dey were tryin' to ketch slaves. Pap and mammy tole me marster and missus did not 'low any of de slaves to have a book in deir house. Dat if dey caught a slave wid a book in deir house dey whupped 'em. Dey were keerful not to let 'em learn readin' and writin'.

Dey sold my sister Lucy and my brother Fred in slavery time, an' I have never seen 'em in my life. Mother would cry when she was tellin' me 'bout it. She never seen 'em anymore. I jes' couldn't bear to hear her tell it widout cryin'. Dey were carried to Richmond, an' sold by old marster when dey were chillun.

We tried to get some news of brother and sister. Mother kept 'quiring 'bout 'em as long as she lived and I have hoped dat I could hear from 'em. Dey are dead long ago I recons, and I guess dare aint no use ever expectin' to see 'em. Slavery wus bad and Mr. Lincoln did a good thing when he freed de niggers. I caint express my love for Roosevelt. He has saved so many lives. I think he has saved mine. I want to see him face to face. I purely love him and I feel I could do better to see him and tell him so face to face.

LE

N.C. District:	No. 2
Worker:	Mary A. Hicks
No. Words:	339
Subject:	VINEY BAKER
Person Interviewed:	Viney Baker
Editor:	Daisy Bailey Waitt

VINEY BAKER

My mammy wuz Hannah Murry an' so fur as I know I ain't got no father, do' I reckon dat he wuz de plantation stock nigger. I wuz borned in Virginia as yo' mought say ter my marster Mr. S. L. Allen.

We moved when I wuz little ter Durham County whar we fared bad. We ain't had nothin' much ter eat an' ter w'ar. He had a hundert slaves an' I reckon five hundert acres o' lan'. He made us wuck hard, de little ones included.

One night I lay down on de straw mattress wid my

mammy, an' de nex' mo'nin' I woked up an' she wuz gone. When I axed 'bout her I fin's dat a speculator comed dar de night before an' wanted ter buy a 'oman. Dey had come an' got my mammy widout wakin' me up. I has always been glad somehow dat I wuz asleep.

Dey uster tie me ter a tree an' beat me till de blood run down my back, I doan 'member nothin' dat I done, I jist 'members de whuppin's. Some of de rest wuz beat wuser dan I wuz too, an' I uster scream dat I wuz sho' dyin'.

Yes'um I seed de Yankees go by, but dey ain't bodder us none, case dey knows dat 'hind eber' bush jist about a Confederate soldier pints a gun.

I warn't glad at de surrender, case I doan understand hit, an' de Allen's keeps me right on, an' whups me wuser den dan eber.

I reckon I wuz twelve years old when my mammy come ter de house an' axes Mis' Allen ter let me go spen' de week en' wid her. Mis' Allen can't say no, case Mammy mought go ter de carpet baggers so she lets me go fer de week-en'. Mammy laughs Sunday when I says somethin' 'bout goin' back. Naw, I stayed on wid my mammy, an' I ain't seed Mis' Allen no mo'.

AC

N.C. District:	No. 2
Worker:	Mary A. Hicks
No. Words:	733
Subject:	EX-SLAVE STORY
Person Interviewed:	Charlie Barbour
Editor:	Daisy Bailey Waitt
Date Stamp:	"JUN 7 1937"

A (circled)

CHARLIE BARBOUR

I belonged ter Mr. Bob Lumsford hyar in Smithfield from de time of my birth. My mammy wuz named Candice an' my pappy's name wuz Seth. My brothers wuz Rufus, William an' George, an' my sisters wuz Mary an' Laura.

I 'minds me of de days when as a youngin' I played marbles an' hide an' seek. Dar wuzn't many games den, case nobody ain't had no time fer 'em. De grown folkses had dances an' sometimes co'n shuckin's, an' de little niggers patted dere feets at de dances an' dey he'p ter shuck de co'n. At Christmas we had a big dinner, an' from den through New Year's Day we feast, an' we dance, an' we sing. De fust one what said Christmas gift ter anybody else got a gif', so of cou'se we all try ter ketch de marster.

On de night 'fore de first day of Jinuary we had a dance what lasts all night. At midnight when de New Year comes in marster makes a speech an' we is happy dat he thanks us fer our year's wuck an' says dat we is good, smart slaves.

Marster wucked his niggers from daylight till dark, an' his thirteen grown slaves had ter ten' 'bout three hundred acres o' land. Course dey mostly planted co'n, peas an' vege'ables.

I can 'member, do' I wuz small, dat de slaves wuz whupped fer disobeyin' an' I can think of seberal dat I got. I wuz doin' housewuck at de time an' one of de silber knives got misplaced. Dey 'cused me of misplacin' it on purpose, so I got de wust beatin' dat I eber had. I wuz beat den till de hide wuz busted hyar an' dar.

We little ones had some time ter go swimmin' an' we did; we also fished, an' at night we hunted de possum an' de coon sometimes. Ole Uncle Jeems had some houn's what would run possums or coons an' he uster take we boys 'long wid him.

I 'members onct de houn's struck a trail an' dey tree de coon. Uncle Jeems sen's Joe, who wuz bigger den I wuz, up de tree ter ketch de coon an' he warns him dat coons am fightin' fellers. Joe doan pay much mind he am so happy ter git der chanct ter ketch de coon, but when he ketched dat coon he couldn't turn loose, an' from de way he holler yo' would s'pose dat he ain't neber wanted ter ketch a coon. When Joe Barbour wuz buried hyar las' winter dem coon marks wuz still strong on his arms an' han's an' dar wuz de long scar on his face.

I 'members onct a Yankee 'oman from New York looks at him an' nigh 'bout faints. 'I reckon', says she, dat am what de cruel slave owner or driver done ter him'.

Yes mam, I knows when de Yankees comed ter Smithfield. Dey comed wid de beatin' of drums an' de wavin' of flags. Dey says dat our governor wuz hyar makin' a speech but he flewed 'fore dey got hyar. Anyhow, we libed off from de main path of march, an' so we ain't been trouble so much 'cept by 'scootin' parties, as my ole missus call' em.

Dey am de darndest yo' eber seed, dey won't eat no hog meat 'cept hams an' shoulders an' dey goes ter de smoke house an' gits 'em 'thout no permission. Dey has what dey calls rammin' rods ter dere guns an' dey knock de chickens in de haid wid dat. I hyard dem say dat dar warn't no use wastin' powder on dem chickens.

Dey went ober de neighborhood stealin' an' killin' stock. I hyard 'bout 'em ketchin' a pig, cuttin' off his hams an' leave him dar alive. De foun' all de things we done hid, not dat I thinks dat dey am witches, but dat dey has a money rod, an' 'cides dat some of de slaves tol' 'em whar marster had hid de things.

Yes 'um, I reckon I wuz glad ter git free, case I knows den dat I won't wake up some mornin' ter fin' dat my mammy or some ob de rest of my family am done sold. I left de day I hyard 'bout de surrender an' I fared right good too, do' I knows dem what ain't farin' so well.

I ain't neber learn ter read an' write an' I knows now dat I neber will. I can't eben write a letter ter Raleigh 'bout my ole man's pension.

I 'members de days when mammy wored a blue hankerchief 'round her haid an' cooked in de great house. She'd sometimes sneak me a cookie or a cobbler an' fruits. She had her own little gyardin an' a few chickens an' we w'oud ov been happy 'cept dat we wuz skeered o' bein' sold.

I'se glad dat slavery am ober, case now de nigger has got a chanct ter live an' larn wid de whites. Dey won't neber be as good as de whites but dey can larn ter live an' enjoy life more.

Speakin' 'bout de Ku Klux dey ain't do nothin' but scare me back in '69, but iffen we had some now I thinks dat some of dese young niggers what has forgot what dey mammies tol' 'em would do better.

MH:EH

N.C. District:	No. 2
Worker:	Mary A. Hicks
No. Words:	678
Subject:	MARY BARBOUR
Person Interviewed:	Mary Barbour
Editor:	Daisy Bailey Waitt

MARY BARBOUR

I reckon dat I wuz borned in McDowell County, case dat's whar my mammy, Edith, lived. She 'longed ter Mr. Jefferson Mitchel dar, an' my pappy 'longed ter er Mr. Jordan in Avery County, so he said.

'Fore de war, I doan know nothin' much 'cept dat we lived on a big plantation an' dat my mammy wucked hard, but wuz treated pretty good.

We had our little log cabin off ter one side, an' my mammy had sixteen chilluns. Fas' as dey got three years old de marster sol' 'em till we las' four dat she had wid her durin' de war. I wuz de oldes' o' dese four; den dar wuz Henry an' den de twins, Liza an' Charlie.

One of de fust things dat I 'members wuz my pappy wakin' me up in de middle o' de night, dressin' me in de dark, all de time tellin' me ter keep quiet. One o' de twins hollered some an' pappy put his hand ober its mouth ter keep it quiet.

Atter we wuz dressed he went outside an' peeped roun' fer a minute den he comed back an' got us. We snook out o' de house an' long de woods path, pappy totin' one of de twins an' holdin' me by de han' an' mammy carryin' de udder two.

I reckons dat I will always 'member dat walk, wid de bushes slappin' my laigs, de win' sighin' in de trees, an' de hoot owls an' whippoorwills hollerin' at each other frum de big trees. I wuz half asleep an' skeered stiff, but in a little while we pass de plum' thicket an' dar am de mules an' wagin.

Dar am er quilt in de bottom o' de wagin, an' on dis dey lays we youngins. An' pappy an' mammy gits on de board cross de front an' drives off down de road.

I wuz sleepy but I wuz skeered too, so as we rides 'long I lis'ens ter pappy an' mammy talk. Pappy wuz tellin' mammy 'bout de Yankees comin' ter dere plantation, burnin' de co'n cribs, de smokehouses an' 'stroyin' eber'thing. He says right low dat dey done took marster Jordan ter de Rip Raps down nigh Norfolk, an' dat he stol' de mules an' wagin an' 'scaped.

We wuz skeerd of de Yankees ter start wid, but de more we thinks 'bout us runnin' way frum our marsters de skeerder we gits o' de Rebs. Anyhow pappy says dat we is goin' ter jine de Yankees.

We trabels all night an' hid in de woods all day fer a long time, but atter awhile we gits ter Doctor Dillard's place, in Chowan County. I reckons dat we stays dar seberal days.

De Yankees has tooked dis place so we stops ober, an'

has a heap o' fun dancin' an' sich while we am dar. De Yankees tells pappy ter head fer New Bern an' dat he will be took keer of dar, so ter New Bern we goes.

When we gits ter New Bern de Yankees takes de mules an' wagin, dey tells pappy something, an' he puts us on a long white boat named Ocean Waves an' ter Roanoke we goes.

Later I larns dat most o' de reffes[2] is put in James City, nigh New Bern, but dar am a pretty good crowd on Roanoke. Dar wuz also a ole Indian Witch 'oman dat I 'members.

Atter a few days dar de Ocean Waves comes back an' takes all ober ter New Bern. My pappy wuz a shoemaker, so he makes Yankee boots, an' we gits 'long pretty good.

I wuz raised in New Bern an' I lived dar till forty years ago when me an' my husban' moved ter Raleigh an' do' he's been daid a long time I has lived hyar ober since an' eben if'en I is eighty-one years old I can still outwuck my daughter an' de rest of dese young niggers.

[2] refugees

N.C. District:	No. 2
Worker:	Mary A. Hicks
No. Words:	927
Subject:	Plantation Times
Person Interviewed:	Alice Baugh
Editor:	Daisy Bailey Waitt
Date Stamp:	"JUN 1 1937"

PLANTATION TIMES

My mammy Ferbie, an' her brother Darson belonged ter Mr. David Hinnant in Edgecombe County till young Marster Charlie got married. Den dey wuz drawed an' sent wid him down hyar ter Wendell. De ole Hinnant home am still standin' dar ter dis day.

Marster Charlie an' Missus Mary wuz good ter de hundred slaves what belonged ter' em. Dey gib 'em good houses, good feed, good clothes an' plenty uv fun. Dey had dere co'n shuckin's, dere barn dances, prayer meetin's an' sich like all de year, an' from Christmas till de second day o' January dey had a holiday wid roast oxes, pigs, turkey an' all de rest o' de fixin's. From Saturday till Monday de slaves wuz off an' dey had dere Sunday clothes, which wuz nice. De marster always gib 'em a paper so's de patterollers won't git 'em.

Dey went up de riber to other plantations ter dances an' all dem things, an' dey wuz awful fond uv singin' songs. Dat's whut dey done atter dey comes ter dere cabins at de end o' de day. De grown folkses sings an' somebody pickin' de banjo. De favorite song wuz 'Swing Low Sweet Chariot' an' 'Play on yo' Harp Little David'. De chilluns uster play Hide an' Seek, an' Leap Frog, an' ever'body wuz happy.

Dey had time off ter hunt an' fish an' dey had dere own chickens, pigs, watermillons an' gyardens. De fruits from de big orchard an' de honey from de hives wuz et at home, an' de slave et as good as his marster et. Dey had a whole heap o' bee hives an' my mammy said dat she had ter tell dem bees when Mis' Mary died. She said how she wuz cryin' so hard dat she can't hardly tell 'em, an' dat dey hum lak dey am mo'nin' too.

My mammy marry my pappy dar an' she sez dat de preacher from de Methodis' Church marry 'em, dat she w'ar Miss Mary's weddin' dress, all uv white lace, an' dat my pappy w'ar Mr. Charlie's weddin' suit wid a flower in de button hole. Dey gived a big dance atter de supper dey had, an' Marster Charlie dance de first set wid my mammy.

I jist thought of a tale what I hyard my mammy tell 'bout de Issue Frees of Edgecombe County when she wuz a little gal. She said dat de Issue Frees wuz mixed wid de white folks, an' uv cou'se dat make 'em free. Sometimes dey stay on de plantation, but a whole heap uv dem, long wid niggers who had done runned away from dere marster, dugged caves in de woods, an' dar dey lived an' raised dere families dar. Dey ain't wored much clothes an' what dey got to eat an' to w'ar dey swiped from de white folkses. Mammy said dat she uster go ter de spring fer water, an' dem ole Issue Frees up in de woods would yell at her, 'Doan yo' muddy dat spring, little gal'. Dat scared her moughty bad.

Dem Issue Frees till dis day shows both bloods. De white folkses won't have 'em an' de niggers doan want 'em but will have ter have 'em anyhow.

My uncle wuz raised in a cave an' lived on stold stuff an' berries. My cousin runned away 'cause his marster wuz mean ter him, but dey put de blood hounds on his trail, ketched him. Atter he got well from de beatin' dey gib him, dey sold him.

I'se hyard ole lady Prissie Jones who died at de age of 103 las' winter tell 'bout marsters dat when dere slaves runned away dey'd set de bloodhounds on dere trail an' when dey ketched 'em dey'd cut dere haids off wid de swords.

Ole lady Prissie tole 'bout slaves what ain't had nothin' ter eat an' no clothes 'cept a little strip uv homespun, but my mammy who died four months ago at de age 106 said dat she ain't knowed nothin' 'bout such doin's.

When de Yankees come, dey come a burnin' an' a-stealin' an' Marster Charlie carried his val'ables ter mammy's cabin, but dey found 'em. Dey had a money rod an' dey'd find all de stuff no matter whar it wuz. Mammy said dat all de slaves cried when de Yankees come, an' dat most uv 'em stayed on a long time atter de war. My mammy plowed an' done such work all de time uv slavery, but she done it case she wanted to do it an' not 'cause dey make her.

All de slaves hate de Yankees an' when de southern soldiers comed by late in de night all de niggers got out of de bed an' holdin' torches high dey march behin' de soldiers, all of dem singin', 'We'll Hang Abe Lincoln on de Sour Apple Tree.' Yes mam, dey wuz sorry dat dey wuz free, an' dey ain't got no reason to be glad, case dey wuz happier den dan now.

I'se hyard mammy tell 'bout how de niggers would sing as dey picked de cotton, but yo' ain't hyard none uv dat now. Den dey ain't had to worry 'bout nothin'; now dey has ter study so much dat dey ain't happy nuff ter sing no mo'.

"Does yo' know de cause of de war?" Aunt Alice went to a cupboard and returned holding out a book. "Well hyar's de cause, dis Uncle Tom's Cabin wuz de cause of it all; an' its' de biggest lie what ever been gived ter de public."

N.C. District:	No. 2
Worker:	Mary A. Hicks
No. Words:	341
Subject:	WHEN THE YANKEES CAME
Person Interviewed:	John Beckwith
Editor:	Daisy Bailey Waitt

JOHN BECKWITH

I reckon dat I wuz 'bout nine years old at de surrender, but we warn't happy an' we stayed on dar till my parents died. My pappy wuz named Green an' my mammy wuz named Molly, an' we belonged ter Mr. Joe Edwards, Mr. Marion Gully, an' Mr. Hilliard Beckwith, as de missus married all of 'em. Dar wuz twenty-one other slaves, an' we got beat ever' onct in a while.

When dey told us dat de Yankees wuz comin' we wuz also told dat iffen we didn't behave dat we'd be shot; an' we believed it. We would'uv behaved anyhow, case we had good plank houses, good food, an' shoes. We had Saturday an' Sunday off an' we wuz happy.

De missus, she raised de nigger babies so's de mammies could wuck. I 'members de times when she rock me ter sleep an' put me ter bed in her own bed. I wuz happy den as I thinks back of it, until dem Yankees come.

Dey come on a Chuesday; an' dey started by burnin' de cotton house an' killin' most of de chickens an' pigs. Way atter awhile dey fin's de cellar an' dey drinks brandy till dey gits wobbly in de legs. Atter dat dey comes up on de front porch an' calls my missus. When she comes ter de do' dey tells her dat dey am goin' in de house ter look things over. My missus dejicts, case ole marster am away at de war, but dat doan do no good. Dey cusses her scan'lous an' dey dares her ter speak. Dey robs de house, takin' dere knives an' splittin' mattresses, pillows an' ever' thing open lookin' fer valerables, an' ole missus dasen't open her mouth.

Dey camped dar in de grove fer two days, de officers takin' de house an' missus leavin' home an' goin' ter de neighbor's house. Dey make me stay dar in de house wid 'em ter tote dere brandy frum de cellar, an' ter make 'em some mint jelup. Well, on de secon' night dar come de wust storm I'se eber seed. De lightnin' flash, de thunder roll, an' de house shook an' rattle lak a earthquake had struck it.

Dem Yankees warn't supposed ter be superstitious, but lemmie tell yo', dey wuz some skeered dat night; an' I hyard a Captain say dat de witches wuz abroad. Atter awhile lightnin' struck de Catawba tree dar at de side of de house an' de soldiers camped round about dat way marched off ter de barns, slave cabins an' other places whar dey wuz safter dan at dat place. De next mornin' dem Yankees moved frum dar an' dey ain't come back fer nothin'.

We wuzn't happy at de surrender an' we cussed ole Abraham Lincoln all ober de place. We wuz told de disadvantages of not havin' no edercation, but shucks, we doan need no book larnin' wid ole marster ter look atter us.

My mammy an' pappy stayed on dar de rest of dere lives, an' I stayed till I wuz sixteen. De Ku Klux Klan got atter me den' bout fightin' wid a white boy. Dat night I slipped in de woods an' de nex' day I went ter Raleigh. I got a job dar an' eber' since den I'se wucked fer myself, but now I can't wuck an' I wish dat yo' would apply fer my ole aged pension fer me.

I went back ter de ole plantation long as my pappy, mammy, an' de marster an' missus lived. Sometimes, when I gits de chanct I goes back now. Course now de slave cabins am gone, ever' body am dead, an' dar ain't nothin' familiar 'cept de bent Catawba tree; but it 'minds me of de happy days.

N.C. District: No. 2
Worker: T. Pat Matthews
No. Words: 1,566
Subject: JOHN C. BECTOM
Story Teller: John C. Bectom
Editor: Daisy Bailey Waitt
Date Stamp: "JUN 1 1937"
N. C.

JOHN C. BECTOM

My name is John C. Bectom. I was born Oct. 7, 1862, near Fayetteville, Cumberland County, North Carolina. My father's name was Simon Bectom. He was 86 years of age when he died. He died in 1910 at Fayetteville, N. C. My mother's name was Harriet Bectom. She died in 1907, May 23, when she was seventy years old. My brother's were named Ed, Kato and Willie. I was third of the boys. My sisters were Lucy, Anne and Alice. My father first belonged to Robert Wooten of Craven County, N. C. Then he was sold by the Wootens to the Bectoms of Wayne County, near Goldsboro, the county seat. My mother first belonged to the McNeills of Cumberland County. Miss Mary McNeill married a McFadden, and her parents gave my mother to Mis' Mary. Mis' Mary's daughter in time married Ezekial King and my mother was then given to her by Mis' Mary McFadden, her mother. Mis' Lizzie McFadden became a King. My grandmother was named

Lucy Murphy. She belonged to the Murpheys. All the slaves were given off to the children of the family as they married.

My father and mother told me stories of how they were treated at different places. When my grandmother was with the Murpheys they would make her get up, and begin burning logs in new grounds before daybreak. They also made her plow, the same as any of the men on the plantation. They plowed till dusk-dark before they left the fields to come to the house. They were not allowed to attend any dances or parties unless they slipped off unknowin's. They had candy pullings sometimes too. While they would be there the patterollers would visit them. Sometimes the patterollers whipped all they caught at this place, all they set their hands on, unless they had a pass.

They fed us mighty good. The food was well cooked. They gave the slaves an acre of ground to plant and they could sell the crop and have the money. The work on this acre was done on moonshiny nights and holidays. Sometimes slaves would steal the marster's chickens or a hog and slip off to another plantation and have it cooked. We had plenty of clothes, and one pair o' shoes a year. You had to take care of them because you only got one pair a year. They were given at Christmas every year. The clothes were made on the plantation.

There were corn mills on the plantation, and rice mills, and threshing machines. The plantation had about 300 acres in farm land. The enclosure was three miles. My marster lived in a fine house. It took a year to build it. There were about 16 rooms in it. We slaves called it the great house. Some of the slaves ran away and finally reached Ohio. There was no jail on the plantation. Sometimes the overseer would whip us.

The Kings had no overseers. King beat his slaves with a stick. I remember seeing him do this as well as I can see that house over there. He became blind. An owl scratched him in the face when he was trying to catch him, and his face got into sich a fix he went to Philadelphia for treatment, but they could not cure him. He finally went blind. I have seen him beat his slaves after he was blind. I remember it well. He beat 'em with a stick. He was the most sensitive man you ever seed. He ran a store. After he was blind you could han' him a piece of money and he could tell you what it was.

There were no churches on the plantation but prayer meeting' were held in the quarters. Slaves were not allowed to go to the white folk's church unless they were coach drivers, etc. No sir, not in that community. They taught the slaves the Bible. The children of the marster would go to private school. We small Negro children looked after the babies in the cradles and other young children. When the white children studied their lessons I studied with them. When they wrote in the sand I wrote in the sand too. The white children, and not the marster or mistress, is where I got started in learnin' to read and write.

We had corn shuckings, candy pullings, dances, prayer meetings. We went to camp meetin' on Camp Meeting days in August when the crops were laid by. We played games of high jump, jumping over the pole held by two people, wrestling, leap frog, and jumping. We sang the songs, 'Go tell Aunt Patsy'. 'Some folks says a nigger wont steal, I caught six in my corn field' 'Run nigger run, the patteroller ketch you, Run nigger run like you did the other day'.

When slaves got sick marster looked after them. He gave them blue mass and caster oil. Dr. McDuffy also treated us. Dr. McSwain vaccinated us for small pox. My sister died with it. When the slaves died marster buried them. They dug a grave with a tomb in it. I do not see any of them now. The slaves were buried in a plain box.

The marsters married the slaves without any papers. All they did was to say perhaps to Jane and Frank, 'Frank, I pronounce you and Jane man and wife.' But the woman did not take the name of her husband, she kept the name of the family who owned her.

I remember seeing the Yankees near Fayetteville. They shot a bomb shell at Wheeler's Calvary, and it hit near me and buried in the ground. Wheeler's Calvary came first and ramsaked the place. They got all the valuables they could, and burned the bridge, the covered bridge over Cape Fear river, but when the Yankees got there they had a pontoon bridge to cross on,—all those provision wagons and such. When they passed our place it was in the morning. They nearly scared me to death. They passed right by our door, Sherman's army. They began passing, so the white folks said, at 9 o'clock in the mornin'. At 9 o'clock at night they were passin' our door on foot. They said there were two hundred and fifty thousan' o' them passed. Some camped in my marster's old fiel'. A Yankee caught one of my marster's shoats and cut off one of the hind quarters, gave it to me, and told me to carry and give it to my mother. I was so small I could not tote it, so I drug it to her. I called her when I got in hollering distance of the house and she came and got it. The Yankees called us Johnnie, Dinah, Bill and other funny names. They beat their drums and sang songs. One of the Yankees sang 'Rock a Bye Baby'. At that time Jeff Davis money was plentiful. My mother had about $1000. It was so plentiful it was called Jeff Davis shucks. My mother had bought a pair of shoes, and had put them in a chest. A Yankee came and took the shoes and wore them off, leaving his in their place. They tol' us we were free. Sometimes the marster would get cruel to the slaves if they acted like they were free.

Mat Holmes, a slave, was wearing a ball and chain as a punishment for running away. Marster Ezekial King put it on him. He has slept in the bed with me, wearing that ball and chain. The cuff had embedded in his leg, it was swollen so. This was right after the Yankees came through. It was March, the 9th of March, when the Yankees came through. Mat Holmes had run away with the ball and chain on him and was in the woods then. He hid out staying with us at night until August. Then my mother took him to the Yankee garrison at Fayetteville. A Yankee officer then took him to a black smith shop and had the ball and chain cut off his leg. The marsters would tell the slaves to go to work that they were not free, that they still belonged to them, but one would drop out and leave, then another. There was little work done on the farm, and finally most of the slaves learned they were free.

Abraham Lincoln was one of the greatest men that ever lived. He was the cause of us slaves being free. No doubt about that. I didn't think anything of Jeff Davis. He tried to keep us in slavery. I think slavery was an injustice, not right. Our privilege is to live right, and live according to the teachings of the Bible, to treat our fellowman right. To do this I feel we should belong to some religious organization and live as near right as we know how.

The overseers and patterollers in the time of slavery were called poor white trash by the slaves.

On the plantations not every one, but some of the slave holders would have some certain slave women reserved for their own use. Sometimes children almost white would be born to them. I have seen many of these children. Sometimes the child would be said to belong to the overseer, and sometimes it would be said to belong to the marster.

N.C. District:	No. 2
Worker:	Mary A. Hicks
No. Words:	610
Subject:	AUNT LAURA
Story Teller:	LAURA BELL
Editor:	Geo. L. Andrews
Date Stamp:	"AUG 6 1937"

LAURA BELL

• An interview with Laura Bell, 73 years old, of 2 Bragg Street, Raleigh, North Carolina.

Being informed that Laura Bell was an old slavery Negro, I went immediately to the little two-room shack with its fallen roof and shaky steps. As I approached the shack I noticed that the storm had done great damage to the chaney-berry tree in her yard, fallen limbs litterin' the ground, which was an inch deep in garbage and water.

The porch was littered with old planks and huge tubs and barrels of stagnant water. There was only room for one chair and in that sat a tall Negro woman clad in burlap bags and in her lap she held a small white flea-bitten dog which growled meaningly.

When I reached the gate, which swings on one rusty hinge, she bade me come in and the Carolina Power and Light Company men, who were at work nearby, laughed as I climbed over the limbs and garbage and finally found room for one foot on the porch and one on the ground.

"I wus borned in Mount Airy de year 'fore de Yankees come, bein' de fourth of five chilluns. My mammy an' daddy Minerva Jane an' Wesley 'longed ter Mr. Mack Strickland an' we lived on his big place near Mount Airy."

"Mr. Mack wus good ter us, dey said. He give us enough ter eat an' plenty of time ter weave clothes fer us ter wear. I've hearn mammy tell of de corn shuckin's an' dances dey had an' 'bout some whuppin's too."

"Marse Mack's overseer, I doan know his name, wus gwine ter whup my mammy onct, an' pappy do' he ain't neber make no love ter mammy comes up an' takes de whuppin' fer her. Atter dat dey cou'ts on Sadday an' Sunday an' at all de sociables till dey gits married."

"I'se hearn her tell' bout how he axed Marse Mack iffen he could cou't mammy an' atter Marse Mack sez he can he axes her ter marry him."

"She tells him dat she will an' he had 'em married by de preacher de nex' time he comes through dat country."

"I growed up on de farm an' when I wus twelve years old I met Thomas Bell. My folks said dat I wus too young fer ter keep company so I had ter meet him 'roun' an' about fer seberal years, I think till I wus fifteen."

"He axed me ter marry him while he wus down on de creek bank a fishin' an' I tol' him yes, but when he starts ter kiss me I tells him dat der's many a slip twixt de cup an' de lip an' so he has ter wait till we gits married."

"We runned away de nex' Sadday an' wus married by a Justice of de Peace in Mount Airy."

"Love ain't what hit uster be by a long shot," de ole woman reflected, "'Cause dar ain't many folks what loves all de time. We moved ter Raleigh forty years ago, an' Tom has been daid seberal years now. We had jest one chile but hit wus borned daid."

"Chilluns ain't raised ter be clean lak we wus. I knows dat de house ain't so clean but I doan feel so much lak doin' nothin', I jest went on a visit 'bout seben blocks up de street dis mo'nin' an' so I doan feel lak cleanin' up none."

I cut the interview short thereby missing more facts, as the odor was anything but pleasant and I was getting tired of standing in that one little spot.

"Thank you for comin'", she called, and her dog growled again.

N.C. District:	No. 2
Worker:	T. Pat Matthews
No. Words:	1153
Subject:	EMMA BLALOCK
Story Teller:	Emma Blalock
Editor:	Geo. L. Andrews
Date Stamp:	"AUG 6 1937"

EMMA BLALOCK

- **88 years old 529 Bannon Avenue Raleigh, N.C.**

I shore do 'member de Yankees wid dere blue uniforms wid brass buttons on 'em. I wus too small to work any but I played in de yard wid my oldes' sister, Katie. She is dead long ago. My mother belonged to ole man John Griffith an' I belonged to him. His plantation wus down here at Auburn in Wake County. My father wus named Edmund Rand. He belonged to Mr. Nat Rand. He lived in Auburn. De plantations wus not fur apart. Dere wus about twenty-five slaves on de plantation whur mother an' me stayed.

Marse John used ter take me on his knee an' sing, 'Here is de hammer, Shing ding. Gimme de Hammer, shing ding.' Marster loved de nigger chilluns on his plantation. When de war ended father come an' lived with us at Marse John's plantation. Marster John Griffith named me Emmy. My grandfather on my fathers side wus named Harden Rand, an' grandmother wus named Mason Rand. My grandfather on my mother's side wus named Antny Griffiths an' grandmother wus named Nellie.

Our food wus a plenty and well cooked. Marster fed his niggers good. We had plenty of homespun dresses and we got shoes once a year, at Christmas Eve. I ken 'member it just as good. We got Christmas Holidays an' a stockin' full of candy an' peanuts. Sometimes we got ginger snaps at Christmas. My grandmother cooked' em. She wus a good cook. My mother's missus wus Miss Jetsy Griffith and my father's missus wus Lucy Rand. Dey wus both mighty good women. You know I am ole. I ken 'member all dem good white folks. Dey give us Fourth July Holidays. Dey come to town on dat day. Dey wore, let me tell you what dey wore, dey wore dotted waist blouses an' white pants. Dat wus a big day to ever'body, de Fourth of July. Dey begun singing at Auburn an' sung till dey reached Raleigh. Auburn is nine miles from Raleigh. Dere wus a lot of lemonade. Dey made light bread in big ovens an' had cheese to eat wid it. Some said just goin' on de fofe to git lemonade an' cheese.

In the winter we had a lot of possums to eat an' a lot of rabbits too. At Christmas time de men hunted and caught plenty game. We barbecued it before de fire. I 'members seein' mother an' grandmother swinging rabbits 'fore de fire to cook 'em. Dey would turn an' turn 'em till dey wus done. Dey hung some up in de chimbly an' dry 'em out an' keep 'em a long time an' dat is de reason I won't eat a rabbit today. No Sir! I won't eat a rabbit. I seed 'em mess wid 'em so much turned me 'ginst eatin' 'em.

I don't know how much lan' Marster John owned but, Honey, dat wus some plantation. It reached from Auburn to de Neuse River. Yes Sir, it did, 'cause I been down dere in corn hillin' time an' we fished at twelve o'clock in Neuse River. Marster John had overseers. Dere wus six of 'em. Dey rode horses over de fields but I don't 'member dere names.

I never seen a slave whupped but dey wus whupped on de plantation an' I heard de grown folks talkin' 'bout it. My uncles Nat an' Bert Griffiths wus both whupped. Uncle Nat would not obey his missus rules an' she had him whupped. Dey whupped Uncle Bert 'cause he stayed drunk so much. He loved his licker an' he got drunk an' cut up bad, den dey whupped him. You could git plenty whiskey den. Twon't like it is now. No sir, it won't. Whiskey sold fur ten cents a quart. Most ever' body drank it but you hardly ever seed a man drunk. Slaves wus not whupped for drinkin'. Dere Marsters give 'em whiskey but dey wus whupped for gittin' drunk. Dere wus a jail, a kind of stockade built of logs, on de farm to put slaves in when dey wouldn't mind. I never say any slave put on de block an' sold, but I saw Aunt Helen Rand cryin' because her Marster Nat Rand sold her boy, Fab Rand.

No Sir, no readin' an' writin'. You had to work. Ha! ha! You let your marster or missus ketch you wid a book. Dat wus a strict rule dat no learnin' wus to be teached. I can't read an' write. If it wus not fur my mother wit don't know what would become of me. We had prayer meetings around at de slave houses. I 'member it well. We turned down pots on de inside of de house at de door to keep marster an' missus from hearin' de singin' an' prayin'. Marster an' his family lived in de great house an' de slave quarters wus 'bout two hundred yards away to the back of de great house. Dey wus arranged in rows. When de war ended we all stayed on wid de families Griffiths an' Rands till dey died, dat is all 'cept my father an' me. He lef' an' I lef'. I been in Raleigh forty-five years. I married Mack Blalock in Raleigh. He been dead seven years.

My mother had two boys, Antny an' Wesley. She had four girls, Katie, Grissie, Mary Ella an' Emma. I had three chilluns, two are livin' yet. They both live in Raleigh.

We had big suppers an' dinners at log rollin's an' corn shuckin's in slavery time ha! ha! plenty of corn licker for ever'body, both white an' black. Ever'body helped himself. Dr. Tom Busbee, one good ole white man, looked after us when we got sick, an' he could make you well purty quick, 'cause he wus good an' 'cause he wus sorry fer you. He wus a feelin' man. Course we took erbs. I tell you what I took. Scurrey grass, chana balls dey wus for worms. Scurrey grass worked you out. Dey give us winter green to clense our blood. We slaves an' a lot of de white folks drank sassafras tea in de place of coffee. We sweetened it wid brown sugar, honey, or molasses, just what we had in dat line. I think slavery wus a right good thing. Plenty to eat an' wear.

When you gits a tooth pulled now it costs two dollars, don't it? Well in slavery time I had a tooth botherin' me. My mother say, Emma, take dis egg an' go down to Doctor Busbee an' give it to him an' git your tooth pulled. I give him one egg. He took it an' pulled my tooth. Try dat now, if you wants to an' see what happens. Yes, slavery wus a purty good thing.

N.C. District:	No. 2
Worker:	Mary A. Hicks
No. Words:	1430
Subject:	Days on the Plantation
Person Interviewed:	Uncle David Blount
Editor:	Daisy Bailey Waitt
Date Stamp:	"JUN 1 1937"

HW notes

DAVID BLOUNT

As told by Uncle David Blount, formerly of Beaufort County, who did not know his age. "De Marster" he refers to was Major Wm. A. Blount, who owned plantations in several parts of North Carolina.

Yes mam, de days on de plantation wuz de happy days. De marster made us wuck through de week but on Sadays we uster go swimmin' in de riber an' do a lot of other things dat we lak ter do.

We didn't mind de wuck so much case de ground wuz soft as ashes an' de marster let us stop and rest when we got tired. We planted 'taters in de uplan's and co'n in de lowgroun's nex' de riber. It wuz on de Cape Fear an' on hot days when we wuz a-pullin' de fodder we'd all stop wuck 'bout three o'clock in de ebenin' an' go swimmin'. Atter we come out'n de water we would wuck harder dan eber an' de marster wuz good to us, case we did wuck an' we done what he ast us.

I 'members onct de marster had a oberseer dar dat wuz meaner dan a mean nigger. He always hired good oberseers an' a whole lot of times he let some Negro slave obersee. Well, dis oberseer beat some of de half grown boys till de blood run down ter dar heels an' he tole de rest of us dat if we told on him dat he'd kill us. We don't dasen't ast de marster ter git rid of de man so dis went on fer a long time.

It wuz cold as de debil one day an' dis oberseer had a gang of us a-clearin' new groun'. One boy ast if he could warm by de bresh heap. De oberseer said no, and atter awhile de boy had a chill. De oberseer don't care, but dat night de boy am a sick nigger. De nex' mornin' de marster gits de doctor, an' de doctor say dat de boy has got pneumonia. He tells 'em ter take off de boys shirt an' grease him wid some tar, turpentine, an' kerosene, an' when dey starts ter take de shirt off dey fin's dat it am stuck.

Dey had ter grease de shirt ter git it off case de blood whar de oberseer beat him had stuck de shirt tight ter de skin. De marster wuz in de room an' he axed de boy how come it, an' de boy tole him.

De marster sorta turns white an' he says ter me, 'Will yo' go an' ast de oberseer ter stop hyar a minute, please?'

When de oberseer comes up de steps he axes sorta sassy-like, 'What yo' want?'

De marster says, 'Pack yo' things an' git off'n my place as fast as yo' can, yo' pesky varmit.'

De oberseer sasses de marster some more, an' den I sees de marster fairly loose his temper for de first time. He don't say a word but he walks ober, grabs de oberseer by de shoulder, sets his boot right hard 'ginst de seat of his pants an' sen's him, all drawed up, out in de yard on his face. He close up lak a umbrella for a minute den he pulls hisself all tergether an' he limps out'n dat yard an' we ain't neber seed him no more.

No mam, dar wuzent no marryin' on de plantation dem days, an' as one ole 'oman raised all of de chilluns me an' my brother Johnnie ain't neber knowed who our folkses wuz. Johnnie wuz a little feller when de war ended, but I wuz in most of de things dat happen on de plantation fer a good while.

One time dar, I done fergit de year, some white mens comes down de riber on a boat an' dey comes inter de fiel's an' talks ter a gang of us an' dey says dat our masters ain't treatin' us right. Dey tells us dat we orter be paid fer our wuck, an' dat we hadn't ort ter hab passes ter go anywhar. Dey also tells us dat we ort ter be allowed ter tote guns if we wants 'em. Dey says too dat sometime our marsters was gwine ter kill us all.

I laughs at 'em, but some of dem fool niggers listens ter 'em; an' it 'pears dat dese men gib de niggers some guns atter I left an' promised ter bring 'em some more de nex' week.

I fin's out de nex' day 'bout dis an' I goes an' tells de marster. He sorta laughs an' scratches his head, 'Dem niggers am headed fer trouble, Dave, 'he says ter me, 'an I wants yo' ter help me.'

I says, 'Yas sar, marster.'

An' he goes on, 'Yo' fin's out when de rest of de guns comes Dave, an' let me know.'

When de men brings back de guns I tells de marster, an' I also tells him dat dey wants ter hold er meetin'.

'All right,' he says an' laughs, 'dey can have de meetin'. Yo' tell 'em, Dave, dat I said dat dey can meet on Chuesday night in de pack house.'

Chuesday ebenin' he sen's dem all off to de low groun's but me, an' he tells me ter nail up de shutters ter de pack house an' ter nail 'em up good.

I does lak he tells me ter do an' dat night de niggers marches in an' sneaks dar guns in too. I is lyin' up in de loft an' I hyars dem say dat atter de meetin' dey is gwine ter go up ter de big house an' kill de whole fambly.

I gits out of de winder an' I runs ter de house an tells de marster. Den me an' him an' de young marster goes out an' quick as lightnin', I slams de pack house door an' I locks it. Den de marster yells at dem, 'I'se got men an' guns out hyar, he yells, 'an' if yo' doan throw dem guns out of de hole up dar in de loft, an' throw dem ebery one out I'se gwine ter stick fire ter dat pack house.'

De niggers 'liberates for a few minutes an' den dey throws de guns out. I knows how many dey has got so I counts till dey throw dem all out, den I gathers up dem guns an' I totes 'em off ter de big house.

Well sar, we keeps dem niggers shet up fer about a week on short rations; an' at de end of dat time dem niggers am kyored for good. When dey comes out dey had three oberseers 'stid of one, an' de rules am stricter dan eber before; an' den de marster goes off ter de war.

I reckon I was 'bout fifteen or sixteen den; an' de marster car's me 'long fer his pusonal sarvant an' body guard an' he leabes de rest of dem niggers in de fiel's ter wuck like de dickens while I laughs at dem Yankees.

Jim belonged to Mr. Harley who lived in New Hanover County during de war, in fac' he was young Massa Harley's slave; so when young Massa Tom went to de war Jim went along too.

Dey wuz at Manassas, dey tells me, when Massa Tom got kilt, and de orders wuz not to take no bodies off de field right den.

Course ole massa down near Wilmington, doan know 'bout young Massa Tom, but one night dey hears Jim holler at de gate. Dey goes runnin' out; an' Jim has brung Massa Tom's body all dat long ways home so dat he can be buried in de family burian ground.

De massa frees Jim dat night; but he stays on a time atter de war, an' tell de day he died he hated de Yankees for killing Massa Tom. In fact we all hated de Yankees, 'specially atter we hear 'bout starve dat first winter. I tried ter make a libin' fer me an' Johnnie but it was bad goin'; den I comes ter Raleigh an' I gits 'long better. Atter I gits settled I brings Johnnie, an' so we done putty good.

Dat's all I can tell yo' now Miss, but if'n yo'll come back sometime I'll tell yo' de rest of de tales.

Shortly after the above interview Uncle Dave who was failing fast was taken to the County Home, where he died. He was buried on May 4th, 1937, the rest of the tale remaining untold.

N.C. District:	No. 2
Worker:	Mary A. Hicks
No. Words:	459
Subject:	Ex-Slave Story
Person Interviewed:	Clay Bobbit
Editor:	Daisy Bailey Waitt
Date Stamp:	"JUN 17 1937"

CLAY BOBBIT

I wuz borned May 2, 1837 in Warren County to Washington an' Delisia Bobbit. Our Marster wuz named Richard Bobbit, but we all calls him Massa Dick.

Massa Dick ain't good ter us, an' on my arm hyar, jist above de elbow am a big scar dis day whar he whupped me wid a cowhide. He ain't whupped me fer nothin' 'cept dat I is a nigger. I had a whole heap of dem whuppin's, mostly case I won't obey his orders an' I'se seed slaves beat 'most ter deff.

I wuz married onct 'fore de war by de broom stick ceremony, lak all de rest of de slaves wuz but shucks dey sold away my wife 'fore we'd been married a year an' den de war come on.

I had one brother, Henry who am wuckin' fer de city, an' one sister what wuz named Deliah. She been daid dese many years now.

Massa Dick owned a powerful big plantation an' ober a hundert slaves, an' we wucked on short rations an' went nigh naked. We ain't gone swimmin' ner huntin' ner nothin' an' we ain't had no pleasures 'less we runs away ter habe 'em. Eben when we sings we had ter turn down a pot in front of de do' ter ketch de noise.

I knowed some pore white trash; our oberseer wuz one, an' de shim shams[3] wuz also nigh 'bout also. We ain't had no use fer none of 'em an' we shorely ain't carin' whe'her dey has no use fer us er not.

De Ku Kluxes ain't done nothin' fer us case dar ain't many in our neighborhood. Yo' see de Yankees ain't come through dar, an' we is skeerd of dem anyhow. De white folks said dat de Yankees would kill us if'en dey ketched us.

I ain't knowed nothin' 'bout de Yankees, ner de surrender so I stays on fer seberal months atter de wahr wuz ober, den I comes ter Raleigh an' goes ter wuck fer de city. I wucks fer de city fer nigh on fifty years, I reckon, an' jis' lately I retired.

I'se been sick fer 'bout four months an' on, de second day of May. De day when I wuz a hundert years old I warn't able ter git ter de city lot, but I got a lot uv presents.

Dis 'oman am my third lawful wife. I married her three years ago.[4]

[3] Shim Sham, Free Issues or Negroes of mixed blood.

[4] The old man was too ill to walk out on the porch for his picture, and his mind wandered too much to give a connected account of his life.

N.C. District:	No. 2
Worker:	Mary A. Hicks
No. Words:	793
Subject:	Ex-Slave Story
Story Teller:	Henry Bobbitt
Editor:	Daisy Bailey Waitt

HENRY BOBBITT

I wuz borned at Warrenton in Warren County in 1850. My father wuz named Washington, atter General Washington an' my mamma wuz named Diasia atter a woman in a story. Us an' 'bout forty or fifty other slaves belonged ter Mr. Richard Bobbitt an' we wucked his four hundred acres o' land fer him. I jist had one brother named Clay, atter Henry Clay, which shows how Massa Dick voted, an' Delilah, which shows dat ole missus read de Bible.

We farmed, makin' tobacco, cotton, co'n, wheat an' taters. Massa Dick had a whole passel o' fine horses an' our Sunday job wuz ter take care of 'em, an' clean up round de house. Yes mam, we wucked seben days a week, from sunup till sundown six days, an' from seben till three or four on a Sunday.

We didn't have many tear-downs an' prayer meetin's an' sich, case de fuss sturbed ole missus who wuz kinder sickly. When we did have sompin' we turned down a big wash-pot in front of de do', an' it took up de fuss, an' folkses in de yard can't hyar de fuss. De patterollers would git you iffen you went offen de premises widout a pass, an' dey said dat dey would beat you scandelous. I seed a feller dat dey beat onct an' he had scars as big as my fingers all ober his body.

I got one whuppin' dat I 'members, an' dat wuz jist a middlin' one. De massa told me ter pick de cotton an' I sot down in de middle an' didn't wuck a speck. De oberseer come an' he frailed me wid a cotton-stalk; he wuz a heap meaner ter de niggers dan Massa Dick wuz. I saw some niggers what wuz beat bad, but I ain't neber had no bad beatin'.

We libed in log houses wid sand floors an' stick an' dirt chimneys an' we warn't 'lowed ter have no gyarden, ner chickens, ner pigs. We ain't had no way o' makin' money an' de fun wuz only middlin'. We had ter steal what rabbits we et from somebody elses boxes on some udder plantation, case de massa won't let us have none o' our own, an' we ain't had no time ter hunt ner fish.

Now talkin' 'bout sompin' dat we'd git a whuppin' fer, dat wuz fer havin' a pencil an' a piece of paper er a slate. Iffen you jist looked lak you wanted ter larn ter read er write you got a lickin'.

Dar wuz two colored women lived nigh us an' dey wuz called "free issues," but dey wuz really witches. I ain't really seen 'em do nothin' but I hyard a whole lot 'bout 'em puttin' spells on folkses an' I seed tracks whar day had rid Massa Dick's hosses an' eber mo'nin' de hosses manes an' tails would be all twisted an' knotted up. I know dat dey done dat case I seed it wid my own eyes. Dey doctored lots of people an' our folkses ain't neber had no doctor fer nothin' dat happen.

You wuz axin' 'bout de slave sales, an' I want ter tell you dat I has seen some real sales an' I'se seed niggers, whole bunches of' em, gwin' ter Richmond ter be sold. Dey wuz mostly chained, case dey wuz new ter de boss, an' he doan know what ter 'spect. I'se seed some real sales in Warrenton too, an' de mammies would be sold from deir chilluns an' dare would be a whole heap o' cryin' an' mou'nin' 'bout hit. I tell you folkses ain't lak dey uster be, 'specially niggers. Uster be when a nigger cries he whoops an' groans an' hollers an' his whole body rocks, an' dat am de way dey done sometime at de sales.

Speakin' 'bout haints: I'se seed a whole lot o' things, but de worst dat eber happen wuz 'bout twenty years ago when a han'ts hand hit me side o' de haid. I bet dat hand weighed a hundred pounds an' it wuz as cold as ice. I ain't been able ter wuck fer seben days an' nights an' I still can't turn my haid far ter de left as you sees.

I reckon 'bout de funniest thing 'bout our plantation wuz de marryin'. A couple got married by sayin' dat dey wuz, but it couldn't last fer longer dan five years. Dat wuz so iffen one of 'em got too weakly ter have chilluns de other one could git him another wife or husban'.

I 'members de day moughty well when de Yankees come. Massa Dick he walked de floor an' cussed Sherman fer takin' his niggers away. All o' de niggers lef', of course, an' me, I walked clean ter Raleigh ter find out if I wuz really free, an' I couldn't unnerstan' half of it.

Well de first year I slept in folkses woodhouses an'

barns an' in de woods or any whar else I could find. I wucked hyar an' dar, but de folkses' jist give me sompin' ter eat an' my clothes wuz in strings' fore de spring o' de year.

Yo' axes me what I thinks of Massa Lincoln? Well, I thinks dat he wuz doin' de wust thing dat he could ter turn all dem fool niggers loose when dey ain't got no place ter go an' nothin' ter eat. Who helped us out den? Hit wuzn't de Yankees, hit wuz de white folkses what wuz left wid deir craps in de fiel's, an' wuz robbed by dem Yankees, ter boot. My ole massa, fur instance, wuz robbed uv his fine hosses an' his feed stuff an' all dem kaigs o' liquor what he done make hisself, sides his money an' silver.

Slavery wuz a good thing den, but de world jist got better an' outgrowed it.

EH

N.C. District: No. 2
Worker: Mary A. Hicks
No. Words: 863
Subject: HERNDON BOGAN
Story Teller: Herndon Bogan
Editor: Daisy Bailey Waitt

HERNDON BOGAN

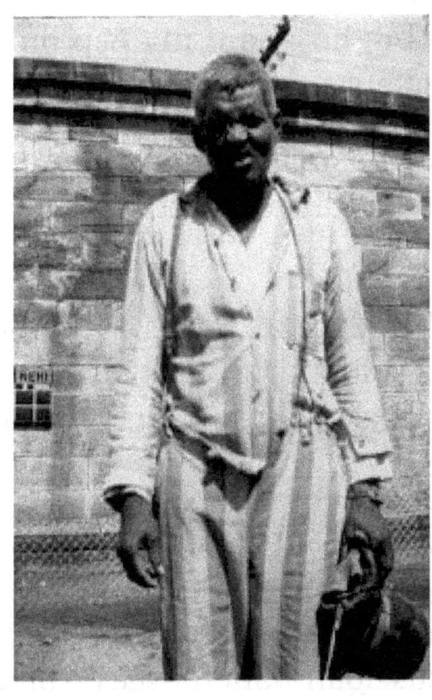

I wus bawned in Union County, South Carolina on de plantation o' Doctor Bogan, who owned both my mammy Issia, an' my pap Edwin. Dar wus six o' us chilluns; Clara, Lula, Joe, Tux, Mack an' me.

I doan' member much 'bout slavery days 'cept dat my white folkses wus good ter us. Dar wus a heap o' slaves, maybe a hundert an' fifty. I 'members dat we wucked hard, but we had plenty ter eat an' w'ar, eben iffen we did w'ar wood shoes.

I kin barely recolleck 'fore de war dat I'se seed a heap o' cocks fightin' in pits an' a heap o' horse racin'. When de marster winned he 'ud give us niggers a big dinner or a dance, but if he lost, oh!

My daddy wus gived ter de doctor when de doctor wus married an' dey shore loved each other. One day marster, he comes in an' he sez dat de Yankees am aimin' ter try ter take his niggers way from him, but dat dey am gwine ter ketch hell while dey does hit. When he sez dat he starts ter walkin' de flo'. 'I'se gwine ter leave yore missus in yore keer, Edwin,' he sez.

But pa 'lows, 'Wid all respec' fer yore wife sar, she am a Yankee too, an' I'd ruther go wid you ter de war. Please sar, massa, let me go wid you ter fight dem Yanks.'

At fust massa 'fuses, den he sez, 'All right.' So off dey goes ter de war, massa on a big hoss, an' my pap on a strong mule 'long wid de blankets an' things.

Dey tells me dat ole massa got shot one night, an' dat pap grabs de gun 'fore hit hits de earth an' lets de Yanks have hit.

I 'members dat dem wus bad days fer South Carolina, we gived all o' de food ter de soldiers, an' missus, eben do' she has got some Yankee folks in de war, l'arns ter eat cabbages an' kush an' berries.

I 'members dat on de day of de surrender, leastways de day dat we hyard 'bout hit, up comes a Yankee an' axes ter see my missus. I is shakin', I is dat skeerd, but I bucks up an' I tells him dat my missus doan want ter see no blue coat.

He grins, an' tells me ter skedaddle, an' 'bout den my missus comes out an' so help me iffen she doan hug dat dratted Yank. Atter awhile I gathers dat he's her brother, but at fust I ain't seed no sense in her cryin' an' sayin' 'thank God', over an' over.

Well sar, de massa an' pap what had gone off mad an' healthy an' ridin' fine beastes comes back walkin' an' dey looked sick. Massa am white as cotton, an' so help me, iffen my pap, who wuz black as sin, ain't pale too.

Atter a few years I goes ter wuck in Spartanburg as a houseboy, den I gits a job wid de Southern Railroad an' I goes ter Charlotte ter night-watch de tracks.

I stays dar eighteen years, but one night I kills a white hobo who am tryin' ter rob me o' my gol' watch an' chain, an' dey gives me eighteen months. I'se been hyar six already. He wus a white man, an' jist a boy, an' I is sorry, but I comes hyar anyhow.

I hyard a ole 'oman in Charlotte tell onct 'bout witchin' in slavery times, dar in Mecklenburg County. She wus roun' ninety, so I reckon she knows. She said dat iffen anybody wanted ter be a witch he would draw a circle on de groun' jist at de aidge o' dark an' git in de circle an' squat down.

Dar he had ter set an' talk ter de debil, an' he mus' say, 'I will have nothin' ter do wid 'ligion, an' I wants you ter make me a witch.' Atter day he mus' bile a black cat, a bat an' a bunch of herbs an' drink de soup, den he wuz really a witch.

When you wanted ter witch somebody, she said dat you could take dat stuff, jist a little bit of hit an' put hit under dat puson's doorsteps an' dey'd be sick.

You could go thru' de key hole or down de chimney or through de chinks in a log house, an' you could ride a puson jist lak ridin' a hoss. Dat puson can keep you outen his house by layin' de broom 'fore de do' an' puttin' a pin cushion full of pins side of de bed do', iffen he's a mind to.

Dat puson can kill you too, by drawin' yore pitcher an' shootin' hit in de haid or de heart too.

Dar's a heap o' ways ter tell fortunes dat she done tol' me but I'se done forgot now 'cept coffee groun's an' a little of de others. You can't tell hit wid 'em do', case hit takes knowin' how, hit shore does.

N.C. District:	No. 2
Worker:	T. Pat Matthews
No. Words:	1,741
Subject:	ANDREW BOONE
Story Teller:	Andrew Boone
Editor:	G. L. Andrews
Date Stamp:	"OCT 23 1937"

ANDREW BOONE

I been living in dese backer barns fifteen years. I built this little shelter to cook under. Dey cut me off the WPA cause dey said I wus too ole to work. Dey tole us ole folks we need not put down our walkin' sticks to git work cause dey jes' won't goin' to put us on.

Well, I had some tomatoes cooked widout any grease for my breakfast. I had a loaf of bread yesterday, but I et it. I ain't got any check from the ole age pension an' I have nothin' to eat an' I am hongry. I jes' looks to God. I set down by de road thinkin' bout how to turn an' what to do to git a meal, when you cum along. I thanks you fer dis dime. I guess God made you give it to me.

I wus glad to take you down to my livin' place to give you my story. Dis shelter, an ole tobacco barn, is better dan no home at all. I is a man to myself an' I enjoy livin' out here if I could git enough to eat.

Well de big show is coming to town. It's de Devil's wurk. Yes sir, it's de Devil's wurk. Why dem show folks ken make snakes an' make 'em crawl too. Dere wus one in Watson Field in de edge of Raleigh not long ago an' he made snakes an' made 'em crawl too. All shows is de Devil's wurk.

I never done anything fer myself in all my life. I always wurked fer de Rebels. I stuck right to 'em. Didn't have no sense fer doin' dat I guess.

One time a Rebel saw a Yankee wid one eye, one leg an' one arm. De Yankee wus beggin'. De Rebel went up to him an' give him a quarter. Den he backed off an' jes' stood a-lookin' at de Yankee, presently he went back an' give him anudder quarter, den anudder, den he said, 'You take dis whole dollar, you is de first Yankee I eber seed trimmed up jes' to my notion, so take all dis, jes' take de whole dollar, you is trimmed up to my notion'.

I belonged to Billy Boone in Slavery time. He wus a preacher. He lived on an' owned a plantation in Northampton County. The plantation wus near woodland. The nearest river to the place wus the Roanoke. My ole missus' name wus Nancy. When ole marster died I stayed around wid fust one then another of the chilluns, cause marster tole me jes' fore he died fer me to stay wid any of 'em I wanted to stay with. All dem ole people done dead an' gone on.

Niggers had to go through thick an' thin in slavery time, with rough rations most of de time, wid jes' enough clothin' to make out wid. Our houses were built of logs an' covered wid slabs. Dey wus rived out of blocks of trees about 3-6 and 8ft in length. De chimleys wus built of sticks and mud, den a coat of clay mud daubed over ‘em. De cracks in de slave houses wus daubed wid mud too.

We wurked from sun to sun. If we had a fire in cold weather where we wus wurkin’ marster or de overseer would come an’ put it out. We et frozen meat an’ bread many times in cold weather. After de day’s wurk in de fields wus over we had a task of pickin’ de seed from cotton till we had two ounces of lint or spin two ounces of cotton on a spinnin’ wheel. I spun cotton on a spinnin’ wheel. Dats de way people got clothes in slavery time.

I can’t read an’ write but dey learned us to count. Dey learned us to count dis way. ‘Ought is an’ ought, an’ a figger is a figger, all for de white man an’ nothin’ fer de nigger’. Hain’t you heard people count dat way?

Dey sold slaves jes’ like people sell hosses now. I saw a lot of slaves sold on de auction block. Dey would strip ‘em stark naked. A nigger scarred up or whaled an’ welted up wus considered a bad nigger an’ did not bring much. If his body wus not scarred, he brought a good price. I saw a lot of slaves whupped an’ I was whupped myself. Dey whupped me wid de cat o’ nine tails. It had nine lashes on it. Some of de slaves wus whupped wid a cabbin paddle. Dey had forty holes in’ em an’ when you wus buckled to a barrel dey hit your naked flesh wid de paddle an’ every whur dere wus a hole in de paddle it drawed a blister. When de whuppin’ wid de paddle wus over, dey took de cat o’ nine tails an’ busted de blisters. By dis time de blood sometimes would be runnin’ down dere heels. Den de next thing wus a wash in salt water strong enough to hold up an egg. Slaves wus punished dat way fer runnin’ away an’ sich.

If you wus out widout a pass dey would shore git you. De paterollers shore looked after you. Dey would come to de house at night to see who wus there. If you wus out of place, dey would wear you out.

Sam Joyner, a slave, belonged to marster. He wus runnin' from de paterollers an' he fell in a ole well. De pateroller went after marster. Marster tole' em to git ole Sam out an' whup him jes' as much as dey wanted to. Dey got him out of de well an' he wus all wet an' muddy. Sam began takin' off his shoes, den he took off his pants an' got in his shirt tail. Marster, he say, 'What you takin' off you clothes fer Sam?' Sam, he say, 'Marster, you know you all can't whup dis nigger right over all dese wet clothes.' Den Sam lit out. He run so fas' he nearly flew. De paterollers got on dere hosses an' run him but dey could not ketch him. He got away. Marster got Sam's clothes an' carried 'em to de house. Sam slipped up next morning put his clothes on an' marster said no more about it.

I wus a great big boy when de Yankees come through. I wus drivin' a two mule team an' doin' other wurk on de farm. I drove a two hoss wagon when dey carried slaves to market. I went to a lot of different places.

My marster wus a preacher, Billy Boone. He sold an' bought niggers. He had fifty or more. He wurked the grown niggers in two squads. My father wus named Isham Boone and my mother wus Sarah Boone. Marster Boone whupped wid de cobbin paddle an' de cat o' nine tails an' used the salt bath an' dat wus 'nough. Plenty besides him whupped dat way.

Marster had one son, named Solomon, an' two girls, Elsie an' Alice. My mother had four children, three boys an' one girl. The boys were named Sam, Walter and Andrew, dats me, an' de girl wus Cherry.

My father had several children cause he had several women besides mother. Mollie and Lila Lassiter, two sisters, were also his women. Dese women wus given to him an' no udder man wus allowed to have anything to do wid 'em. Mollie an' Lila both had chilluns by him. Dere names wus Jim, Mollie, Liza, Rosa, Pete an' I can't remember no more of 'em.

De Yankees took jes' what dey wanted an' nothin' stopped 'em, cause de surrender had come. Before de surrender de slave owners begun to scatter de slaves 'bout from place to place to keep de Yankees from gittin' 'em. If de Yankees took a place de slaves nearby wus moved to a place further off.

All I done wus fer de Rebels. I wus wid 'em an' I jes' done what I wus tole. I wus afraid of de Yankees 'cause de Rebels had told us dat de Yankees would kill us. Dey tole us dat de Yankees would bore holes in our shoulders an' wurk us to carts. Dey tole us we would be treated a lot worser den dey wus treating us. Well, de Yankees got here but they treated us fine. Den a story went round an' round dat de marster would have to give de slaves a mule an' a year's provisions an' some lan', about forty acres, but dat was not so. Dey nebber did give us anything. When de war ended an' we wus tole we wus free, we stayed on wid marster cause we had nothin' an' nowhere to go.

We moved about from farm to farm. Mother died an' father married Maria Edwards after de surrender. He did not live wid any of his other slave wives dat I knows of.

I have wurked as a han' on de farm most of de time since de surrender and daddy worked most of de time as a han', but he had gardens an' patches most everywhere he wurked. I wurked in New York City for fifteen years with Crawford and Banhay in de show business. I advertised for 'em. I dressed in a white suit, white shirt, an' white straw hat, and wore tan shoes. I had to be a purty boy. I had to have my shoes shined twice a day. I lived at 18 Manilla Lane, New York City. It is between McDougall Street and 6th Avenue. I married Clara Taylor in New York City. We had two children. The oldest one lives in New York. The other died an' is buried in Raleigh.

In slavery time they kept you down an' you had to wurk, now I can't wurk, an' I am still down. Not allowed to wurk an' still down. It's all hard, slavery and freedom, both bad when you can't eat. The ole bees makes de honey comb, the young bee makes de honey, niggers makes de cotton an' corn an' de white folks gets de money. Dis wus de case in Slavery time an' its de case now. De nigger do mos' de hard wurk on de farms now, and de white folks still git de money dat de nigger's labor makes.

LE

STATE:	North Carolina
RECEIVED FROM:	(State office) Asheville
MS:	Interview with W. L. Bost, Ex-Slave.
WORDS:	2000
DATE:	Sept. 27, 1937

W. L. BOST

My Massa's name was Jonas Bost. He had a hotel in Newton, North Carolina. My mother and grandmother both belonged to the Bost family. My ole Massa had two large plantations one about three miles from Newton and another four miles away. It took a lot of niggers to keep the work a goin' on them both. The women folks had to work in the hotel and in the big house in town. Ole Missus she was a good woman. She never allowed the Massa to buy or sell any slaves. There never was an overseer on the whole plantation. The oldest colored man always looked after the niggers. We niggers lived better than the niggers on the other plantations.

Lord child, I remember when I was a little boy, 'bout ten years, the speculators come through Newton with droves of slaves. They always stay at our place. The poor critters nearly froze to death. They always come 'long on the last of December so that the niggers would be ready for sale on the first day of January. Many the time I see four or five of them chained together. They never had enough clothes on to keep a cat warm. The women never wore anything but a thin dress and a petticoat and one underwear. I've seen the ice balls hangin' on to the bottom of their dresses as they ran along, jes like sheep in a pasture 'fore they are sheared. They never wore any shoes. Jes run along on the ground, all spewed up with ice. The speculators always rode on horses and drove the pore niggers. When they get cold, they make 'em run 'til they are warm again.

The speculators stayed in the hotel and put the niggers in the quarters jes like droves of hogs. All through the night I could hear them mournin' and prayin'. I didn't know the Lord would let people live who were so cruel. The gates were always locked and they was a guard on the outside to shoot anyone who tried to run away. Lord miss, them slaves look jes like droves of turkeys runnin' along in front of them horses.

I remember when they put 'em on the block to sell 'em. The ones 'tween 18 and 30 always bring the most money. The auctioneer he stand off at a distance and cry 'em off as they stand on the block. I can hear his voice as long as I live.

If the one they going to sell was a young Negro man this is what he say: "Now gentlemen and fellow-citizens here is a big black buck Negro. He's stout as a mule. Good for any kin' o' work an' he never gives any trouble. How much am I offered for him?" And then the sale would commence, and the nigger would be sold to the highest bidder.

If they put up a young nigger woman the auctioneer cry out: "Here's a young nigger wench, how much am

I offered for her?" The pore thing stand on the block a shiverin' an' a shakin' nearly froze to death. When they sold many of the pore mothers beg the speculators to sell 'em with their husbands, but the speculator only take what he want. So meybe the pore thing never see her husban' agin.

Ole' Massa always see that we get plenty to eat. O' course it was no fancy rashions. Jes corn bread, milk, fat meat, and 'lasses but the Lord knows that was lots more than other pore niggers got. Some of them had such bad masters.

Us pore niggers never 'lowed to learn anything. All the readin' they ever hear was when they was carried through the big Bible. The Massa say that keep the slaves in they places. They was one nigger boy in Newton who was terrible smart. He learn to read an' write. He take other colored children out in the fields and teach 'em about the Bible, but they forgit it 'fore the nex' Sunday.

Then the paddyrollers they keep close watch on the pore niggers so they have no chance to do anything or go anywhere. They jes' like policemen, only worser. 'Cause they never let the niggers go anywhere without a pass from his master. If you wasn't in your proper place when the paddyrollers come they lash you til' you was black and blue. The women got 15 lashes and the men 30. That is for jes bein' out without a pass. If the nigger done anything worse he was taken to the jail and put in the whippin' post. They was two holes cut for the arms stretch up in the air and a block to put your feet in, then they whip you with cowhide whip. An' the clothes shore never get any of them licks.

I remember how they kill one nigger whippin' him with the bull whip. Many the pore nigger nearly killed with the bull whip. But this one die. He was a stubborn Negro and didn't do as much work as his Massa thought he ought to. He been lashed lot before. So they take him to the whippin' post, and then they strip his clothes off and then the man stan' off and cut him with the whip. His back was cut all to pieces. The cuts about half inch apart. Then after they whip him they tie him down and put salt on him. Then after he lie in the sun awhile they whip him agin. But when they finish with him he was dead.

Plenty of the colored women have children by the white men. She know better than to not do what he say. Didn't have much of that until the men from South Carolina come up here and settle and bring slaves. Then they take them very same children what have they own blood and make slaves out of them. If the Missus find out she raise revolution. But she hardly find out. The white men not going to tell and the nigger women were always afraid to. So they jes go on hopin' that thing won't be that way always.

I remember how the driver, he was the man who did most of the whippin', use to whip some of the niggers. He would tie their hands together and then put their hands down over their knees, then take a stick and stick it 'tween they hands and knees. Then when he take hold of them and beat 'em first on one side then on the other.

Us niggers never have chance to go to Sunday School and church. The white folks feared for niggers to get any religion and education, but I reckon somethin' inside jes told us about God and that there was a better place hereafter. We would sneak off and have prayer meetin'.

Sometimes the paddyrollers catch us and beat us good but that didn't keep us from tryin'. I remember one old song we use to sing when we meet down in the woods back of the barn. My mother she sing an' pray to the Lord to deliver us out o' slavery. She always say she thankful she was never sold from her children, and that our Massa not so mean as some of the others. But the old song it went something like this:

> "Oh, mother lets go down, lets go down, lets go down, lets go down.
>
> Oh, mother lets go down, down in the valley to pray.
>
> As I went down in the valley to pray
>
> Studyin' about that good ole way
>
> Who shall wear that starry crown.
>
> Good Lord show me the way."

Then the other part was just like that except it said 'father' instead of 'mother', and then 'sister' and then 'brother'.

Then they sing sometime:

> "We camp a while in the wilderness, in the wilderness, in the wilderness.
>
> We camp a while in the wilderness, where the Lord makes me happy
>
> And then I'm a goin' home."

I don't remember much about the war. There was no fightin' done in Newton. Jes a skirmish or two. Most of the people get everything jes ready to run when the Yankee sojers come through the town. This was toward the las' of the war. Cose the niggers knew what all the fightin' was about, but they didn't dare say anything. The man who owned the slaves was too mad as it was, and if the niggers say anything they get shot right then and thar. The sojers tell us after the war that we get food, clothes, and wages from our Massas else we leave. But they was very few that ever got anything. Our ole Massa say he not gwine pay us anything, corse his money was no good, but he wouldn't pay us if it had been.

Then the Ku Klux Klan come 'long. They were terrible dangerous. They wear long gowns, touch the ground. They ride horses through the town at night and if they find a Negro that tries to get nervy or have a little bit for himself, they lash him nearly to death and gag him and leave him to do the bes' he can. Some time they put sticks in the top of the tall thing they wear and then put an extra head up there with scary eyes and great big mouth, then they stick it clear up in the air to scare the poor Negroes to death.

They had another thing they call the 'Donkey Devil' that was jes as bad. They take the skin of a donkey and get inside of it and run after the pore Negroes. Oh, Miss them was bad times, them was bad times. I know folks think the books tell the truth, but they shore don't. Us pore niggers had to take it all.

Then after the war was over we was afraid to move. Jes like tarpins or turtles after 'mancipation. Jes stick our heads out to see how the land lay. My mammy stay with Marse Jonah for 'bout a year after freedom then ole Solomon Hall made her an offer. Ole man Hall was a good man if there ever was one. He freed all of his slaves about two years 'fore 'mancipation and gave each of them so much money when he died, that is he put that in his will. But when he die his sons and daughters never give anything to the pore Negroes. My mother went to live on the place belongin' to the nephew of Solomon Hall. All of her six children went with her. Mother she cook for the white folks an' the children make crop. When the first year was up us children got the first money we had in our lives. My mother certainly was happy.

We live on this place for over four years. When I was 'bout twenty year old I married a girl from West Virginia but she didn't live but jes 'bout a year. I stayed down there for a year or so and then I met Mamie. We came here and both of us went to work, we work at the same place. We bought this little piece of ground 'bout forty-two years ago. We gave $125 for it. We had to buy the lumber to build the house a little at a time but finally we got the house done. Its been a good home for us and the children. We have two daughters and one adopted son. Both of the girls are good cooks. One of them lives in New Jersey and cooks in a big hotel. She and her husband come to see us about once a year. The other one is in Philadelphia. They both have plenty. But the adopted boy, he was part white. We took him when he was a small and did the best we could by him. He never did like to 'sociate with colored people. I remember one time when he was a small child I took him to town and the conductor made me put him in the front of the street car cause he thought I was just caring for him and that he was a white boy. Well, we sent him to school until he finished. Then he joined the navy. I ain't seem him in several years. The last letter I got from him he say he ain't spoke to a colored girl since he has been there. This made me mad so I took his insurance policy and cashed it. I didn't want nothin' to do with him, if he deny his own color.

Very few of the Negroes ever get anywhere; they never have no education. I knew one Negro who got to be a policeman in Salisbury once and he was a good one too. When my next birthday comes in December I will be eighty-eight years old. That is if the Lord lets me live and I shore hope He does.

N.C. District: No. 3
Worker: Travis Jordan
No. Words: 1384
Subject: Mary Wallace Bowe
Ex-slave 81 Years
Durham County Home
Durham, N.C.
Lovely story about Abraham Lincoln

[TR: This interview was heavily corrected by hand. i.e. wuz to was, er to a, etc. Changes made without comment.]

MARY WALLACE BOWE

My name is Mary Wallace Bowe. I was nine years ole at de surrender.

My mammy an' pappy, Susan an' Lillman Graves, first belonged to Marse Fountain an' Mis' Fanny Tu'berville, but Marse Fountain sold me, my mammy an' my brother George to Mis' Fanny's sister, Mis' Virginia Graves. Mis' Virginia's husban' was Marse Doctor Graves. Dey lived on de ole Elijah Graves estate not far from Marse Fountain's plantation here in Durham county, an' Mis' Virginia an' Mis' Fanny seed each other near 'bout every day.

I was little when Marse Fountain an' Marse Doctor went to de war but I remembers it. I remembers it kaze Mis' Fanny stood on de po'ch smilin' an' wavin' at Marse Fountain 'til he went 'roun' de curve in de road, den she fell to de floor like she was dead. I thought she was dead 'till Mis' Virginia th'owed some water in her face an' she opened her eyes.

De nex day Mis' Virginia took me an' mammy an' we all went over an' stayed wid Mis' Fanny kaze she was skeered, an' so dey'd be company for each other. Mammy waited on Mis' Virginia an' he'ped Surella Tu'berville, Mis' Fanny's house girl, sweep an' make up de beds an' things. I was little but mammy made me work. I shook de rugs, brung in de kindlin' an run 'roun' waitin' on Mis' Virginia an' Mis' Fanny, doin' things like totin' dey basket of keys, bringin' dey shawls and such as dat. Dey was all de time talkin' about de folks fightin' an' what dey would do if de Yankees come.

Every time dey talk Mis' Fanny set an' twist her han's an' say: "What is we gwine do, Sister, what is we gwine do?"

Mis' Virginia try to pacify Mis' Fanny. She say, 'Don' yo' worry none, Honey, I'll fix dem Yankees when dey come.' Den she set her mouf. When she done dat I run an' hid behin' Mis' Fanny's chair kaze I done seed Mis' Virginia set her mouf befo' an' I knowed she meant biznes'.

I didn' have sense enough to be skeered den kaze I hadn' never seed no Yankee sojers, but 'twaren't long befo' I wuz skeered. De Yankees come one mornin', an' dey ripped, Oh, Lawd, how dey did rip. When dey rode up to de gate an' come stompin' to de house, Mis' Fanny 'gun to cry. 'Tell dem somethin', Sister, tell dem somethin'; she tole Mis' Virginia.

Mis' Virginia she ain' done no cryin'. When she seed dem Yankees comin' 'cross de hill, she run 'roun' an' got all de jewelry. She took off de rings an' pins she an' Mis' Fanny had on an' she got all de things out of de jewelry box an' give dem to pappy. "Hide dem, Lillmam" she tole pappy, 'hide dem some place whare dem thieves won't find dem'.

Pappy had on high top boots. He didn' do nothin but stuff all dat jewelry right down in dem boots, den he strutted all' roun' dem Yankees laughin' to heself. Dey cussed when dey couldn' fin' no jewelry a tall. Dey didn' fin' no silver neither kaze us niggers done he'p Mis' Fanny an' Mis' Virginia hide dat. We done toted it all down to de cottin gin house an' hid it in de loose cotton piled on de floor. When dey couldn' fin' nothin' a big sojer went up to Mis' Virginia who wuz standin' in de hall. He look at her an' say: 'Yo's skeered of me, ain' yo'?'

Mis' Virginia ain' batted no eye yet. She tole him, "If I was gwine to be skeered, I'd be skeered of somethin'. I sho ain' of no ugly, braggin' Yankee."

De man tu'ned red an he say: "If you don' tell me where you done hide dat silver I'se gwine to make' you skeered."

Mis' Virginia's chin went up higher. She set her mouf an' look at dat sojer twell he drap his eyes. Den she tole him dat some folks done come an' got de silver, dat dey done toted it off. She didn' tell him dat it wuz us niggers dat done toted it down to de cotton gin house.

In dem days dey wuz peddlers gwine 'roun' de country sellin' things. Dey toted big packs on dey backs filled wid everythin' from needles an' thimbles to bed spreads an' fryin' pans. One day a peddler stopped at Mis' Fanny's house. He was de uglies' man I ever seed. He was tall an' bony wid black whiskers an' black bushy hair an' curious eyes dat set way back in his head. Dey was dark an' look like a dog's eyes after you done hit him. He set down on de po'ch an' opened his pack, an' it was so hot an' he looked so tired, dat Mis' Fanny give him er cool drink of milk dat done been settin' in de spring house. All de time Mis' Fanny was lookin' at de things in de pack an' buyin', de man kept up a runnin' talk. He ask her how many niggers dey had; how many men dey had fightin' on de 'Federate side, an' what wuz was she gwine do if de niggers wuz was set free. Den he ask her if she knowed Mistah Abraham Lincoln.

'Bout dat time Mis' Virginia come to de door an' heard what he said. She blaze up like a lightwood fire an' told dat peddler dat dey didn't want to know nothin' 'bout Mistah Lincoln; dat dey knowed too much already, an' dat his name wuzn 'lowed called in dat house. Den she say he wuzn nothin' but a black debil messin' in other folks biznes', an' dat she'd shoot him on sight if she had half a chance.

De man laughed. "Maybe he ain't so bad,' he told her. Den he packed his pack an' went off down de road, an' Mis' Virginia watched him 'till he went out of sight 'roun' de bend."

Two or three weeks later Mis' Fanny got a letter. De letter was from dat peddler. He tole her dat he was Abraham Lincoln hese'f; dat he wuz peddlin' over de country as a spy, an' he thanked her for de res' on her shady po'ch an' de cool glass of milk she give him.

When dat letter come Mis' Virginia got so hoppin' mad dat she took all de stuff Mis' Fanny done bought from Mistah Lincoln an' made us niggers burn it on de ash pile. Den she made pappy rake up de ashes an' th'ow dem in de creek.

N.C. District:	No. 2
Worker:	Mary A. Hicks
No. Words:	377
Subject:	Ex-Slave Recollections
Person Interviewed:	Lucy Brown
Editor:	Daisy Bailey Waitt
Date Stamp:	"JUN 7 1937"

LUCY BROWN

I wuz jist a little thing when de war wuz over an' I doan 'member much ter tell yo'. Mostly what I does know I hyard my mammy tell it.

We belonged to John Neal of Person County. I doan know who my pappy wuz, but my mammy wuz named Rosseta an' her mammy's name 'fore her wuz Rosseta. I had one sister named Jenny an' one brother named Ben.

De marster wuz good ter us, in a way, but he ain't 'lowin' no kinds of frolickin' so when we had a meetin' we had ter do it secret. We'd turn down a wash pot outside de do', an' dat would ketch de fuss so marster neber knowed nothin' 'bout hit.

On Sundays we went ter church at de same place de white folkses did. De white folkses rid an' de niggers walked, but eben do' we wored wooden bottomed shoes we wuz proud an' mostly happy. We had good clothes an' food an' not much abuse. I doan know de number of slaves, I wuz so little.

My mammy said dat slavery wuz a whole lot wuser 'fore I could 'member. She tol' me how some of de slaves had dere babies in de fiel's lak de cows done, an' she said dat 'fore de babies wuz borned dey tied de mammy down on her face if'en dey had ter whup her ter keep from ruinin' de baby.

She said dat dar wuz ghostes an' some witches back den, but I doan know nothin' 'bout dem things.

Naw. I can't tell yo' my age but I will tell yo' dat eber'body what lives in dis block am either my chile or gran'chile. I can't tell yo' prexackly how many dar is o' 'em, but I will tell you dat my younges' chile's baby am fourteen years old, an' dat she's got fourteen youngin's , one a year jist lak I had till I had sixteen.

I'se belonged ter de church since I wuz a baby an' I tells dem eber'day dat dey shore will miss me when I'se gone.

N.C. District:	No. 2
Worker:	Mary Hicks
No. Words:	462
Subject:	PLANTATION LIFE IN GEORGIA
Reference:	Midge Burnett
Editor:	George L. Andrews
Date Stamp:	"AUG 6 1937"

MIDGE BURNETT

I wus borned in Georgia eighty years ago, de son of Jim an' Henretta Burnett an' de slave of Marse William Joyner.

I wurked on de farm durin' slavery times, among de cotton, corn, an' sugar cane. De wurk wusn't so hard an' we had plenty of time ter have fun an' ter git inter meanness, dat's why Marse William had ter have so many patterollers on de place.

Marse William had near three hundret slaves an' he kept seben patterollers ter keep things goin' eben. De slaves ain't run away. Naw sir, dey ain't, dey knows good things when dey sees dem an' dey ain't leavin' dem nother. De only trouble wus dat dey wus crazy 'bout good times an' dey'd shoot craps er bust.

De patterollers 'ud watch all de paths leadin' frum de plantation an' when dey ketched a nigger leavin' dey whupped him an' run him home. As I said de patterollers watched all paths, but dar wus a number of little paths what run through de woods dat nobody ain't watched case dey ain't knowed dat de paths wus dar.

On moonlight nights yo' could hear a heap of voices an' when yo' peep ober de dike dar am a gang of niggers a-shootin' craps an' bettin' eber'thing dey has stold frum de plantation. Sometimes a pretty yaller gal er a fat black gal would be dar, but mostly hit would be jist men.

Dar wus a ribber nearby de plantation an' we niggers swum dar ever' Sadday an' we fished dar a heap too. We ketched a big mess of fish ever' week an' dese come in good an' helped ter save rations ter boot. Dat's what Marse William said, an' he believed in havin' a good time too.

We had square dances dat las' all night on holidays an' we had a Christmas tree an' a Easter egg hunt an' all dat, case Marse William intended ter make us a civilized bunch of blacks.

Marse William ain't eber hit one of us a single lick till de day when we heard dat de Yankees wus a-comin'. One big nigger jumps up an' squalls, 'Lawd bless de Yankees'.

Marse yells back, 'God damn de Yankees', an' he slaps big Mose a sumerset right outen de do'. Nobody else wanted ter git slapped soe ever'body got outen dar in a hurry an' nobody else dasen't say Yankees ter de marster.

Eben when somebody seed de Yankees comin' Mose wont go tell de' marster 'bout hit, but when Marster William wus hilt tight twixt two of dem big husky Yankees he cussed 'em as hard as he can. Dey carries him off an' dey put him in de jail at Atlanta an' dey keeps him fer a long time.

Atter de surrender we left dar an' we moves ter Star, South Carolina, whar I still wurks 'roun' on de farm. I stayed on dar' till fifty years ago when I married Roberta Thomas an' we moved ter Raliegh. We have five chilluns an' we's moughty proud of 'em, but since I had de stroke we has been farin' bad, an' I'se hopin' ter git my ole aged pension.

EH

N.C. District: No. 3
Worker: Travis Jordan
No. Words: [TR Added: 1,444
Subject: Fanny Cannady
Ex-Slave 79 Years
Durham County

FANNY CANNADY

I don' 'member much 'bout de sojers an' de fightin' in de war kaze I wuzn' much more den six years ole at de surrender, but I do 'member how Marse Jordan Moss shot Leonard Allen, one of his slaves. I ain't never forgot dat.

My mammy an' pappy, Silo an' Fanny Moss belonged to Marse Jordan an' Mis' Sally Moss. Dey had 'bout three hundred niggahs an' mos' of dem worked in de cotton fields.

Marse Jordan wuz hard on his niggahs. He worked dem over time an' didn' give den enough to eat. Dey didn' have good clothes neither an' dey shoes wuz made out of wood. He had 'bout a dozen niggahs dat didn' do nothin' else but make wooden shoes for de slaves. De chillun didn' have no shoes a tall; dey went barefooted in de snow an' ice same as 'twuz summer time. I never had no shoes on my feets 'twell I wuz pas' ten years ole, an' dat wuz after de Yankees done set us free.

I wuz skeered of Marse Jordan, an' all of de grown niggahs wuz too 'cept Leonard an' Burrus Allen. Dem niggahs wuzn' skeered of nothin'. If de debil hese'f had come an' shook er stick at dem dey'd hit him back. Leonard wuz er big black buck niggah; he wuz de bigges niggah I ever seed, an' Burrus wuz near 'bout as big, an' dey 'spized Marse Jordan wus'n pizen.

I wuz sort of skeered of Mis' Polly too. When Marse Jordan wuzn' 'roun' she wuz sweet an' kind, but when he wuz 'roun', she wuz er yes, suh, yes, suh, woman. Everythin' he tole her to do she done. He made her slap Marmy one time kaze when she passed his coffee she spilled some in de saucer. Mis' Sally hit Mammy easy, but Marse Jordan say: 'Hit her, Sally, hit de black bitch like she 'zerve to be hit.' Den Mis' Sally draw back her hand an' hit Mammy in de face, pow, den she went back to her place at de table an' play like she eatin' her breakfas'. Den when Marse Jordan leave she come in de kitchen an' put her arms 'roun' Mammy an' cry, an' Mammy pat her on de back an' she cry too. I loved Mis' Sally when Marse Jordan wuzn' 'roun'.

Marse Jordan's two sons went to de war; dey went all dressed up in dey fightin' clothes. Young Marse Jordan wuz jus' like Mis' Sally but Marse Gregory wuz like Marse Jordan, even to de bully way he walk. Young Marse Jordan never come back from de war, but 'twould take more den er bullet to kill Marse Gregory; he too mean to die anyhow kaze de debil didn' want him an' de Lawd wouldn' have him.

One day Marse Gregory come home on er furlo'. He think he look pretty wid his sword clankin' an' his boots shinin'. He wuz er colonel, lootenent er somethin'. He wuz struttin' 'roun' de yard showin' off, when Leonard Allen say under his breath, 'Look at dat God damn sojer. He fightin' to keep us niggahs from bein' free.'

'Bout dat time Marse Jordan come up. He look at Leonard an' say: 'What yo' mumblin' 'bout?'

Dat big Leonard wuzn' skeered. He say, I say, 'Look at dat God damn sojer. He fightin' to keep us niggahs from bein' free.'

Marse Jordan's face begun to swell. It turned so red dat de blood near 'bout bust out. He turned to Pappy an' tole him to go an' bring him dis shot gun. When Pappy come back Mis' Sally come wid him. De tears wuz streamin' down her face. She run up to Marse Jordan an' caught his arm. Ole Marse flung her off an' took de gun from Pappy. He leveled it on Leonard an' tole him to pull his shirt open. Leonard opened his shirt an' stood dare big as er black giant sneerin' at Ole Marse.

Den Mis' Sally run up again an' stood 'tween dat gun an' Leonard.

Ole Marse yell to pappy an' tole him to take dat woman out of de way, but nobody ain't moved to touch Mis' Sally, an' she didn' move neither, she jus' stood dare facin' Ole Marse. Den Ole Marse let down de gun. He reached over an' slapped Mis' Sally down, den picked up de gun an' shot er hole in Leonard's ches' big as yo' fis'. Den he took up Mis' Sally an' toted her in de house. But I wuz so skeered dat I run an' hid in de stable loft, an' even wid my eyes shut I could see Leonard layin' on de groun' wid dat bloody hole in his ches' an' dat sneer on his black mouf.

After dat Leonard's brother Burrus hated Ole Marse wus' er snake, den one night he run away. Mammy say he run away to keep from killin' Ole Marse. Anyhow, when Ole Marse foun' he wuz gone, he took er bunch of niggahs an' set out to find him. All day long dey tromped de woods, den when night come dey lit fat pine to'ches an' kept lookin', but dey couldn' find Burrus. De nex' day Ole Marse went down to de county jail an' got de blood houn's. He brung home er great passel of dem yelpin' an' pullin' at de ropes, but when he turned dem loose dey didn' find Burrus, kaze he done grease de bottom of his feets wid snuff an' hog lard so de dogs couldn' smell de trail. Ole Marse den tole all de niggahs dat if anybody housed an' fed Burrus on de sly, dat he goin' to shoot dem like he done shot Leonard. Den he went every day an' searched de cabins; he even looked under de houses.

One day in 'bout er week Mis' Sally wuz feedin' de chickens when she heard somethin' in de polk berry bushes behin' de hen house. She didn' go 'roun' de house but she went inside house an' looked through de crack. Dare wuz Burrus layin' down in de bushes. He wuz near 'bout starved kaze he hadn' had nothin' to eat since he done run away.

Mis' Sally whisper an' tole him to lay still, dat she goin' to slip him somethin' to eat. She went back to de house an' made up some more cawn meal dough for de chickens, an' under de dough she put some bread an' meat. When she went 'cross de yard she met Marse Jordan. He took de pan of dough an' say he goin' to feed de chickens. My mammy say dat Mis' Sally ain't showed no skeer, she jus' smile at Ole Marse an' pat his arm, den while she talk she take de pan an' go on to de chicken house, but Ole Marse he go too. When dey got to de hen house Ole Marse puppy begun sniffin' 'roun'. Soon he sta'ted to bark; he cut up such er fuss dat Ole Marse went to see what wuz wrong. Den he foun' Burrus layin' in de polk bushes.

Ole Marse drag Burrus out an' drove him to de house. When Mis' Sally seed him take out his plaited whip, she run up stairs an' jump in de bed an' stuff er pillow over her head.

Dey took Burrus to de whippin' post. Dey strip off his shirt, den dey put his head an' hands through de holes in de top, an' tied his feets to de bottom, den, Ole Marse took de whip. Dat lash hiss like col' water on er red hot iron when it come through de air, an' every time it hit Burrus it lef' er streak of blood. Time Ole Marse finish, Burrus' back look like er piece of raw beef.

Dey laid Burrus face down on er plank den dey poured turpentine in all dem cut places. It burned like fire but dat niggah didn' know nothin' 'bout it kaze he done passed out from pain. But, all his life dat black man toted dem scares on his back.

When de war ended Mis' Sally come to Mammy an' say: 'Fanny, I's sho glad yo's free. Yo' can go now an' yo' won' ever have to be er slave no more.'

But Mammy, she ain't had no notion of leavin' Mis' Sally. She put her arms' roun' her an' call her Baby, an' tell her she goin' to stay wid her long as she live. An' she did stay wid her. Me an' Mammy bof stayed Mis' Sally 'twell she died.

N.C. District:	No. 3
Field Worker:	Esther S. Pinnix
Word Total:	3199
Editor:	P. G. Cross
Subject:	"Negro Folklore of the Piedmont".
Consultants:	Mrs. P. G. Cross
	Miss Kate Jones,
	Descendants of Dr. Beverly Jones.

BETTY COFER

The ranks of negro ex-slaves are rapidly thinning out, but, scattered here and there among the ante-bellum families of the South, may be found a few of these picturesque old characters. Three miles north of Bethania, the second oldest settlement of the "Unitas Fratrum" in Wachovia, lies the 1500 acre Jones plantation. It has been owned for several generations by the one family, descendants of Abraham Conrad. Conrad's daughter, Julia, married a physician of note, Dr. Beverly Jones, whose family occupied the old homestead at the time of the Civil War.

Here, in 1856, was born a negro girl, Betty, to a slave mother. Here, today, under the friendly protection of this same Jones family, surrounded by her sons and her sons' sons, lives this same Betty in her own little weather-stained cottage. Encircling her house are lilacs, althea, and flowering trees that soften the bleak outlines of unpainted out-buildings. A varied collection of old-fashioned plants and flowers crowd the neatly swept dooryard. A friendly German-shepherd puppy rouses from his nap on the sunny porch to greet visitors enthusiastically. In answer to our knock a gentle voice calls, "Come in." The door opens directly into a small, low-ceilinged room almost filled by two double beds. These beds are conspicuously clean and covered by homemade crocheted spreads. Wide bands of hand-made insertion ornament the stiffly starched pillow slips. Against the wall is a plain oak dresser. Although the day is warm, two-foot logs burn on the age-worn andirons of the wide brick fire place. From the shelf above dangles a leather bag of "spills" made from twisted newspapers.

In a low, split-bottom chair, her rheumatic old feet resting on the warm brick hearth, sits Aunt Betty Cofer. Her frail body stoops under the weight of four-score years but her bright eyes and alert mind are those of a woman thirty years younger. A blue-checked mob cap covers her grizzled hair. Her tiny frame, clothed in a motley collection of undergarments, dress, and sweaters, is adorned by a clean white apron. Although a little shy of her strange white visitors, her innate dignity, gentle courtesy, and complete self possession indicate long association with "quality folks."

Her speech shows a noticeable freedom from the usual heavy negro dialect and idiom of the deep south. "Yes, Ma'am, yes, Sir, come in. Pull a chair to the fire. You'll have to 'scuse me. I can't get around much, 'cause my feet and legs bother me, but I got good eyes an' good ears an' all my own teeth. I aint never had a bad tooth in my head. Yes'm, I'm 81, going on 82. Marster done wrote my age down in his book where he kep' the names of all his colored folks. Muh (Mother) belonged to Dr. Jones but Pappy belonged to Marse Israel Lash over yonder. (Pointing northwest.) Younguns always went with their mammies so I belonged to the Joneses.

Muh and Pappy could visit back and forth sometimes but they never lived together 'til after freedom. Yes'm, we was happy. We got plenty to eat. Marster and old Miss Julia (Dr. Jones' wife, matriarch of the whole plantation) was mighty strict but they was good to us. Colored folks on some of the other plantations wasn't so lucky. Some of' em had overseers, mean, cruel men. On one plantation the field hands had to hustle to git to the end of the row at eleven o'clock dinner-time 'cause when the cooks brought their dinner they had to stop just where they was and eat, an' the sun was mighty hot out in those fields. They only had ash cakes (corn pone baked in ashes) without salt, and molasses for their dinner, but we had beans an' grits an' salt an' sometimes meat.

I was lucky. Miss Ella (daughter of the first Beverly Jones) was a little girl when I was borned and she claimed me. We played together an' grew up together. I waited on her an' most times slept on the floor in her room. Muh was cook an' when I done got big enough I helped to set the table in the big dinin' room. Then I'd put on a clean white apron an' carry in the victuals an' stand behind Miss Ella's chair. She'd fix me a piece of somethin' from her plate an' hand it back over her shoulder to me (eloquent hands illustrate Miss Ella's making of a sandwich.) I'd take it an' run outside to eat it. Then I'd wipe my mouth an' go back to stand behind Miss Ella again an' maybe get another snack.

Yes'm, there was a crowd of hands on the plantation. I mind 'em all an' I can call most of their names. Mac, Curley, William, Sanford, Lewis, Henry, Ed, Sylvester, Hamp, an' Juke was the men folks. The women was Nellie, two Lucys, Martha, Nervie, Jane, Laura, Fannie, Lizzie, Cassie, Tensie, Lindy, an' Mary Jane. The women mostly, worked in the house. There was always two washwomen, a cook, some hands to help her, two sewin' women, a house girl, an' some who did all the weavin' an' spinnin'. The men worked in the fields an' yard. One was stable boss an' looked after all the horses an' mules. We raised our own flax an' cotton an' wool, spun the thread, wove the cloth, made all the clothes. Yes'm, we made the mens' shirts an' pants an' coats. One woman knitted all the stockin's for the white folks an' colored folks too. I mind she had one finger all twisted an' stiff from holdin' her knittin' needles. We wove the cotton an' linen for sheets an' pillow-slips an' table covers. We wove the wool blankets too. I use to wait on the girl who did the weavin' when she took the cloth off the loom she done give me the 'thrums' (ends of thread left on the loom.) I tied 'em all together with teensy little knots an' got me some scraps from the sewin' room and I made me some quilt tops. Some of 'em was real pretty too! (Pride of workmanship evidenced by a toss of Betty's head.)

All our spinnin' wheels and flax wheels and looms was hand-made by a wheel wright, Marse Noah Westmoreland. He lived over yonder. (A thumb indicates north.) Those old wheels are still in the family'. I got one of the flax wheels. Miss Ella done give it to me for a present. Leather was tanned an' shoes was made on the place. 'Course the hands mostly went barefoot in warm weather, white chillen too. We had our own mill to grind the wheat and corn an' we raised all our meat. We made our own candles from tallow and beeswax. I 'spect some of the old candle moulds are over to 'the house' now. We wove our own candle wicks too. I never saw a match 'til I was a grown woman. We made our fire with flint an' punk (rotten wood). Yes'm, I was trained to cook an' clean an' sew. I learned to make mens' pants an' coats. First coat I made, Miss Julia told me to rip the collar off, an' by the time I picked out all the teensy stitches an' sewed it together again I could set a collar right! I can do it today, too! (Again there is manifested a good workman's pardonable pride of achievement)

Miss Julia cut out all the clothes herself for men and women too. I 'spect her big shears an' patterns an' old cuttin' table are over at the house now. Miss Julia cut out all the clothes an' then the colored girls sewed 'em up but she looked 'em all over and they better be sewed right! Miss Julia bossed the whole plantation. She looked after the sick folks and sent the doctor (Dr. Jones) to dose 'em and she carried the keys to the store-rooms and pantries.

HW Yes'm, I'm some educated. Muh showed me my 'a-b-abs' and my numbers and when I was fifteen I went to school in the log church built by the Moravians. They give it to the colored folks to use for their own school and church. (This log house is still standing near Bethania). Our teacher was a white man, Marse Fulk. He had one eye, done lost the other in the war. We didn't have no colored teachers then. They wasn't educated. We 'tended school four months a year. I went through the fifth reader, the

'North Carolina Reader'. I can figger a little an' read some but I can't write much 'cause my fingers 're—all stiffened up. Miss Julia use to read the bible to us an' tell us right an' wrong, and Muh showed me all she could an' so did the other colored folks. Mostly they was kind to each other.

No'm, I don't know much about spells an' charms. Course most of the old folks believed in 'em. One colored man use to make charms, little bags filled with queer things. He called 'em 'jacks' an' sold 'em to the colored folks an' some white folks too.

Yes'm, I saw some slaves sold away from the plantation, four men and two women, both of 'em with little babies. The traders got 'em. Sold 'em down to Mobile, Alabama. One was my pappy's sister. We never heard from her again. I saw a likely young feller sold for $1500. That was my Uncle Ike. Marse Jonathan Spease bought him and kept him the rest of his life.

Yes'm, we saw Yankee soldiers. (Stoneman's Cavalry in 1865.) They come marchin' by and stopped at 'the house. I wasn't scared 'cause they was all talkin' and laughin' and friendly but they sure was hongry. They dumped the wet clothes out of the big wash-pot in the yard and filled it with water. Then they broke into the smokehouse and got a lot of hams and biled 'em in the pot and ate 'em right there in the yard. The women cooked up a lot of corn pone for 'em and coffee too. Marster had a barrel of 'likker' put by an' the Yankees knocked the head in an' filled their canteens. There wasn't ary drop left. When we heard the soldiers comin' our boys turned the horses loose in the woods. The Yankees said they had to have 'em an' would burn the house down if we didn't get 'em. So our boys whistled up the horses an' the soldiers carried 'em all off. They carried off ol' Jennie mule too but let little Jack mule go. When the soldiers was gone the stable boss said,'if ol' Jennie mule once gits loose nobody on earth can catch her unless she wants. She'll be back!' Sure enough, in a couple of days she come home by herself an' we worked the farm jus' with her an' little Jack.

Some of the colored folks followed the Yankees away. Five or six of our boys went. Two of 'em travelled as far as Yadkinville but come back. The rest of 'em kep' goin' an' we never heard tell of' em again.

Yes'm, when we was freed Pappy come to get Muh and me. We stayed around here. Where could we go? These was our folks and I couldn't go far away from Miss Ella. We moved out near Rural Hall (some 5 miles from Bethania) an' Pappy farmed, but I worked at the home place a lot. When I was about twenty-four Marse R. J. Reynolds come from Virginia an' set up a tobacco factory. He fotched some hands with 'im. One was a likely young feller, named Cofer, from Patrick County, Virginia. I liked 'im an' we got married an' moved back here to my folks. (the Jones family) We started to buy our little place an' raise a family. I done had four chillen but two's dead. I got grandchillen and great-grandchillen close by. This is home to us. When we talk about the old home place (the Jones residence, now some hundred years old) we just say 'the house' 'cause there's only one house to us. The rest of the family was all fine folks and good to me but I loved Miss Ella better'n any one or anythin' else in the world. She was the best friend I ever had. If I ever wanted for anythin' I just asked her an she give it to me or got it for me somehow. Once when Cofer was in his last sickness his sister come from East Liverpool, Ohio, to see 'im. I went to Miss Ella to borrow a little money. She didn't have no change but she just took a ten dollar bill from her purse an' says 'Here you are, Betty, use what you need and bring me what's left'.

I always did what I could for her too an' stood by her—but one time. That was when we was little girls goin' together to fetch the mail. It was hot an' dusty an' we stopped to cool off an' wade in the 'branch'. We heard a horse trottin' an' looked up an' there was Marster switchin' his ridin' whip an' lookin' at us. 'Git for home, you two, and I'll 'tend to you,' he says, an' we got! But this time I let Miss Ella go to 'the house' alone an' I sneaked aroun' to Granny's cabin an' hid. I was afraid I'd git whupped! 'Nother time, Miss Ella went to town an' told me to keep up her fire whilst she was away. I fell asleep on the hearth and the fire done burnt out so's when Miss Ella come home the room was cold. She was mad as hops. Said she never had hit me but she sure felt like doin' it then.

Yes'm, I been here a right smart while. I done lived to see three generations of my white folks come an' go, an' they're the finest folks on earth. There use to be a reg'lar buryin' ground for the plantation hands. The colored chillen use to play there but I always played with the white chillen. (This accounts for Aunt Betty's gentle manner and speech.) Three of the old log cabins (slave cabins) is there yet. One of 'em was the 'boys cabin'. (house for boys and unmarried men) They've got walls a foot thick an' are used for store-rooms now. After freedom we buried out around our little churches but some of th' old grounds are plowed under an' turned into pasture cause the colored folks didn't get no deeds to 'em. It won't be long 'fore I go too but I'm gwine lie near my old home an' my folks.

Yes'm, I remember Marse Israel Lash, my Pappy's Marster. He was a low, thick-set man, very jolly an' friendly. He was real smart an' good too, 'cause his colored folks all loved 'im. He worked in the bank an' when the Yankees come, 'stead of shuttin' the door 'gainst 'em like the others did, he bid 'em welcome. (Betty's nodding head, expansive smile and wide-spread hands eloquently pantomime the banker's greeting.) So the Yankees done took the bank but give it back to 'im for his very own an' he kep' it but there was lots of bad feelin' 'cause he never give folks the money they put in the old bank. (Possibly this explains the closing of the branch of the Cape Fear Bank in Salem and opening of Israel Lash's own institution, the First National Bank of Salem, 1866.)

I saw General Robert E. Lee, too. After the war he come with some friends to a meeting at Five Forks Baptist Church. All the white folks gathered 'round an' shook his hand an' I peeked 'tween their legs an' got a good look at' im. But he didn't have no whiskers, he was smooth-face! (Pictures of General Lee all show him with beard and mustache)

Miss Ella died two years ago. I was sick in the hospital but the doctor come to tell me. I couldn't go to her buryin'. I sure missed her. (Poignant grief moistens Betty's eyes and thickens her voice). There wasn't ever no one like her. Miss Kate an' young Miss Julia still live at 'the house' with their brother, Marse Lucian (all children of the first Beverly Jones and 'old Miss Julia',) but it don't seem right with Miss Ella gone. Life seems dif'rent, some how, 'though there' lots of my young white folks an' my own kin livin' round an' they're real good to me. But Miss Ella's gone!

"Goodday, Ma'am. Come anytime. You're welcome to. I'm right glad to have visitors 'cause I can't get out much." A bobbing little curtsy accompanies Betty's cordial farewell.

Although a freed woman for 71 years, property owner for half of them, and now revered head of a clan of self respecting, self-supporting colored citizens, she is still at heart a "Jones negro," and all the distinguished descendants of her beloved Marse Beverly and Miss Julia will be her "own folks" as long as she lives.

N.C. District:	No. 2
No. Words:	340
Worker:	Mary A. Hicks
Subject:	Ex-Slave Story
Person Interviewed:	John Coggin
Editor:	Daisy Bailey Waitt

JOHN COGGIN

When the interviewer first visited Uncle John he was busy cutting hay for a white family nearby, swinging the scythe with the vigor of a young man. In late afternoon he was found sitting on the doorsteps of his granddaughter's house after a supper which certainly had onions on the menu and was followed by something stronger than water.

"I was borned on March 1, 1852 in Orange County. My mammy wuz named Phillis Fenn an' she wuz from

Virginia. I ain't neber had no paw an' I ain't wanted none, I ain't had no brothers nar sisters nother."

"We 'longed ter Doctor Jim Leathers, an' de only whuppin' I eber got wuz 'bout fightin' wid young Miss Agnes, who wuz sommers long' bout my age. Hit wuz jist a little whuppin' but I' members hit all right."

"We wucked de fiel's, I totin' water fer de six or seben han's that wucked dar. An' we jist wucked moderate like. We had plenty ter eat an' plenty ter w'ar, do' we did go barefooted most of de year. De marster shore wuz good ter us do'."

"I 'members dat de fust I hyard of de Yankees wuz when young marster come in an' says, 'Lawd pa, de Yankees am in Raleigh.'"

"Dat ebenin' I wuz drawin' water when all of a sudden I looks up de road, an' de air am dark wid Yankees. I neber seed so many mens, hosses an' mules in my life. De band wuz playin' an' de soldiers wuz hollerin' an' de hosses wuz prancin' high. I done what all of de rest o' de slaves done, I run fer de woods."

"Atter de surrender we moved ter a place nigh Dix Hill hyar in Raleigh an' my mammy married a Coggin, dar's whar I gits my name. All of us slaves moved dar an' farmed."

"Way long time atter dat ole Marster Jim come ter visit his niggers, an' we had a big supper in his honor. Dat night he died, an' 'fore he died his min' sorta wanders an' he thinks dat hit am back in de slave days an' dat atter a long journey he am comin' back home. Hit shore wuz pitiful an' we shore did hate it."

"Yes 'um honey, we got 'long all right atter de war. You knows dat niggers ain't had no sense den, now dey has. Look at dese hyar seben chilluns, dey am my great gran'chillun an' dey got a heap mo' sense dan I has right now."

EH

N.C. District:	No. 2
Worker:	Mary A. Hicks
No. Words:	433
Subject:	MANDY COVERSON
Story Teller:	Mandy Coverson
Editor:	Daisy Bailey Waitt
Date Stamp:	"JUN 7 1937"

MANDY COVERSON

I wuz borned in Union County to Sarah an' Henderson Tomberlin. My mother belonged to Mr. Moses Coverson, an' my pappy belonged to Mr. Jackie Tom Tomberlin. I stayed wid my mammy, of course, an' Marster Moses wuz good ter me. Dey warn't so good ter my mammy, case dey makes her wuck frum sunup till sundown in de hot summertime, an' she ain't had no fun at all. She plowed two oxes, an' if'en yo' has eber been around a steer yo' knows what aggravatin' things dey is.

De oberseer, whose name I'se plumb forget, wuz pore white trash an' he wuz meaner dan de meanest nigger. Anyhow I wuz too little ter do much wuck so I played a heap an' I had a big time.

My mammy, died 'fore I wuz very old an' missus kept me in de house. I wuz petted by her, an' I reckon spoiled. Yo' knows dat den de niggers ain't neber eat no biscuits but missus always gimmie one eber meal an' in dat way she got me interested in waitin' on de table.

I wuzn't old enough ter know much, but I does 'member how de fambly hid all de valuables 'fore de Yankees come, an' dat Marster Moses in pickin' up de big brass andirons hurt his back an' dey said dat dat wuz de cause of his death a little while atterwards. Anyhow de andirons wuz saved an' dar warn't no trouble wid de Yankees who comed our way, an' dey ain't hurt nobody dar.

Dey did kill all de things dat dey could eat an' dey stold de rest of de feed stuff. Dey make one nigger boy draw water fer dere hosses fer a day an' night. De Yankees wuz mean 'bout cussin', but de southern soldiers wuz jist as bad. Wheeler's Cavalry wuz de meanest in de whole bunch, I thinks.

De Ku Kluxes wuz pretty mean, but dey picked dere spite on de Free Issues. I doan know why dey done dis 'cept dat dey ain't wantin' no niggers a-favorin' dem nigh by, now dat slavery am ober. Dey done a heap of beatin' an' chasin' folkses out'n de country but I 'specks dat de Carpet Bagger's rule wuz mostly de cause of it.

I married Daniel Coverson, a slave on de same plantation I wuz on, an' forty years ago we moved ter Raleigh. We had a hard time but I'se glad dat he an' me am free an' doan belong ter two diff'ent famblies.

AC

N.C. District:	No. 2
Worker:	Mary A. Hicks
No. Words:	914
Subject:	Ex-Slave Story
Person Interviewed:	Willie Cozart
Editor:	Daisy Bailey Waitt

WILLIE COZART

No mam, Mistress, I doan want ter ride in no automobile, thank you, I'se done walked these three miles frum Zebulon an' walkin' is what has kept me goin' all dese years.

Yes'm I'se a bachelor an' I wuz borned on June 11, 1845 in Person County. My papa wuz named Ed an' my maw wuz named Sally. Dar wuz ten of us youngins, Morris, Dallas, Stephen, Jerry, Florence, Polly, Lena, Phillis, Caroline, an' me. Mr. Starling Oakley of Person County, near Roxboro wuz my master an' as long as him an' ole mistress lived I went back ter see dem.

He wuz right good to de good niggers an' kinder strick wid de bad ones. Pusonly he ain't never have me whupped but two or three times. You's hyard 'bout dese set down strikes lately, well dey ain't de fust ones. Onct when I wuz four or five years old, too little to wuck in de fiel's, my master sot me an' some more little chilluns ter wuck pullin' up weeds roun' de house. Well, I makes a speech and I tells dem le's doan wuck none so out we sprawls on de grass under de apple tree. Atter awhile ole master found us dar, an' when he fin's dat I wuz de ring-leader he gives me a little whuppin'.

Hit wuz a big plantation, round 1,200 acres o' land, I reckon, an' he had 'bout seventy or eighty slaves to wuck de cotton, corn, tobacco an' de wheat an' vege'bles. De big house wuz sumpin to look at, but de slave cabins wuz jist log huts wid sand floors, and stick an' dirt chimneys. We wuz 'lowed ter have a little patch o' garden stuff at de back but no chickens ner pigs. De only way we had er' makin' money wuz by pickin' berries an' sellin' 'em. We ain't had much time to do dat, case we wucked frum sunup till sundown six days a week.

De master fed us as good as he knowed how, but it wuz mostly on bread, meat, an' vege'bles.

I 'members seberal slave sales whar dey sold de pappy or de mammy 'way frum de chillums an' dat wuz a sad time. Dey led dem up one at de time an' axed dem questions an' dey warn't many what wuz chained, only de bad ones, an' sometime when dey wuz travelin' it wuz necessary to chain a new gang.

I'se seed niggers beat till da blood run, an' I'se seed plenty more wid big scars, frum whuppin's but dey wuz de bad ones. You wuz whupped 'cordin ter de deed yo' done in dem days. A moderate whuppin' wuz thirty-nine or forty lashes an' a real whuppin' wuz a even hundred; most folks can't stand a real whuppin'.

Frum all dis you might think dat we ain't had no good times, but we had our co'n shuckin's, candy pullin's an' sich like. We ain't felt like huntin' much, but I did go on a few fox hunts wid de master. I uster go fishin' too, but I ain't been now since 1873, I reckon. We sometimes went ter de neighborhood affairs if'n we wuz good, but if we wuzn't an' didn't git a pass de patter-rollers would shore git us. When dey got through whuppin' a nigger he knowed he wuz whupped too.

De slave weddin's in dat country wuz sorta dis way: de man axed de master fer de 'oman an' he jist told dem ter step over de broom an' dat wuz de way dey got married dem days; de pore white folks done de same way.

Atter de war started de white folks tried ter keep us niggers frum knowin' 'bout it, but de news got aroun' somehow, an' dar wuz some talk of gittin' shet of de master's family an' gittin' rich. De plans didn't 'mout to nothin' an' so de Yankees come down.

I 'members moughty well when de Yankees come through our country. Dey stold ever'thing dey could find an' I 'members what ole master said. He says, 'Ever' one dat wants ter wuck fer me git in de patch ter pullin' dat forty acres of fodder an' all dat don't git up de road wid dem d—— Yankees.' Well we all went away.

Dat winter wuz tough, all de niggers near 'bout starved ter death, an' we ain't seed nothin' of de forty acres of land an' de mule what de Yankees done promise us nother. Atter awhile we had ter go ter our ole masters an' ax 'em fer bread ter keep us alive.

De Klu Klux Klan sprung right up out of de earth, but de Yankees put a stop ter dat by puttin' so many of dem in jail. Dey do say dat dat's what de State Prison wus built fer.

I never believed in witches an' I ain't put much stock in hain'ts but I'se seed a few things durin' my life dat I can't 'splain, like de thing wid de red eyes dat mocked me one night; but shucks I ain't believin' in dem things much. I'se plowed my lan', tended it year atter year, lived by myself an' all, an' I ain't got hurted yet, but I ain't never rid in a automobile yet, an' I got one tooth left.

B. N.

N.C. District: No. 2
Worker: T. Pat Matthews
No. Words: 1453
Subject: HANNAH CRASSON
Story Teller: Hannah Crasson
Editor: Daisy Bailey Waitt
HW notes at bottom of page illegible

HANNAH CRASSON

My name is Hannah Crasson. I wuz born on John William Walton's plantation 4 miles from Garner and 13 miles from Raleigh, N. C. in the County of Wake. I am 84 years ole the 2nd day uv dis las' gone March. I belonged to Mr. John William Walton in slavery time. My missus wuz named Miss Martha.

My father wuz named Frank Walton. My mother wuz named Flora Walton. Grandma wuz 104 years when she died. She died down at de old plantation. My brothers were named

Johnnie and Lang. My sisters were Adeline, Violet, Mary, Sarah, Ellen, and Annie. Four of us are livin', Ellen, Mary, Sarah and me.

De old boss man wuz good to us. I wuz talkin' about him the udder night. He didn't whup us and he said, he didn't want nobody else to whup us. It is jis like I tell you; he wuz never cruel to us. One uv his sons wuz cruel to us. We had a plenty to eat, we shore did, plenty to eat. We had nice houses to live in too. Grandma had a large room to live in, and we had one to live in. Daddy stayed at home with mother. They worked their patches by moonlight; and worked for the white folks in the day time.

They sold what they made. Marster bought it and paid for it. He made a barrel o' rice every year, my daddy did.

Mr. Bell Allen owned slaves too. He had a plenty o' niggers. His plantation wuz 5 miles from ourn. We went to church at the white folks church. When Mr. Bell Allen seed us cummin' he would say, 'Yonder comes John Walton's free niggers.'

Our marster would not sell his slaves. He give dem to his children when they married off do'. I swept yards, churned, fed the chickens. In de ebening I would go with my missus a fishin'. We eat collards, peas, corn bread, milk, and rice. We got biskit and butter twice a week. I thought dat de best things I ever et wuz butter spread on biskit. We had a corn mill and a flour mill on the plantation. There wuz about 24 slaves on de place. Dey had brandy made on de plantation, and de marster gib all his slaves some for dere own uses.

My grandmother and mother wove our clothes.

Dey were called homespun. Dey made de shoes on de plantation too. I wuz not married til atter de surrender. I did not dress de finest in the world; but I had nice clothes. My wedding dress wuz made of cream silk, made princess with pink and cream bows. I wore a pair of morocco store bought shoes. My husband was dressed in a store bought suit of clothes, the coat wuz made pigen tail. He had on a velvet vest and a white collar and tie. Somebody stole de ves' atter dat.

One of our master's daughters wuz cruel. Sometimes she would go out and rare on us, but old marster didn't want us whupped.

Our great grand mother wuz named granny Flora. Dey stole her frum Africa wid a red pocket handkerchief. Old man John William got my great grandmother. De people in New England got scured of we niggers. Dey were afrid me would rise aginst em and dey pushed us on down South. Lawd, why didn't dey let us stay whur we wuz, dey nebber wouldn't a been so menny half white niggers, but the old marster wuz to blame for that.

We never saw any slaves sold. They carried them off to sell 'em. The slaves travelled in droves. Fathers and mothers were sold from their chilluns. Chilluns wuz sold from their parents on de plantations close to us. Where we went to church, we sat in a place away from de white folks. The slaves never did run away from marster, because he wuz good to 'em; but they run away from other plantations.

Yes, we seed the patterollers, we called 'em pore white trash, we also called patterollers pore white pecks. They had ropes around their necks. They came to our house one night when we were singin' and prayin'. It wuz jist before the surrender. Dey were hired by de slave owner. My daddy told us to show 'em de brandy our marster gib us, den dey went on a way, kase dey knowed John Walton wuz a funny man about his slaves. Dey gave us Christmas and other holidays. Den dey, de men, would go to see dere wives. Some of the men's wives belong to other marsters on other plantations. We had corn shuckin's at night, and candy pullin's. Sometimes we had quiltings and dances.

One of the slaves, my aint, she wuz a royal slave. She could dance all over de place wid a tumbler of water on her head, widout spilling it. She sho could tote herself. I always luved to see her come to church. She sho could tote herself.

My oldest sister Violet died in slavery time. She wuz ten years old when she died. Her uncles were her pall bearers. Uncle Hyman and Uncle Handy carried her to the grave yard. If I makes no mistake my daddy made her coffin. Dere wuz no singin'. There were seven of the family dere, dat wuz all. Dey had no funeral. Dere were no white folks dere.

Dey baptized people in creeks and ponds.

We rode corn stalks, bent down small pine trees and rode' em for horses. We also played prison base. Colored and white played, yes sir, whites and colored. We played at night but we had a certain time to go to bed. Dat wuz nine o'clock. HW:

De boss man looked atter us when we wuz sick. He got doctors. I had the typhoid fever. All my hair came out. Dey called it de "mittent fever." Dr. Thomas Banks doctored me. He been dead a long time. Oh! I don't know how long he been dead. Near all my white folks were found dead. Mr. John died outside.

Walton died in bed. Marster Joe Walton died sitting under a tree side de path. Miss Hancey died in bed.

I 'member the day de war commenced. My marster called my father and my two uncles Handy and Hyman, our marster called 'em. Dey had started back to the field to work in the afternoon. He said, 'Cum here boys,' that wuz our young marster, Ben Walton, says 'cum here boys. I got sumptin' to tell you.' Uncle Hyman said, 'I can't. I got to go to work.' He said 'Come here and set down, I got sumptin' to tell you.'

The niggers went to him and set down. He told them; 'There is a war commenced between the North and the South. If the North whups you will be as free a man as I is. If the South whups you will be a slave all your days.'

Mr. Joe Walton said when he went to war dat dey could eat breakfast at home, go and whup the North, and be back far dinner. He went away, and it wuz four long years before he cum back to dinner. De table wuz shore set a long time for him. A lot of de white folks said dey wouldn't be much war, dey could whup dem so easy. Many of dem never did come back to dinner. I wuz afraid of the Yankees because Missus had told us the Yankees were going to kill every nigger in the South. I hung to my mammy when dey come through.

I thought Abraham Lincoln wuz the Medicine man, with grip in his han', cause he said every borned man must be free.

I did not think anything of Jeff Davis. I thank de will of God for setting us free. He got into Abraham Lincoln and the Yankees. We are thankful to the Great Marster dat got into Lincoln and the Yankees. Dey say Booker Washington wuz fine, I don't know.

The white folks did not allow us to have nuthing to do wid books. You better not be found, tryin' to learn to read. Our marster wuz harder down on dat den anything else. You better not be ketched wid a book. Day read the Bible and told us to obey our marster for de Bible said obey your marster.

The first band of music I ever herd play the Yankees wuz playin' it. They were playin' a song. 'I am tired of seeing de homespun dresses the southern women wear'.

I thinks Mr. Roosevelt is a fine man. Jus' what we need.

N.C. District: No. 2
Worker: Mary A. Hicks
No. Words: 130
Subject: EX-SLAVE STORY
Story Teller: Julia Crenshaw
Editor: Daisy Bailey Waitt
[TR: HW circled "I"]

JULIA CRENSHAW

My mammy wuz named Jane an' my pappy wuz named Richard. Dey belonged ter Lawyer R. J. Lewis in Raleigh, dar whar Peace Institute am ter day. Mammy said dat de white folkses wuz good ter dem an' gib 'em good food an' clothes. She wuz de cook, an' fer thirty years atter de war she cooked at Peace.

Before de Yankees come Mr. Lewis said, dat he dreamed dat de yard wuz full uv dem an' he wuz deef. When dey comed he played deef so dat he won't have ter talk ter 'em. Him he am dat proud.

Mammy said dat she ain't cared 'bout been' free case she had a good home, but atter all slavery wusn't de thing fer America.

N.C. District:	No. 2
Worker:	T. Pat Matthews
No. Words:	1,414
Subject:	ZEB CROWDER
Story Teller:	Zeb Crowder
Editor:	Daisy Bailey Waitt
Date Stamp:	"JUN 30 1937"

ZEB CROWDER

I wont nuthin' in slavery time and I aint nuthin' now. All de work I am able ter do now is a little work in de garden. Dey say I is too ole ter work, so charity gives me a little ter go upon every week. For one weeks 'lowance o' sumptin' ter eat dey gives me, hold on, I will show you, dat beats guessin'. Here it is: ½ peck meal (corn meal), 2 lbs oat meal, 2 lb dry skim milk, and 1 lb plate meat. Dis is what I gits fer one week 'lowance. I can't work much, but de white folks gib me meals fur washin' de woodwork in dere houses, de white folks in Hayes's Bottom. What little I do, I does fer him. He gives me meals for workin'. De charity gives me about 80 cts worth o' rations a week.

I wus seven years old when de Yankees come through. All de niggers 'cept me an' de white folks ran to de woods. I didn't have sense enough ter run, so I stayed on de porch where dey were passin' by. One of 'em pointed his gun at me. I remember it as well as it was yisterday.

Yes sir, I seed de Yankees and I remember de clothes dey wore. Dey were blue and dere coats had capes on' em and large brass buttons. De niggers and white folks were afraid of' em. De ole house where dey came by, an' me on de porch is still standin', yes sir, and dey are livin' in it now. It belongs to Ralph Crowder, and he has a fellow by de name o' Edward, a colored man, livin' dere now. De house is de udder side o' Swift Creek, right at Rands Mill. I belonged ter ole man William Crowder durin' slavery, Tom Crowder's daddy. Ralph is Tom's son. My missus wus named Miss Melvina an' if I lives ter be a hundred years old I will never forget dem white folks. Yes sir, dey shore wus good ter us. We had good food, good clothes and a good place ter sleep.

My mother died before de war, but Miss Melvina wus so good ter us we didn't know so much difference. Mother wus de first person I remember seein' dead. When she died Miss Melvina, marster's wife, called us chillun in and says, 'Chillun your mother is dead, but anything in dis kitchen you wants ter eat go take it, but don't slip nuthin'. If you slip it you will soon be stealin' things.' I had four brothers and one sister, and none of us never got into trouble 'bout stealin'. She taught us ter let other people's things alone.

My father wus named Waddy Crowder. My mother wus named Neelie Crowder. Grandpa was named Jacob Crowder and grandma was named Sylvia Crowder. I know dem jist as good as if it wus yisterday.

Never went ter school a day in my life. I can't read an' write. Dey would not 'low slaves ter have books, no sir reee, no, dat dey wouldn't. We went wid de white folks to church; dey were good ter us, dat's de truth. Dere aint many people dat knows 'bout dem good times. Dey had a lot o' big dinners and when de white folks got through I would go up and eat all I wanted.

I 'member choppin' cotton on Clabber branch when I wus a little boy before de surrender. When de surrender come I didn't like it. Daddy an' de udders didn't like it, 'cause after de surrender dey had to pay marster fer de meat an' things. Before dat dey didn't have nuthin' to do but work. Dere were eight slaves on de place in slavery time. Clabber branch run into Swift Creek. Lord have mercy, I have caught many a fish on dat branch. I also piled brush in de winter time. Birds went in de brush ter roost. Den we went bird blindin'. We had torches made o' lightwood splinters, and brushes in our han's, we hit de piles o' brush after we got 'round 'em. When de birds come out we would kill 'em. Dere were lots o' birds den. We killed' em at night in the sage fields[5] where broom grass was thick. Dem were de good times. No sich times now. We killed robins, doves, patridges and other kinds o' birds. Dey aint no such gangs o' birds now. We briled 'em over coals o' fire and fried 'em in fryin' pans, and sometimes we had a bird stew, wid all de birds we wanted. De stew wus de bes' o' all. Dere aint no sich stews now. We put flour in de stew. It was made into pastry first, and we called it slick. When we cooked chicken wid it we called it chicken slick.

Dere were no overseers on our plantation. Marster wouldn't let you have any money on Sunday. He would not trade on Sunday. He would not handle money matters on Monday, but 'ceptin' dese two days if you went to him he would keep you. He was who a good ole man. Dat's de truf.

The Ku Klux would certainly work on you. If dey caught you out of your place dey would git wid you. I don't remember anything 'bout de Freedman's Bureau but de Ku Klux Klan was something all niggers wus scared of. Yes sir, dey would get wid you. Dats right. Ha! Ha! Dat's right.

I never seen a slave whupped, no sir, I never see a slave sold. I saw de speculators do'. I saw de patterollers, but dey didn't never whup my daddy. Dey run him one time, but dey couldn't cotch him. Marster Crowder allus give daddy a pass when he asked fer it.

I believe ole marster an' ole missus went right on ter Heaven, Yes, I do believe dat. Dat's de truf. Yes, my Lawd, I would like to see' em right now. Dere is only one o' de old crowd livin', an' dat is Miss Cora. She stays right here in Raleigh.

We used to have candy pullin's, an' I et more ash cakes den anybody. We cooked ash cakes out o' meal. We had dances in de winter time, and other plays. I played marbles an' runnin' an' jumpin' when I wus a chile. Dey give us sasafrac tea sweetened to eat wid bread. It shore wus mighty good. My father never married enny more. He settled right down after de war and farmed fer his old marster and all we chillun stayed. We didn't want ter leave, an' I would be wid 'em right now if dey wus livin'.

I got married when I wus 21 years old, and moved ter myself in a little house on de plantation. De house is standin' dere now, de house where I lived den. I seed it de udder day when I went out dere to clean off my wife's grave. I married Lula Hatcher. She died 'bout ten years ago. I married her in Georgia. I stayed dere a long time when missus' brother, Wiley Clemmons, went ter Georgia ter run turpentine an' tuck me wid him. I stayed dere till he died; an' Mr. Tom Crowder went after him an' brought him back home an' buried him at de ole home place. He is buried right dere at de Crowder place.

I have worked wid some o' de Crowders mos' all my life and I miss dem people, when one of 'em dies. Dey allus give my daddy outside patches, and he made good on it. He cleaned up seven acres, and do you know how he fenced it? Wid nuthin' but bresh. An' hogs an' cows didn't go in dere neither. We had lots o' game ter eat. Marster 'lowed my daddy ter hunt wid a gun, and he killed a lot o' rabbits, squirrels, an' game. We trapped birds an' caught rabbits in boxes. Daddy caught possums an' coons wid dogs. One o' my brothers is livin' at Garner, N.C. I am four years older den he is. From what little judgment I got I thought a right smart o' Abraham Lincoln, but I tells you de truf Mr. Roosevelt has done a lot o' good. Dats de truf. I likes him.

[5] The Negroes call the tall grass sage.

AC

N.C. District:	No. 2
Worker:	T. Pat Matthews
No. Words:	585
Subject:	ADELINE CRUMP
Person Interviewed:	Adeline Crump
Editor:	Daisy Bailey Waitt

ADELINE CRUMP

My name is Adeline Crump, and I am 73 years old. My husband's name wus James Crump. My mother's wus Marie Cotton and my father's name wus Cotton. My mother belonged to the Faucetts; Rich Faucett wus her marster. Father belonged to the Cottons; Wright Cotton wus his marster. My maiden name wus Cotton. Mother and father said they were treated all right and that they loved their white folks. They gave them patches, clothed them tolerably well, and seed that they got plenty to eat. The hours of work wus long. Nearbout everybody worked long hours then, but they said they wus not mistreated 'bout nothing. When they got sick marster got a doctor, if they wus bad off sick.

They wus allowed holidays Christmas and at lay-by time, an' they wus 'lowed to hunt possums an' coons at night an' ketch rabbits in gums. They also caught birds in traps made of splinters split from pine wood.

Mother and father had no learnin'. They would not

allow them to learn to read and write. Marster wus keerful 'bout that. I cannot read an' write. My mother and father told me many stories 'bout the patterollers and Ku Klux. A nigger better have a pass when he went visitin' or if they caught him they tore up his back. The Ku Klux made the niggers think they could drink a well full of water. They carried rubber things under their clothes and a rubber pipe leadin' to a bucket o' water. The water bag helt the water they did not drink it. Guess you have heard people tell 'bout they drinking so much water.

Marster didn't have no overseers to look after his slaves. He done that hisself with the help o' some o' his men slaves. Sometimes he made 'em foreman and my mother and father said they all got along mighty fine. The colored folks went to the white folk's church and had prayer meeting in their homes.

Mother lived in the edge o' marster's yard. When the surrender come after the war they stayed on the plantation right on and lived on marster's land. They built log houses after de war cause marster let all his slaves stay right on his plantation. My mother had twenty-one chillun. She had twins five times. I was a twin and Emaline wus my sister. She died 'bout thirty years ago. She left 11 chillun when she died. I never had but four chillun. All my people are dead, I is de only one left.

Marster's plantation was 'bout six miles from Merry Oaks in Chatham County. We moved to Merry Oaks when I wus fourteen years old. I married at seventeen. I have lived in North Carolina all my life. We moved to Raleigh from Merry Oaks long time ago. My husband died here seventeen years ago. I worked after my husband died, washin' and ironin' for white folks till I am not able to work no more. Hain't worked any in fo' years. Charity don't help me none. My chillun gives me what I gits.

Slavery wus a bad thing, cause from what mother and father tole me all slaves didn't fare alike. Some fared good an' some bad. I don't know enough 'bout Abraham Lincoln an' Mr. Roosevelt to talk about 'em. No, I don't know just what to say. I sho' hopes you will quit axin' me so many things cause I forgot a lot mother and father tole me.

N.C. District:	No. 2
Worker:	Mary A. Hicks
No. Words:	844
Subject:	BILL CRUMP
Person Interviewed:	Bill Crump
Editor:	Daisy Bailey Waitt

HW: "photo"

BILL CRUMP

I reckon dat I wus borned in Davidson County on de plantation of Mr. Whitman Smith, my mammy's marster.

My daddy wus named Tom an' he 'longed ter Mr. Ben Murry fust an' later ter Mr. Jimmy Crump. Daddy wus named atter his young marster. Dey lived in Randolph, de county next ter Davidson whar me mammy an' de rest of de chilluns, Alt, George, Harriet, Sarah, Mary an' de baby libed.

Both of de marsters wus good ter us, an' dar wus plenty ter eat an' w'ar, an' right many jubilees. We ain't none of de dozen er so of us eber got a whuppin', case we ain't desarved no whuppin'; why, dar wusn't eben a cowhide whup anywhar on de place. We wucked in de fie'ls from sunup ter sundown mos' o' de time, but we had a couple of hours at dinner time ter swim or lay on de banks uv de little crick an' sleep. Ober 'bout sundown marster let us go swim ag'in iff'en we wanted ter do it.

De marster let us have some chickens, a shoat an' a gyarden, an' 'tater patch, an' we had time off ter wuck 'em. In season we preserved our own fruits fer de winter an' so we larned not ter be so heaby on de marster's han's.

My daddy wus a fiddler, an' he sometimes played fer de dances at de Cross Roads, a little village near de marster's place. All what ain't been mean could go, but de mean ones can't, an' de rest o' us has ter habe a pass ter keep de patterollers from gittin us.

Yes mam, we had our fun at de dances, co'n chuckin's, candy pullin's, an' de gatherin's an' we sarbed de marster better by habin' our fun.

I'se seed a bunch o' slaves sold a heap of times an' I neber seed no chains on nobody. Dey jist stood dem on de table front of de post office at Cross Roads an' sol' 'em ter de one what bids de highes'.

We hyard a whisper 'bout some slaves bein' beat ter death, but I ain't neber seed a slave git a lick of no kin', course atter de war I seed de Ku Klux runnin' mean niggers.

Dar wus no marryin' on de plantation, iffen a nigger wants a 'oman he has got ter buy her or git her marster's permit, den dey am married.

When one o' de slaves wus sick he had a doctor fast as lightnin', an' when de died he wus set up wid one night. De marster would gibe de mourners a drink o' wine mebbe, an' dey'd mo'n, an' shout, an' sing all de night long, while de cop'se laid out on de coolin' board, which 'minds me of a tale.

Onct we wus settin' up wid a nigger, 'fore de war an' hit bein' a hot night de wine wus drunk an' de mo'ners wus settin' front o' de do' eatin' watermillons while de daid man laid on de coolin' board. Suddenly one of de niggers looks back in at de do', an' de daid man am settin' up on de coolin' board lookin right at him. De man what sees hit hollers, an' all de rest what has been wishin 'dat de daid man can enjoy de wine an' de watermillons am sorry dat he has comed back.

Dey doan take time ter say hit do', case dey am gone ter de big house. De marster am brave so he comes ter see, an' he says dat hit am only restrictions o' de muscles.

De nex' mornin', as am de way, dey puts de man in a pine box made by 'nother slave an' dey totes him from de cabin ter de marster's buryin' groun' at de cedars; an' de slaves bury's him while de marster an' his fambly looks on.

I doan know much 'bout de Yankees case de warn't none 'cept de skirtin' parties comed our way.

Atter de war we stays on fer four or five years mebbe, an' I goes ter school two weeks. De teacher wus Mr. Edmund Knights from de No'th.

I'se sarbed four years an' ten months of a eight ter twelve stretch fer killin' a man. Dis man an' a whole gang o' us wus at his house gamblin'. I had done quit drinkin' er mont' er so 'fore dat, but dey 'sists on hit, but I 'fuses. Atter 'while he pours some on me an' I cusses him, den he cusses me, an' he says dat he am gwine ter kill me, an' he follers me down de road. I turns roun' an' shoots him.

Dat am all of my story 'cept dat I has seen a powerful heap of ghostes an' I knows dat dey comes in white an' black, an' dat dey am in de shape er dogs, mens, an' eber'thing dat you can have a mind to.

LE

N.C. District:	No. 2
Worker:	Mary A. Hicks
No. Words:	652
Subject:	CHARLIE CRUMP
Person Interviewed:	Charlie Crump
Editor:	Daisy Bailey Waitt
Date Stamp:	"— 11 1937"

CHARLIE CRUMP

I wuz borned at Evan's Ferry in Lee or Chatham County, an' I belonged ter Mr. Davis Abernathy an' his wife Mis' Vick. My pappy wuz named Ridge, an' my mammy wuz named Marthy. My brothers wuz Stokes an' Tucker, an' my sisters wuz Lula an' Liddy Ann. Dar wuz nine o' us in all, but some o' dem wuz sold, an' some o' dem wuz dead.

De Abernathy's wuzn't good ter us, we got very little ter eat, nothin' ter wear an' a whole lot o' whuppin's. Dey ain't had no slaves 'cept seben or eight, in fact, dey wuz pore white trash tryin' ter git rich; so dey make us wuck.

Dey wucks us from daylight till dark, an' sometimes we jist gits one meal a day. De marster says dat empty niggers am good niggers an' dat full niggers has got de debil in dem. An' we ain't 'lowed ter go nowhar at night, dat is if dey knowed it. I'se seed de time dat niggers from all ober de neighborhood gang up an' have fun anyhow, but if dey hyard de patterollers comin' gallopin' on a hoss dey'd fly. Crap shootin' wuz de style den, but a heap of times dey can't find nothin ter bet.

I toted water, case dat's all I wuz big enough ter do, an' lemmie tell yo' dat when de war wuz ober I ain't had nary a sprig of hair on my haid, case de wooden buckets what I toted on it wored it plumb off.

When we got hongry an' could fin' a pig, a calf or a chicken, no matter who it had belonged to, it den belonged ter us. We raised a heap o' cane an' we et brown sugar. Hit 's funny dat de little bit dey gibed us wuz what dey now calls wholesome food, an' hit shore make big husky niggers.

My mammy had more grit dan any gal I now knows of has in her craw. She plowed a hateful little donkey dat wuz about as hongry as she wuz, an' he wuz a cuss if'en dar eber wuz one. Mammy wuz a little brown gal, den, tough as nails an' she ain't axin' dat donkey no odds at all. She uster take him out at twelve an' start fer de house an' dat donkey would hunch up his back an' swear dat she wuzn't gwine ter ride him home. Mammy would swear dat she would, an' de war would be on. He'd throw her, but she'd git back on an' atter she'd win de fight he'd go fer de house as fast as a scaulded dog.

When we hyard dat de Yankees wuz comin' we wuz skeerd, case Marse Abernathy told us dat dey'd skin us alive. I'members hit wuz de last o' April or de fust o' May when dey comed, an' I had started fer de cane fil' wid a bucket o' water on my haid, but when I sees dem Yankees comin' I draps de bucket an' runs.

De folks thar 'bouts burnt de bridge crost de ribber, but de Yankees carried a rope bridge wid 'em, so dey crossed anyhow.

Dem Yankees tuck eber thing dat dey saw eben to our kush, what we had cooked fer our supper. Kush wuz cornmeal, onions, red pepper, salt an' grease, dat is if we had any grease. Dey killed all de cows, pigs, chickens an' stold all de hosses an' mules.

We wuz glad ter be free, an' lemmie tell yo', we shore cussed ole marster out 'fore we left dar; den we comed ter Raleigh. I'se always been a farmer an' I'se made right good. I lak de white folkses an' dey laks me but I'll tell yo' Miss, I'd ruther be a nigger any day dan to be lak my ole white folks wuz.

L. E.

N.C. District:	No. 2
Worker:	Mary Hicks
No. Words:	10,018
Subject:	BEFORE AND AFTER THE WAR
Story Teller:	Mattie Curtis
Editor:	George L. Andrews
Date Stamp:	**HW: 8/31/37**

MATTIE CURTIS

I wus borned on de plantation of Mr. John Hayes in Orange County ninety-eight years ago. Seberal of de chilluns had been sold 'fore de speculator come an' buyed mammy, pappy an' we three chilluns. De speculator wus named Bebus an' he lived in Henderson, but he meant to sell us in de tobacco country.

We come through Raleigh an' de fust thing dat I 'members good wus goin' through de paper mill on Crabtree. We traveled on ter Granville County on de Granville Tobacco path till a preacher named Whitfield buyed us. He lived near de Granville an' Franklin County line, on de Granville side.

Preacher Whitfield, bein' a preacher, wus supposed to be good, but he ain't half fed ner clothed his slaves an' he whupped 'em bad. I'se seen him whup my mammy wid all de clothes offen her back. He'd buck her down on a barrel an' beat de blood outen her. Dar wus some difference in his beatin' from de neighbors. De folks round dar 'ud whup in de back yard, but Marse Whitfield 'ud have de barrel carried in his parlor fer de beatin'.

We ain't had no sociables, but we went to church on Sunday an' dey preached to us dat we'd go ter hell alive iffen we sassed our white folks.

Speakin' 'bout clothes, I went as naked as Yo' han' till I wus fourteen years old. I wus naked like dat when my nature come to me. Marse Whitfield ain't carin', but atter dat mammy tol' him dat I had ter have clothes.

Marse Whitfield ain't never pay fer us so finally we wus sold to Mis' Fanny Long in Franklin County. Dat 'oman wus a debil iffen dar eber wus one. When I wus little I had picked up de fruit, fanned flies offen de table wid a peafowl fan an' nussed de little slave chilluns. De las' two or three years I had worked in de fiel' but at Mis' Long's I worked in de backer factory.

Yes mam, she had a backer factory whar backer wus stemmed, rolled an' packed in cases fer sellin'. Dey said dat she had got rich on sellin' chawin' terbacker.

We wus at Mis' Long's when war wus declared, 'fore dat she had been purty good, but she am a debil now. Her son am called ter de war an' he won't go. Dey comes an' arrests him, den his mammy tries ter pay him out, but dat ain't no good.

De officers sez dat he am yaller an' dat day am gwine ter shoot his head off an' use hit fer a soap gourd. De Yankees did shoot him down here at Bentonville an' Mis' Long went atter de body. De Confederates has got de body but dey won't let her have it fer love ner money. Dey laughs an' tells her how yaller he am an' dey buries him in a ditch like a dog.

Mis' Long has been bad enough fore den but atter her son is dead she sez dat she am gwine ter fight till she draps dead. De nex' day she sticks de shot gun in mammy's back an' sez dat she am gwine ter shoot her dead. Mammy smiles an' tells her dat she am ready ter go. Mis' Long turns on me an' tells me ter go ter de peach tree an' cut her ten limbs 'bout a yard long, dis I does an' atter she ties dem in a bundle she wears dem out on me at a hundret licks. Lemmie tell yo', dar wus pieces of de peach tree switches stickin' all in my bloody back when she got through.

Atter dat Mis' Long ain't done nothin' but whup us an' fight till she shore nuff wore out.

De Yankee captain come ter our place an tol' us dat de lan' was goin' ter be cut up an' divided among de slaves, dey would also have a mule an' a house apiece.

I doan know how come hit but jist 'fore de end of de war we come ter Moses Mordicia's place, right up de hill from here. He wus mean too, he'd get drunk an' whup niggers all day off' an' on. He'd keep dem tied down dat long too, sometimes from sunrise till dark.

Mr. Mordicia had his yaller gals in one quarter ter dereselves an' dese gals belongs ter de Mordicia men, dere friends an' de overseers. When a baby wus born in dat quarter dey'd sen' hit over ter de black quarter at birth. Dey do say dat some of dese gal babies got grown an' atter goin' back ter de yaller quarter had more chilluns fer her own daddy or brother. De Thompson's sprung from dat set an' dey say dat a heap of dem is halfwits fer de reason dat I has jist tol' yo'. Dem yaller wimen wus highfalutin' too, dey though dey wus better dan de black ones.

Has yo' ever wondered why de yaller wimen dese days am meaner dan black ones 'bout de men? Well dat's de reason fer hit, dere mammies raised dem to think 'bout de white men.

When de Yankees come dey come an' freed us. De woods wus full of Rebs what had deserted, but de Yankees killed some of dem.

Some sort of corporation cut de land up, but de slaves ain't got none of it dat I ever heard about.

I got married before de war to Joshua Curtis. I loved him too, which is more dam most folks can truthfully say. I always had craved a home an' a plenty to eat, but freedom ain't give us notin' but pickled hoss meat an' dirty crackers, an' not half enough of dat.

Josh ain't really care 'bout no home but through dis land corporation I buyed dese fifteen acres on time. I cut down de big trees dat wus all over dese fields an' I milled out de wood an' sold hit, den I plowed up de fields an' planted dem. Josh did help to build de house an' he worked out some.

All of dis time I had nineteen chilluns an' Josh died, but I kep' on an' de fifteen what is dead lived to be near 'bout grown, ever one of dem.

Right atter de war northern preachers come around wid a little book a-marrying slaves an' I seed one of dem marry my pappy an' mammy. Atter dis dey tried to find dere fourteen oldest chilluns what wus sold away, but dey never did find but three of dem.

But you wants ter find out how I got along. I'll never fergit my first bale of cotton an' how I got hit sold. I wus some proud of dat bale of cotton, an' atter I had hit ginned I set out wid hit on my steercart fer Raleigh. De white folks hated de nigger den, 'specially de nigger what wus makin' somethin' so I dasen't ax nobody whar de market wus.

I thought dat I could find de place by myself, but I rid all day an' had to take my cotton home wid me dat night 'case I can't find no place to sell hit at. But dat night I think hit over an' de nex' day I goes' back an' axes a policeman 'bout de market. Lo an' behold chile, I foun' hit on Blount Street, an' I had pass by hit seberal times de day before.

I done a heap of work at night too, all of my sewin' an' such an' de piece of lan' near de house over dar ain't never got no work 'cept at night. I finally paid fer de land. Some of my chilluns wus borned in de field too. When I wus to de house we had a granny an' I blowed in a bottle to make de labor quick an' easy.

Dis young generation ain't worth shucks. Fifteen years ago I hired a big buck nigger to help me shrub an' 'fore leben o'clock he passed out on me. You know 'bout leben o'clock in July hit gits in a bloom. De young generation wid dere schools an dere divorcing ain't gwine ter git nothin' out of life. Hit wus better when folks jist lived tergether. Dere loafin' gits dem inter trouble an' dere novels makes dem bad husban's an' wives too.

EH

TR Note: No Header Page

No. Words: [TR: 1,165]

Subject: [TR: Charles Lee Dalton]

By Miss Nancy Woodburn Watkins
Rockingham County
Madison, North Carolina

CHARLES LEE DALTON

In July, 1934, the census taker went to the home of Unka Challilee Dalton and found that soft talking old darky on the porch of his several roomed house, a few hundred feet south of the dirt road locally called the Ayersville road because it branches from the hard surfaced highway to Mayodan at Anderson Scales' store, a short distance from Unka Challilie's. Black got its meaning from his face, even his lips were black, but his hair was whitening. His lean body was reclining while the white cased pillows of his night bed sunned on a chair. His granddaughter kept house for him the census taker learned. Unka Challilie said: "I'se got so I ain't no count fuh nuthin. I wuz uh takin' me a nap uh sleepin' (' AM). Dem merry-go-wheels keep up sich a racket all nite, sech a racket all nite, ah cyan't sleep." This disturbance was "The Red Wolfe Medicine Troop of Players and Wheels" near Anderson Scales' store in the forks of the Mayodan and the Ayresville roads.

In 1937 in the home of his son, Unka Challilie ninety-three, told the cause of his no "countness." "I wuz clean-up man in de mill in Mayodan ontill three years ago, I got too trimbly to git amongst de machinery. Daze frade I'd fall and git cut."

I cum tuh Madison forty-five yeah ago, and I bought one acre, and built me a house on it, an' razed my leben chillun dyah. My wife was Ellen Irving of Reidsville. We had a cow, pigs, chickens, and gyardum of vegetables to hope out what I got paid at de mill.

Nome I nevah learned to read an write. Ounct I thought mebbe I'd git sum lunnin but aftah I got married, I didn't think I would.

My old Marse wuz Marse Lee Dalton and I stayed on his plantation till forty-five years ago when I cum tuh Madison. His place wuz back up dyah close tuh. Mt. Herman Church. Nome we slaves ain't learn no letters, but sumtimes young mistis' 'd read de Bible tuh us. Day wuz pretty good tuh us, but sumtimes I'd ketch uh whippin'. I wuz a hoe boy and plow man. My mothers' name wuz Silvia Dalton and my daddy's name wuz Peter Dalton. Day belonged to Marse Lee and his wife wuz Miss Matilda Steeples (Staples). Marse Lee lived on Beaver Island Creek at the John Hampton Price place. Mr. Price bought it. He married Miss Mollie Dalton, Marse Lee's daughter. Dyah's uh ole graveyard dyah whah lots uh Daltons is buried but no culled fokes. Day is buried to the side uh Stoneville wiff no white fokes a-tall berried dyah. De ole Daltons wuz berried on de Ole Jimmy Scales plantation. Day bought hit, an little John Price what runs uh tuhbaccah warehouse in Madison owns hit now. (1937) His tenant is Marse Walt Hill, an hits five miles frum Madison. I knose whah de old Deatherage graveyard is, too, up close to Stoneville whah sum Daltons is berried. Ole Marse Lee's mother was a Deatherage.

Ole Marse was kind to us, an' I stayed on his plantation an' farmed till I kum to Madison. Dee Yankees, day didn't giv us nuthin so we had kinduh to live off'n old Marse.

Fuh ayteen yuz I kin member ah de Mefodis Church byah in Madison. I wuzn't converted unduh de Holiness preachment uh James Foust but duh de revival of Reverend William Scales. William didn't bare much lunnin. His wife wuz Mittie Scales an huh mother wuz Chlocy Scales, sister to Tommie Scales, de shoemaker, what died lase summuh (July, 1936). William jes wanted so much tuh preach, and Mittie hoped him. I'se been uh class leader, an uh stewart, an uh trustee in de church. It's St. Stephen's and de new brick church was built in 1925, an Mistuh John Wilson's son wrote uh peace uh bout hit in de papuh. De fuss chuch wuz down dyah cross de street fum Jim Foust's "tabernacle." But de fuss cullud chuch in Madison wuz a Union chuch over dyah by de Presbyterian graveyard whah now is de Gyartuh factry. An' Jane Richardson wuz de leader.

Yess'm I got so no count, I had to cum live with mah son, Frank Dalton. Frank married Mattie Cardwell. You remembuh Mary Mann? She married Anderson Cardwell. Day's bofe dade long time. Days berried jess up hyuh at Mayodan whah Mr. Bollin's house is on and dem new bungyloes is on top um, too. Uh whole lots uh cullud people berried in dah with de slaves of Ole Miss Nancy (Watkins) Webster on till de Mayo Mills got started and day built Mayhodan at de Mayo Falls. An' dat's whah my daughter-in-law's folks is berried.

My leben chillun—Frank, one died in West Virginia; Cora married Henry Cardwell; Hattie married Roy Current and bafe ob dem in Winston; Della married Arthur Adkins, an' Joe, an' George an' Perry an' Nathaniel Dalton, an'.

Yes'm mah daughter-in-law has de writings about de brick chuch, dem whut started hit, an' she'll put it out whah she can git hit fuh you easy, when you coun back fuh hit.

Nome, up at Marse Lee Dalton's fob de s'renduh us slaves didn't nevuh go tuh chuch. But young Miss'ud read de Bible to us sometimes.

Here in the five room, white painted cottage of his son, Frank, Unka Challilie is kindly cared for by his daughter-in-law, Mattie. A front porch faces the Mayodan hard road a few doors from the "coppubration line." A well made arch accents the entrance to the front walk. A climbing rose flourishes on the arch. Well kept grass with flowers on the edges show Mattie's love. At the right side is the vegetable garden, invaded by several big domineckuh chickens. A kudzu vine keeps out the hot west sun. Unka Challilie sits on the front porch and nods to his friends else back in the kitchen, he sits and watches Mattie iron after he has eaten his breakfast. Several hens come on the back porch and lay in boxes there. One is "uh settin" fuh fried chicken later! A walnut tree, "uh white wawnut", waves its long dangly green blooms as the leaves are half grown in the early May. Well dressed, clean, polite, comforted with his religion, but very "trimbly" even on his stout walking stick, Unka Challilie often dozes away his "no countness" with "uh napuh sleepin" while the mad rush of traffic and tourist wheels stir the rose climbing over the entrance arch. An ex-slave who started wiff nuffin de Yankees gave him, who lived on his old Marse's place ontil he wuz forty-eight, who cleaned the Mayo Mills ontill he wuz too trimbly to get amongst de machinery, who raised eleven children on an acre of red Rockingham county hillside, faces the next move with plenty to eat, wear, plenty time to take a nap uh sleepin.

N.C. District: No. 2
Worker: Mary A. Hicks
No. Words: 386
Subject: JOHN DANIELS
Story Teller: John Daniels
Editor: Daisy Bailey Waitt

JOHN DANIELS

I'se named fer my pappy's ole massa down in Spartanburg, South Carolina, course I doan know nothin' 'bout no war, case I warn't borned. I does 'member seein' de ole 'big house' do', maybe you want me ter tell you how hit looked?

It wuz a big white two-story house at de end uv a magnolia lane an' a-settin' in a big level fiel'. Back o' de big house wuz de ole slave cabins whar my folks uster live.

Dey said dat de massa wuz good ter 'em, but dat sometimes in de mo'nin' dey jist has lasses an' co'nbread fer breakfas'.

I started ter tell you 'bout de Joe Moe do'.

You mebbe doan know hit, but de prisoners hyar doan git de blues so bad if de company comes on visitin' days, an' de mail comes reg'lar. We's always gittin' up somepin' ter have a little fun, so somebody gits up de Joe Moe.

Yo' sees dat when a new nigger comes in he am skeerd an' has got de blues. Somebody goes ter cheer him up an' dey axes him hadn't he ruther be hyar dan daid. Yo' see he am moughty blue den, so mebbe he says dat he'd ruther be daid; den dis feller what am tryin' ter cheer him tells him dat all right he sho' will die dat he's got de Joe Moe put on him.

Seberal days atter dis de new nigger fin's a little rag full of somepin twix de bed an' mattress an' he axes what hit am. Somebody tells him dat hit am de Joe Moe, an' dey tells him dat de only way he can git de spell off am ter git de bag off on somebody else. Ever'body but him knows' bout hit so de Joe Moe keeps comin' back till a new one comes in an' he l'arns de joke.

Talkin' 'bout ghostes I wants ter tell you dat de air am full of 'em. Dar's a strip from de groun' 'bout four feet high which am light on de darkes' night, case hit can't git dark down dar. Git down an' crawl an' yo'll see a million laigs of eber' kin' an' if'en you lis'ens you'll hyar a little groanin' an' den you has gone through a warm spot.

B. N.

N.C. District:	No. 2
Worker:	T. Pat Matthews
No. Words:	725
Subject:	HARRIET ANN DAVES
Story Teller:	Harriet Ann Daves
Editor:	Daisy Bailey Waitt

HARRIET ANN DAVES

My full name is Harriet Ann Daves, I like to be called Harriet Ann. If my mother called me when she was living, I didn't want to answer her unless she called me Harriet Ann. I was born June 6, 1856. Milton Waddell, my mother's marster was my father, and he never denied me to anybody.

My mother was a slave but she was white. I do not know who my mother's father was. My mother was Mary Collins. She said that her father was an Indian. My mother's mother was Mary Jane Collins, and she was white—maybe part Indian. My grandfather was old man William D. Waddell, a white man. I was born in Virginia near Orange Courthouse. The Waddells moved to Lexington, Missouri, after I was born. I guess some of the family would not like it if they knew I was telling this. We had good food and a nice place to live. I was nothing but a child, but I know, and remember that I was treated kindly. I remember the surrender very well. When the surrender came my grandfather came to mother and told her: ‘Well, you are as free as I am.’ That was William D. Waddell. He was one of the big shots among the white folks.

My white grandmother wanted mother to give me to her entirely. She said she had more right to me than my Indian grandmother that she had plenty to educate and care for me. My mother would not give me to her, and she cried. My mother gave me to my Indian grandmother. I later went back to my mother.

While we were in Missouri some of my father’s people, a white girl, sent for me to come up to the great house. I had long curls and was considered pretty. The girl remarked, ‘Such a pretty child’ and kissed me. She afterwards made a remark to which my father who was there, my white father, took exception telling her I was his child and that I was as good as she was. I remember this incident very distinctly.

My mother had two children by the same white man, my father. The other was a girl. She died in California. My father never married. He loved my mother, and he said if he could not marry Mary he did not want to marry. Father said he did not want any other woman. My father was good to me. He would give me anything I asked him for. Mother would make me ask him for things for her. She said it was no harm for me to ask him for things for her which she could not get unless I asked him for them. When the surrender came my mother told my father she was tired of living that kind of a life, that if she could not be his legal wife she wouldn’t be anything to him, so she left and went to Levenworth, Kansas. She died there in

1935. I do not know where my father is, living or dead, or what became of him.

I can read and write well. They did not teach us to read and write in slavery days. I went to a school opened by the Yankees after the surrender.

I went with my mother to Levenworth, Kansas. She sent me to school in Flat, Nebraska. I met my husband there. My first husband was Elisha Williams; I ran away from school in Flat, and married him. He brought me to Raleigh. He was born and raised in Wake County. We lived together about a year when he died July 1st, 1872. There was one child born to us which died in infancy.

I married the second time Rufus H. Daves in 1875. He was practically a white man. He wouldn't even pass for a mulatto. He used to belong to the Haywoods. He died in 1931 in Raleigh.

I think Abraham Lincoln was a fine, conscientious man; my mother worshipped him, but he turned us out without anything to eat or live on. I don't think Mr. Roosevelt is either hot or cold—just a normal man.

AC

N.C. District: No. 2
Worker: Mary A. Hicks
No. Words: 429
Subject: JERRY DAVIS
Story Teller: Jerry Davis
Editor: Daisy Bailey Waitt
Date Stamp: "JUN 26 1937"

JERRY DAVIS

I wus borned in Warren County ter Mataldia an' Jordan Davis. Dere wus twenty-two o' us chilluns, an' natu'ally Marster Sam Davis laked my mammy an' daddy. He owned two hundert an' sebenty slaves, an' three, four, or five scopes o' lan'.

Marster wus good ter us, he gibe us plenty ter eat, an' w'ar, an' he wus good an' kind in his talkin'. I warn't big 'nuff ter do much 'sides min' de chickens, an' sich lak.

I doan 'member so much 'bout de Yankees comin' 'cept sein' dem, an' dat dey gibe my pappy a new blue overcoat an' dat I slep' on it onct er twict. I knows dat de Yankees wus good ter de niggers but dey warn't so good ter de ole Issues. Dey did 'stroy most eber'thing do'.

I can't 'member, but I'se hyard my mammy tell o' dances, co'n shuckin's, wrestlin' matches, candy pullin's an' sich things dat wus had by de slaves dem days.

My pappy tol' me 'bout de cock fights in de big pits at Warrenton an' how dat when de roosters got killed de owner often gibe de dead bird ter him. I'se also hyard him tell 'bout de hoss races an' 'bout Marster Sam's fine hosses.

I knows dat de marster an' missus wus good case my mammy an' daddy 'sisted on stayin' right on atter de war, an' so dey died an' was buried dar on Marster Sam's place.

I wucked in de Dupont Powder plant durin' de World War but I wus discharged case I had acid injury.

Yessum, I'll tell you de only rale ole tale dat I knows an' dat am de story' bout——Jack.

• JACK

Onct dar wus a white man down in Beaufort County what owned a nigger named Jack. Dis man owned a boat an' he was fer ever more goin' boat ridin', fer days an' nights. He larned Jack how ter steer an' often he'd go ter sleep leavin' Jack at de wheel, wid 'structions ter steer always by de seben stars.

One night as Jack steered for his master to sleep, Jack suddenly fell asleep too. When he awake it wuz jist at de crack of dawn so no stars wus dar.

Jack went flyin' ter de marster hollerin', 'please sur marster, hang up some mo' stars, I done run by dem seben'.

• JACK AND THE DEVIL

Onct Jack an' de debil got inter a 'spute 'bout who can

throw a rock de ferderest. De debil sez dat he can throw a rock so fur dat hit won't come down in three days.

Iffen you can throw a rock furder dan dat, sez de debil, I'll give you yer freedom.

De debil chunks a rock an' hit goes up an' stays fer three days. When hit comes down Jack picks hit up an' he 'lows, 'Good Lawd, move de stars an' de moon case dar's a rock comin' ter heaben'.

De debil sez, 'Iffen you can do dat den you can beat me case I can't throw a rock in a mile o' heaben'.

AC

N.C. District:	No. 2
Worker:	T. Pat Matthews
No. Words:	1025
Subject:	A Slave Story
Story Teller:	W. S. Debnam
Editor:	Daisy Bailey Waitt
Date Stamp:	"JUN 30 1937"

W. SOLOMON DEBNAM

Yes, I remember the Yankees coming to Raleigh. I don't know very much about those times, I was so young, but I remember the Yankees all right in their blue clothes; their horses, and so on. I'll be 78 years old the 8th of this comin' September an' I've heard mother an' father talk about slavery time a whole lot. We belonged to T. R. Debnam at Eagle Rock, Wake County. His wife was named Priscilla Debnam. My father was named Daniel Debnam an' my mother was named Liza Debnam. My master had several plantations an' a lot of slaves. I don't know how many, but I know he had 'em. He fed us well; we had a good place to sleep. We had wove clothes, enough to keep us warm. He treated me just like he had been my father. I didn't know the difference. Marster an' missus never hit me a lick in their lives. My mother was the house girl. Father tended business around the house an' worked in the field sometimes. Our houses were in marster's yard. The slave quarters were in the yard of the great house. I don't remember going to church until after the surrender.

I remember the corn shuckin's, but not the Christmas and the fourth of July holidays. They had a lot of whiskey at corn shuckin's and good things to eat.

I heard pappy talk of patterollers, but I do not know what they were. Pappy said he had to have a pass to visit on, or they would whip him if they could ketch him. Sometimes they could not ketch a nigger they were after. Yes, they taught us to say pappy an' mammy in them days.

I remember the coon and possum hunts an' the rabbits we caught in gums. I remember killin' birds at night with thorn brush. When bird blindin' we hunt 'em at night with lights from big splinters. We went to grass patches, briars, and vines along the creeks an' low groun's where they roosted, an' blinded 'em an' killed 'em when they come out. We cooked 'em on coals, and I remember making a stew and having dumplings cooked with 'em. We'd flustrate the birds in their roostin' place an' when they come out blinded by the light we hit 'em an' killed 'em with thorn brush we carried in our han's.

Marster had a gran'son, the son of Alonza Hodge an' Arabella Hodge, 'bout my age an' I stayed with him most of the time. When Alonza Hodge bought his son anything he bought for me too. He treated us alike. He bought each of us a pony. We could ride good, when we were small. He let us follow him. He let us go huntin' squirrels with him. When he shot an' killed a squirrel he let us race to see which could get him first, while he laughed at us.

I didn't sleep in the great house. I stayed with this white boy till bed time then my mammy come an' got me an' carried me home. When marster wanted us boys to go with him he would say, 'Let's go boys,' an' we would follow him. We were like brothers. I ate with him at the table. What they et, I et. He made the house girl wait on me just like he an' his son was waited on.

My father stayed with marster till he died, when he was 63 an' I was 21; we both stayed right there. My white playmate's name was Richard Hodge. I stayed there till I was married. When I got 25 years old I married Ida Rawlson. Richard Hodge became a medical doctor, but he died young, just before I was married.

They taught me to read an' write. After the surrender I went to free school. When I didn't know a word I went to old marster an' he told me.

During my entire life no man can touch my morals, I was brought up by my white folks not to lie, steal or do things immoral. I have lived a pure life. There is nothing against me.

I remember the Yankees, yes sir, an' somethings they done. Well, I remember the big yeller gobler they couldn't ketch. He riz an' flew an' they shot him an' killed him. They went down to marster's store an' busted the head outen a barrel o' molasses an' after they busted the head out I got a tin bucket an' got it full o' molasses an' started to the house. Then they shoved me down in the molasses. I set the bucket down an' hit a Yankee on the leg with a dogwood stick. He tried to hit me. The Yankees ganged around him, an' made him leave me alone, give me my bucket o' molasses, an' I carried it on to the house. They went down to the lot, turned out all the horses an' tuck two o' the big mules, Kentucky mules, an' carried 'em off. One of the mules would gnaw every line in two you tied him with, an' the other could not be rode. So next morning after the Yankees carried 'em off they both come back home with pieces o' lines on 'em. The mules was named, one was named Bill, an' the other Charles. You could ride old Charles, but you couldn't ride old Bill. He would throw you off as fast as you got on 'im.

After I was married when I was 25 years old I lived there ten years, right there; but old marster had died an' missus had died. I stayed with his son Nathaniel; his wife was named Drusilla.

I had five brothers, Richard, Daniel, Rogene, Lorenzo, Lumus and myself. There wont places there for us all, an' then I left. When I left down there I moved to Raleigh. The first man I worked fer here was George Marsh Company, then W. A. Myatt Company an' no one else. I worked with the Myatt Company twenty-six years; 'till I got shot.

It was about half past twelve o'clock. I was on my way home to dinner on the 20th of December, 1935. When I was passing Patterson's Alley entering Lenoir Street near the colored park in the 500 block something hit me. I looked around an' heard a shot. The bullet hit me before I heard the report of the pistol. When hit, I looked back an' heard it. Capt. Bruce Pool, o' the Raleigh Police force, had shot at some thief that had broken into a A&P Store an' the bullet hit me. It hit me in my left thigh above the knee. It went through my thigh, a 38 caliber bullet, an' lodged under the skin on the other side. I did not fall but stood on one foot while the blood ran from the wound. A car came by in about a half hour an' they stopped an' carried me to St. Agnes Hospital. It was not a police car. I stayed there a week. They removed the bullet, an' then I had to go to the hospital every day for a month. I have not been able to work a day since. I was working with W. A. Myatt Company when I got shot. My leg pains me now and swells up. I cannot stand on it much. I am unable to do a day's work. Can't stand up to do a day's work. The city paid me $200.00, an' paid my hospital bill.

Abraham Lincoln was all right. I think slavery was wrong because birds an' things are free an' man ought to have the same privilege.

Franklin Roosevelt is a wonderful man. Men would have starved if he hadn't helped 'em.

N.C. District:	No. 3
Worker:	Travis Jordan
No. Words:	1384
Subject:	SARAH DEBRO
	EX-SLAVE 90 YEARS
	Durham, N.C.
Date Stamp:	"JUL 24 1937"

SARAH DEBRO

I was bawn in Orange County way back some time in de fifties.

Mis Polly White Cain an' Marse Docter Cain was my white folks. Marse Cain's plantation joined Mistah Paul Cameron's land. Marse Cain owned so many niggers dat he didn' know his own slaves when he met dem in de road. Sometimes he would stop dem an' say: 'Whose niggers am you?' Dey'd say, 'We's Marse Cain's niggers.' Den he would say, 'I'se Marse Cain,' and drive on.

Marse Cain was good to his niggers. He didn' whip dem like some owners did, but if dey done mean he sold dem. Dey knew dis so dey minded him. One day gran'pappy sassed Mis' Polly White an' she told him dat if he didn' 'have hese'f dat she would put him in her pocket. Gran'pappy wuz er big man an' I ax him how Mis' Polly could do dat. He said she meant dat she would sell him den put de money in her pocket. He never did sass Mis' Polly no more.

I was kept at de big house to wait on Mis' Polly, to tote her basket of keys an' such as dat. Whenever she seed a chile down in de quarters dat she wanted to raise be hand, she took dem up to do big house an' trained dem. I wuz to be a house maid. De day she took me my mammy cried kaze she knew I would never be 'lowed to live at de cabin wid her no more Mis' Polly was big an' fat an' she made us niggers mind an' we had to keep clean. My dresses an' aprons was starched stiff. I had a clean apron every day. We had white sheets on de beds an' we niggers had plenty to eat too, even ham. When Mis' Polly went to ride she took me in de carriage wid her. De driver set way up high an' me an' Mis' Polly set way down low. Dey was two hosses with shiney harness. I toted Mis' Polly's bag an' bundles, an' if she dropped her hank'chief I picked it up. I loved Mis' Polly an' loved stayin' at de big house.

I was 'bout wais' high when de sojers mustered. I went wid Mis' Polly down to de musterin' fiel' whare dey was marchin'. I can see dey feets now when dey flung dem up an' down, sayin', hep, hep. When dey was all ready to go an' fight, de women folks fixed a big dinner. Aunt Charity an' Pete cooked two or three days for Mis' Polly. De table was piled wid chicken, ham, shoat, barbecue, young lam', an'all sorts of pies, cakes an' things, but nobody eat nothin much. Mis' Polly an' de ladies got to cryin.' De vittles got cold. I was so sad dat I got over in de corner an' cried too. De men folks all had on dey new sojer clothes, an' dey didn' eat nothin neither. Young Marse Jim went up an' put his arm 'roun' Mis' Polly, his mammy, but dat made her cry harder. Marse Jim was a cavalry. He rode a big hoss, an' my Uncle Dave went wid him to de fiel' as his body guard. He had a hoss too so if Marse Jim's hoss got shot dare would be another one for him to ride. Mis' Polly had another son but he was too drunk to hold a gun. He stayed drunk.

De first cannon I heard skeered me near 'bout to death. We could hear dem goin' boom, boom. I thought it was thunder, den Mis Polly say, 'Lissen, Sarah, hear dem cannons? Dey's killin' our mens.' Den she 'gun to cry.

I run in de kitchen whare Aunt Charity was cookin an' tole her Mis' Polly was cryin. She said: 'She ain't cryin' kaze de Yankees killin' de mens; she's doin' all dat cryin' kaze she skeered we's goin' to be sot free.' Den I got mad an' tole her Mis' Polly wuzn' like dat.

I 'members when Wheelers Cavalry come through. Dey was 'Federates but dey was mean as de Yankees. Dey stold everything dey could find an' killed a pile of niggers. Dey come 'roun' checkin'. Dey ax de niggahs if dey wanted to be free. If dey say yes, den dey shot dem down, but if dey say no, dey let dem alone. Dey took three of my uncles out in de woods an' shot dey faces off.

I 'members de first time de Yankees come. Dey come gallupin' down de road, jumpin' over de palin's, tromplin' down de rose bushes an' messin' up de flower beds. Dey stomped all over de house, in de kitchen, pantries, smoke house, an' everywhare, but dey didn' find much, kaze near 'bout everything done been hid. I was settin' on de steps when a big Yankee come up. He had on a cap an' his eyes was mean.

'Whare did dey hide do gol' an silver, Nigger?' he yelled at me.

I was skeered an my hands was ashy, but I tole him I didn' nothin' 'bout nothin; dat if anybody done hid things dey hid it while I was sleep.

'Go ax dat ole white headed devil,' he said to me.

I got mad den kaze he was tawkin' 'bout Mis' Polly, so I didn' say nothin'. I jus' set. Den he pushed me off de step an' say if I didn' dance he gwine shoot my toes off. Skeered as I was, I sho done some shufflin'. Den he give me five dollers an' tole me to go buy jim cracks, but dat piece of paper won't no good. 'Twuzn nothin' but a shin plaster like all dat war money, you couldn' spend it.

Dat Yankee kept callin' Mis' Polly a white headed devil an' said she done ramshacked 'til dey wuzn' nothin' left, but he made his mens tote off meat, flour, pigs, an' chickens. After dat Mis' Polly got mighty stingy wid de vittles an' de didn' have no more ham.

When de war was over de Yankees was all 'roun' de place tellin' de niggers what to do. Dey tole dem dey was free, dat dey didn' have to slave for de white folks no more. My folks all left Marse Cain an' went to live in houses dat de Yankees built. Dey wuz like poor white folks houses, little shacks made out of sticks an' mud wid stick an' mud chimneys. Dey wuzn' like Marse Cain's cabins, planked up an' warm, dey was full of cracks, an' dey wuzn' no lamps an' oil. All de light come from de lightwood knots burnin' in de fireplace.

One day my mammy come to de big house after me. I didn' want to go, I wanted to stay wid Mis' Polly. I 'gun to cry an' Mammy caught hold of me. I grabbed Mis' Polly an' held so tight dat I tore her skirt bindin' loose an' her skirt fell down 'bout her feets.

'Let her stay wid me,' Mis' Polly said to Mammy.

But Mammy shook her head. 'You took her away from me an' didn' pay no mind to my cryin', so now I'se takin' her back home. We's free now, Mis' Polly, we ain't gwine be slaves no more to nobody.' She dragged me away. I can see how Mis' Polly looked now. She didn' say nothin' but she looked hard at Mammy an' her face was white.

Mammy took me to de stick an' mud house de Yankees done give her. It was smoky an' dark kaze dey wuzn' no windows. We didn' have no sheets an' no towels, so when I cried an' said I didn' want to live on no Yankee house, Mammy beat me an' made me go to bed. I laid on de straw tick lookin' up through de cracks in de roof. I could see de stars, an' de sky shinin' through de cracks looked like long blue splinters stretched 'cross de rafters. I lay dare an' cried kaze I wanted to go back to Mis' Polly.

I was never hungry til we waz free an' de Yankees fed us. We didn' have nothin to eat 'cept hard tack an' middlin' meat. I never saw such meat. It was thin an' tough wid a thick skin. You could boil it allday an' all night an' it wouldn' cook dome, I wouldn' eat it. I thought 'twuz mule meat; mules dat done been shot on de battle field den dried. I still believe 'twuz mule meat.

One day me an' my brother was lookin' for acorns in de woods. We foun' sumpin' like a grave in de woods. I tole Dave dey wuz sumpin' buried in dat moun'. We got de grubbin hoe an' dug. Dey wuz a box wid eleven hams in dat grave. Somebody done hid it from de Yankees an' forgot whare dey buried it. We covered it back up kaze if we took it home in de day time de Yankees an' niggers would take it away from us. So when night come we slipped out an' toted dem hams to de house an' hid dem in de loft.

Dem was bad days. I'd rather been a slave den to been hired out like I was, kaze I wuzn' no fiel' hand, I was a hand maid, trained to wait on de ladies. Den too, I was hungry most of de time an' had to keep fightin' off dem Yankee mens. Dem Yankees was mean folks.

We's come a long way since dem times. I'se lived near 'bout ninety years an' I'se seen an' heard much. My folks don't want me to talk 'bout slavery, day's shame niggers ever was slaves. But, while for most colored folks freedom is de bes, dey's still some niggers dat out to be slaves now. Dese niggers dat's done clean forgot de Lawd; dose dat's always cuttin' an' fightin' an' gwine in white folks houses at night, dey ought to be slaves. Dey ought to have an' Ole Marse wid a whip to make dem come when he say come, an' go when he say go, 'til dey learn to live right.

I looks back now an' thinks. I ain't never forgot dem slavery days, an' I ain't never forgot Mis' Polly an' my white starched aprons.

N.C. District: No. 2
Worker: T. Pat Matthews
No. Words: 805
Subject: CHARLES W. DICKENS
Story Teller: Charles W. Dickens
Editor: Daisy Bailey Waitt
Date Stamp: "JUN 11 1937"

CHARLES W. DICKENS

My name is Charles W. Dickens. I lives at 1115 East Lenoir Street, Raleigh, North Carolina, Wake County. I wuz born August 16, 1861, de year de war started. My mother wuz named Ferebee Dickens. My father wuz named John Dickens. I had nine sisters and brothers. My brothers were named Allen, Douglas, my name, Jake, Johnnie and Jonas. The girls Katie, Matilda Francis, and Emily Dickens.

My grandmother wuz named Charity Dickens. My grandfather wuz Dudley T. Dickens. I do not know where dey came from. No, I don't think I do. My mother belonged to Washington Scarborough, and so did we chilluns. My father he belonged to Obediah Dickens and missus wuz named Silvia Dickens. Dey lowed mother to go by the name of my father after dey wuz married.

We lived in log houses and we had bunks in 'em. Master died, but I 'member missus wuz mighty good to us. We had tolerable fair food, and as fur as I know she wuz good to us in every way. We had good clothing made in a loom, that is de cloth wuz made in de loom. My father lived in Franklin County. My mother lived in Wake County. I 'member hearin' father talk about walkin' so fur to see us. There wuz about one dozen slaves on de plantation. Dere were no hired overseers. Missus done her own bossing. I have heard my father speak about de patterollers, but I never seed none. I heard him say he could not leave the plantation without a strip o' something.

No, sir, the white folks did not teach us to read and write. My mother and father, no sir, they didn't have any books of any kind. We went to white folk's church. My father split slats and made baskets to sell. He said his master let him have all de money he made sellin' de things he made. He learned a trade. He wuz a carpenter. One of the young masters got after father, so he told me, and he went under de house to keep him from whuppin' him. When missus come home she wouldn't let young master whup him. She jist wouldn't 'low it.

I 'members de Yankees comin' through. When mother heard they were comin', she took us chillun and carried us down into an ole field, and after that she carried us back to the house. Missus lived in a two-story house. We lived in a little log house in front of missus' house. My mother had a shoulder of meat and she hid it under a mattress in the house. When the Yankees lef, she looked for it; they had stole the meat and gone. Yes, they stole from us slaves. The road the Yankees wuz travellin' wuz as thick wid' em as your fingers. I 'member their blue clothes, their blue caps. De chickens they were carrying on their horses wuz crowing. Dey wuz driving cows, hogs, and things. Yes sir, ahead of 'em they come first. The barns and lots were on one side de road dey were trabellin' on and de houses on de other. Atter many Yankees had passed dey put a bodyguard at de door of de great house, and didn't 'low no one to go in dere. I looked down at de Yankees and spit at 'em. Mother snatched me back, and said, 'Come back here chile, dey will kill you.'

Dey carried de horses off de plantation and de meat from missus' smokehouse and buried it. My uncle, Louis Scarborough, stayed wid de horses. He is livin' yet, he is over a hundred years old. He lives down at Moores Mill, Wake County, near Youngsville. Before de surrender one of de boys and my uncle got to fightin', one of de Scarborough boys and him. My uncle threw him down. The young Master Scarborough jumped up, and got his knife and cut uncle's entrails out so uncle had to carry 'em to de house in his hands. About a year after de war my father carried us to Franklin County. He carried us on a steer cart. Dat's about all I 'member about de war.

Abraham Lincoln wuz de man who set us free. I think he wuz a mighty good man. He done so much for de colored race, but what he done was intended through de higher power. I don't think slavery wuz right.

I think Mr. Roosevelt is a fine man, one of the best presidents in the world. I voted for him, and I would vote for him ag'in. He has done a lot for de people, and is still doin'. He got a lot of sympathy for 'em. Yas sir, a lot of sympathy for de people.

MM

N.C. District:	No. 2
Worker:	T. Pat Matthews
No. Words:	655
Subject:	MARGARET E. DICKENS
Person Interviewed:	Margaret E. Dickens
Editor:	Daisy Bailey Waitt

MARGARET E. DICKENS

My name is Margaret E. Dickens and I was born on the 5th of June 1861. My mother wuz free born; her name wuz Mary Ann Hews, but my mother wuz colored. I don't remember anything about Marster and Missus. My father was named Henry Byrd. Here is some of father's writing. My mother's father was dark. He had no protection. If he did any work for a white man and the white man didn't like it, he could take him up and whup him. My father was like a stray dog.

My name was Margaret E. Byrd before I got married. Here is some of father's writing—"Margaret Elvira Byrd the daughter of Henry and Mary Ann Byrd was born on the 5th June 1861." My grandfather, my mother's father was a cabinet maker. He made coffins and tables and furniture. If he made one, and it didn't suit the man he would beat him and kick him around and let him go. Dis was told to me. My father was a carpenter. He built houses.

I can read and write. My father could read and write. My mother could read, but couldn't write very much.

I have heerd my mother say when she heerd the Yankees were commin' she had a brand new counterpane, my father owned a place before he married my mother, the counterpane was a woolen woven counterpane. She took it off and hid it. The Yankees took anything they wanted, but failed to find it. We were living in Raleigh, at the time, on the very premises we are living on now. The old house has been torn down, but some of the wood is in this very house. I kin show you part of the old house now. My mother used to pass this place when she wuz a girl and she told me she never expected to live here. She was twenty years younger than my father. My mother, she lived here most of the time except twenty-four years she lived in the North. She died in 1916. My father bought the lan' in 1848 from a man named Henry Morgan. Here is the deed.[6]

When we left Raleigh, and went North we first stopped in Cambridge, Mass. This was with my first husband. His name was Samuel E. Reynolds. He was a preacher. He had a church and preached there. The East winds were so strong and cold we couldn't stan' it. It was too cold for us. We then went to Providence, R. I. From there to Elmira, N. Y. From there we went to Brooklyn, N. Y. He preached in the State of New York; we finally came back South, and he died right here in this house. I like the North very well, but there is nothing like home, the South. Another thing I don't have so many white kin folks up North. I don't like to be called Auntie by anyone, unless they admit bein' kin to me. I was not a fool when I went to the North, and it made no change in me. I was raised to respect everybody and I tries to keep it up. Some things in the North are all right, I like them, but I like the South better. Yes, I guess I like the South better. I was married to Charles W. Dickens in 1920. He is my second husband.

I inherited this place from my father Henry Byrd. I like well water. There is my well, right out here in the yard. This well was dug here when they were building the first house here. I believe in havin' your own home, so I have held on to my home, and I am goin' to try to keep holdin' on to it.

[6] An interesting feature of the deed is the fact that Henry Morgan made his mark while Henry Byrd's signature is his own.

N.C. District:	No. 2
Worker:	T. Pat Matthews
No. Words:	1369
Subject:	REV. SQUIRE DOWD
Story Teller:	Rev. Squire Dowd
Editor:	Daisy Bailey Waitt
Date Stamp:	"JUN 1 1937"

REVEREND SQUIRE DOWD

My name is Squire Dowd, and I was born April 3, 1855. My mother's name was Jennie Dowd. My father's name was Elias Kennedy. My mother died in Georgia at the age of 70, and my father died in Moore County at the age of 82. I attended his funeral. My sister and her husband had carried my mother to Georgia, when my sister's husband went there to work in turpentine. My mother's husband was dead. She had married a man named Stewart. You could hardly keep up with your father during slavery time. It was a hard thing to do. There were few legal marriages. When a young man from one plantation courted a young girl on the plantation, the master married them, sometimes hardly knowing what he was saying.

My master was General W. D. Dowd. He lived three miles from Carthage, in Moore County, North Carolina.

He owned fifty slaves. The conditions were good. I had only ten years' experience, but it was a good experience. No man is fool enough to buy slaves to kill. I have never known a real slave owner to abuse his slaves. The abuse was done by patterollers and overseers.

I have a conservative view of slavery. I taught school for four years and I have been in the ministry fifty years. I was ordained a Christian minister in 1885. I lived in Moore County until 1889, then I moved to Raleigh. I have feeling. I don't like for people to have a feeling that slaves are no more than dogs; I don't like that. It causes people to have the wrong idea of slavery. Here is John Bectom, a well, healthy friend of mine, 75 years of age. If we had been treated as some folks say, these big, healthy niggers would not be walking about in the South now. The great Negro leaders we have now would never have come out of it.

The places we lived in were called cabins. The Negroes who were thrifty had nice well-kept homes; and it is thus now. The thrifty of the colored race live well; the others who are indolent live in hovels which smell foul and are filthy.

Prayer meetings were held at night in the cabins of the slaves. On Sunday we went to the white folk's church. We sat in a barred-off place, in the back of the church or in a gallery.

We had a big time at cornshuckings. We had plenty of good things to eat, and plenty of whiskey and brandy to drink. These shuckings were held at night. We had a good time, and I never saw a fight at a cornshucking in life. If we could catch the master after the shucking was over, we put him in a chair, we darkies, and toted him around and hollered, carried him into the parlor, set him down, and combed his hair. We only called the old master "master". We called his wife "missus." When the white children grew up we called them Mars. John, Miss Mary, etc.

We had some money. We made baskets. On moonlight nights and holidays we cleared land; the master gave us what we made on the land. We had money.

The darkies also stole for deserters during the war. They paid us for it. I ate what I stole, such as sugar. I was not big enough to steal for the deserters. I was a house boy. I stole honey. I did not know I was free until five years after the war. I could not realize I was free. Many of us stayed right on. If we had not been ruined right after the war by carpetbaggers our race would have been, well,—better up by this time, because they turned us against our masters, when our masters had everything and we had nothing. The Freedmen's Bureau helped us some, but we finally had to go back to the plantation in order to live.

We got election days, Christmas, New Year, etc., as holidays. When we were slaves we had a week or more Christmas. The holidays lasted from Christmas Eve to after New Years. Sometimes we got passes. If our master would not give them to us, the white boys we played with would give us one. We played cat, jumping, wrestling and marbles. We played for fun; we did not play for money. There were 500 acres on the plantation. We hunted a lot, and the fur of the animals we caught we sold and had the money. We were allowed to raise a few chickens and pigs, which we sold if we wanted to.

The white folks rode to church and the darkies walked, as many of the poor white folks did. We looked upon the poor white folks as our equals. They mixed with us and helped us to envy our masters. They looked upon our masters as we did.

Negro women having children by the masters was common. My relatives on my mother's side, who were Kellys are mixed blooded. They are partly white. We, the darkies and many of the whites hate that a situation like this exists. It is enough to say that seeing is believing. There were many and are now mixed blooded people among the race.

I was well clothed. Our clothes were made in looms. Shoes were made on the plantation. Distilleries were also located on the plantation. When they told me I was free, I did not notice it. I did not realize it till many years after when a man made a speech at Carthage, telling us we were free.

I did not like the Yankees. We were afraid of them. We had to be educated to love the Yankees, and to know that they freed us and were our friends. I feel that Abraham Lincoln was a father to us. We consider him thus because he freed us. The Freedmen's Bureau and carpet baggers caused us to envy our masters and the white folks. The Ku Klux Klan, when we pushed our rights, came in between us, and we did not know what to do. The Ku Klux were after the carpet baggers and the Negroes who followed them.

It was understood that white people were not to teach Negroes during slavery, but many of the whites taught the Negroes. The children of the white folks made us study.

I could read and write when the war was up. They made me study books, generally a blue-back spelling book as punishment for mean things I done. My Missus, a young lady about 16 years old taught a Sunday School class of colored boys and girls. This Sunday School was held at a different time of day from the white folks. Sometimes old men and old women were in these classes. I remember once they asked Uncle Ben Pearson who was meekest man, 'Moses' he replied. 'Who was the wisest man?' 'Soloman', 'Who was the strongest man?' was then asked him. To this he said 'They say Bill Medlin is the strongest, but Tom Shaw give him his hands full.' They were men of the community. Medlin was white, Shaw was colored.

I do not like the way they have messed up our songs with classical music. I like the songs, 'Roll Jordan Roll', 'Old Ship of Zion', 'Swing Low Sweet Chariot'. Classical singers ruin them, though.

There was no use of our going to town of Saturday afternoon to buy our rations, so we worked Saturday afternoons. When we got sick the doctors treated us. Dr. J. D. Shaw, Dr. Bruce, and Dr. Turner. They were the first doctors I ever heard any tell of. They treated both whites and darkies on my master's plantation.

I married a Matthews, Anna Matthews, August 1881. We have one daughter. Her name is Ella. She married George Cheatam of Henderson, N.C. A magistrate married us, Mr. Pitt Cameron. It was just a quiet wedding on Saturday night with about one-half dozen of my friends present.

My idea of life is to forget the bad and live for the good there is in it. This is my motto.

B. N.

N.C. District:	No. 2
Worker:	T. Pat Matthews
No. Words:	862
Subject:	FANNIE DUNN
Story Teller:	Fannie Dunn
Editor:	G. L. Andrews
Date Stamp:	"AUG 17 1937"

FANNIE DUNN

I don't 'zakly know my age, but I knows and 'members when de Yankees come through Wake County. I wus a little girl an' wus so skeered I run an hid under de bed. De Yankees stopped at de plantation an' along de road fur a rest. I 'members I had diphtheria an' a Yankee doctor come an' mopped my throat. Dey had to pull me outen under de bed so he could doctor me.

One Yankee would come along an' give us sumptin' an another would come on behind him an' take it. Dats de way dey done. One give mother a mule an' when dey done gone she sold it. A Yankee give mother a ham of meat, another come right on behind him an' took it away from her. Dere shore wus a long line of dem Yankees. I can 'member seeing 'em march by same as it wus yisterday. I wus not old enough to work, but I 'members 'em. I don't know 'zackly but I wus 'bout five years old when de surrender wus.

My name before I wus married wus Fannie Sessoms an' mother wus named Della Sessoms. We belonged to Dr. Isaac Sessoms an' our missus wus named Hanna. My father wus named Perry Vick, after his marster who wus named Perry Vick. My missus died durin' de war an' marster never married anymore.

I don't 'member much 'bout missus but mother tole me she wus some good woman an' she loved her. Marster wus mighty good to us an' didn't allow patterollers to whip us none. De slave houses wus warm and really dey wus good houses, an' didn't leak neither.

I don't 'member much 'bout my grandparents, just a little mother tole me 'bout 'em. Grandma 'longed to de Sessoms an' Dr. Isaac Sessoms brother wus mother's father. Mother tole me dat. Look at dat picture, mister, you see you can't tell her from a white woman. Dats my mother's picture. She wus as white as you wid long hair an' a face like a white woman. She been dead 'bout twenty years. My mother said dat we all fared good, but course we wore homemade clothes an' wooden bottomed shoes.

We went to the white folks church at Red Oak an' Rocky Mount Missionary Baptist Churches. We were allowed to have prayer meetings at de slave houses, two an' three times a week. I 'members goin' to church 'bout last year of de war wid mother. I had a apple wid me an' I got hungry an' wanted to eat it in meetin' but mother jest looked at me an' touched my arm, dat wus enough. I didn't eat de apple. I can 'member how bad I wanted to eat it. Don't 'member much 'bout dat sermon, guess I put my mind on de apple too much.

Marster had about twenty slaves an' mother said dey

had always been allowed to go to church an' have prayer meetings 'fore I wus born. Marster had both white an' colored overseers but he would not allow any of his overseers to bulldoze over his slaves too much. He would call a overseer down for bein' rough at de wrong time. Charles Sessoms wus one of marster's colored overseers. He 'longed to marster, an' mother said marster always listened to what Charles said. Dey said marster had always favored him even 'fore he made him overseer. Charles Sessoms fell dead one day an' mother found him. She called Marster Sessoms an' he come an' jest cried. Mother said when Marster come he wus dead shore enough, dat marster jest boohooed an' went to de house, an' wouldn't look at him no more till dey started to take him to de grave. Everybody on de plantation went to his buryin' an' funeral an' some from de udder plantation dat joined ourn.

I 'members but little 'bout my missus, but 'members one time she run me when I wus goin' home from de great house, an' she said, 'I am goin' to catch you, now I catch you'. She pickin' at me made me love her. When she died mother tole me 'bout her bein' dead an' took me to her buryin'. Next day I wanted to go an' get her up. I tole mother I wanted her to come home an' eat. Mother cried an' took me up in her arms, an' said, 'Honey missus will never eat here again.' I wus so young I didn't understand.

Dr. Sessoms an' also Dr. Drake, who married his daughter, doctored us when we wus sick. Dr. Joe Drake married marster's only daughter Harriet an' his only son David died in Mississippi. He had a plantation dere.

I been married only once. I wus married forty years ago to Sidney Dunn. I had one chile, she's dead.

From what I knows of slavery an' what my mother tole me I can't say it wus a bad thing. Mister, I wants to tell de truth an' I can't say its bad 'cause my mother said she had a big time as a slave an' I knows I had a good time an' wus treated right.

LE

N.C. District:	No. 2
Worker:	Mary A. Hicks
No. Words:	382
Subject:	JENNYLIN DUNN
Person Interviewed:	Jennylin Dunn
Editor:	Daisy Bailey Waitt

JENNYLIN DUNN

I wuz borned hyar in Wake County eighty-seben years ago. Me an' my folks an' bout six others belonged ter Mis' Betsy Lassiter who wuz right good ter us, do' she sho' did know dat chilluns needs a little brushin' now an' den.

My papa wuz named Isaac, my mammy wuz named Liza, an' my sisters wuz named Lucy, Candice an' Harriet. Dar wuz one boy what died 'fore I can 'member an' I doan know his name.

We ain't played no games ner sung no songs, but we had fruit ter eat an' a heap of watermillions ter eat in de season.

I seed seberal slabe sales on de block, front of de Raleigh Cou't house, an' yo' can't think how dese things stuck in my mind. A whole heap o' times I seed mammies sold from dere little babies, an' dar wuz no'min' den, as yo' knows.

De patterollers wuz sumpin dat I wuz skeerd of. I know jist two o' 'em, Mr. Billy Allen Dunn an' Mr. Jim Ray, an' I'se hyard of some scandelous things dat dey done. Dey do say dat dey whupped some of de niggers scandelous.

When dey hyard dat de Yankees wuz on dere way ter hyar dey says ter us dat dem Yankees eats little nigger youngins, an' we shore stays hid.

I jist seed squeamishin' parties lookin' fer sumpin' ter eat, an' I'se hyard dat dey tuck ever'thing dey comes 'crost. A whole heap of it dey flunged away, an' atterwards dey got hongry too.

One of 'em tried ter tell us dat our white folks stold us from our country an' brung us hyar, but since den I foun' out dat de Yankees stole us dereselves, an' den dey sold us ter our white folkses.

Atter de war my pappy an' mammy brung us ter Raleigh whar I'se been libin' since dat time. We got along putty good, an' de Yankees sont us some teachers, but most o' us wuz so busy scramblin' roun' makin' a livin' dat we ain't got no time fer no schools.

I reckon dat hit wuz better dat de slaves wuz freed, but I still loves my white folkses, an' dey loves me.

N.C. District:	No. 2
Worker:	Mary A. Hicks
No. Words:	1119
Subject:	AUNT LUCY'S LOVE STORY
Person Interviewed:	Lucy Ann Dunn
Editor:	G. L. Andrews
Date Stamp:	"AUG 1 1937"

LUCY ANN DUNN

My pappy, Dempsey, my mammy, Rachel an' my brothers an' sisters an' me all belonged ter Marse Peterson Dunn of Neuse, here in Wake County. Dar wus five of us chilluns, Allen, Charles, Corina, Madora an' me, all borned before de war.

My mammy wus de cook, an' fur back as I 'members almost, I wus a house girl. I fanned flies offen de table an' done a heap of little things fer Mis' Betsy, Marse Peterson's wife. My pappy worked on de farm, which wus boun' ter have been a big plantation wid two hundert an' more niggers ter work hit.

I 'members when word come dat war wus declared, how Mis' Betsy cried an' prayed an' how Marse Peter quarreled an' walked de floor cussin' de Yankees.

De war comes on jist de same an' some of de men slaves wus sent ter Roanoke ter hep buil' de fort. Yes mam, de war comes ter de great house an' ter de slave cabins jist alike.

De great house wus large an' white washed, wid green blinds an' de slave cabins wus made of slabs wid plank floors. We had plenty ter eat an' enough ter wear an' we wus happy. We had our fun an' we had our troubles, lak little whuppin's, when we warn't good, but dat warn't often.

Atter so long a time de rich folkses tried ter hire, er make de po' white trash go in dere places, but some of dem won't go. Dey am treated so bad dat some of dem cides ter be Ku Kluxes an' dey goes ter de woods ter live. When we starts ter take up de aigs er starts from de spring house wid de butter an' milk dey grabs us an' takes de food fer dereselbes.

Dis goes on fer a long time an' finally one day in de spring I sets on de porch an' I hear a roar. I wus 'sponsible fer de goslins dem days so I sez ter de missus, 'I reckin dat I better git in de goslins case I hear hit a-thunderin'.

'Dat ain't no thunder, nigger, dat am de canon', she sez.

'What canon', I axes?

'Why de canon what dey am fightin' wid', she sez.

Well dat ebenin' I is out gittin' up de goslins when I hears music, I looks up de road an' I sees flags, an' 'bout dat time de Yankees am dar a-killin' as dey goes. Dey kills de geese, de ducks, de chickens, pigs an' ever'thing. Dey goes ter de house an' dey takes all of de meat, de meal, an' ever'thing dey can git dere paws on.

When dey goes ter de kitchen whar mammy am cookin' she cuss dem out an' run dem outen her kitchen. Dey shore am a rough lot.

I aint never fergot how Mis' Betsy cried when de news of de surrender come. She aint said nothin' but Marse Peter he makes a speech sayin' dat he aint had ter sell none of us, dat he aint whupped none of us bad, dat nobody has ever run away from him yet. Den he tells us dat all who wants to can stay right on fer wages.

Well we stayed two years, even do my pappy died de year atter de surrender, den we moves ter Marse Peter's other place at Wake Forest. Atter dat we moves back ter Neuse.

Hit wus in de little Baptist church at Neuse whar I fust seed big black Jim Dunn an' I fell in love wid him den, I reckons. He said dat he loved me den too, but hit wus three Sundays 'fore he axed ter see me home.

We walked dat mile home in front of my mammy an' I wus so happy dat I aint thought hit a half a mile home. We et cornbread an' turnips fer dinner an' hit wus night 'fore he went home. Mammy wouldn't let me walk wid him ter de gate. I knowed, so I jist sot dar on de porch an' sez good night.

He come ever' Sunday fer a year an' finally he proposed. I had told mammy dat I thought dat I ort ter be allowed ter walk ter de gate wid Jim an' she said all right iffen she wus settin' dar on de porch lookin'.

Dat Sunday night I did walk wid Jim ter de gate an' stood under de honeysuckles dat wus a-smellin' so sweet. I heard de big ole bullfrogs a-croakin' by de riber an' de whipper-wills a-hollerin' in de woods. Dar wus a big yaller moon, an' I reckon Jim did love me. Anyhow he said so an' axed me ter marry him an' he squeezed my han'.

I tol' him I'd think hit ober an' I did an' de nex' Sunday I tol' him dat I'd have him.

He aint kissed me yet but de nex' Sunday he axes my mammy fer me. She sez dat she'll have ter have a talk wid me an' let him know.

Well all dat week she talks ter me, tellin' me how serious gittin' married is an' dat hit lasts a powerful long time.

I tells her dat I knows hit but dat I am ready ter try hit an' dat I intends ter make a go of hit, anyhow.

On Sunday night mammy tells Jim dat he can have me an' yo' orter seed dat black boy grin. He comes ter me widout a word an' he picks me up outen dat cheer an' dar in de moonlight he kisses me right 'fore my mammy who am a-cryin'.

De nex' Sunday we wus married in de Baptist church at Neuse. I had a new white dress, do times wus hard.

We lived tergether fifty-five years an' we always loved each other. He aint never whup ner cuss me an' do we had our fusses an' our troubles we trusted in de Lawd an' we got through. I loved him durin' life an' I love him now, do he's been daid now fer twelve years.

The old lady with her long white hair bowed her head and sobbed for a moment then she began again unsteadily.

We had eight chilluns, but only four of dem are livin' now. De livin' are James, Sidney, Helen an' Florence who wus named fer Florence Nightingale.

I can't be here so much longer now case I'se gittin' too old an' feeble an' I wants ter go ter Jim anyhow. The old woman wiped her eyes, 'I thinks of him all de time, but seems lak we're young agin when I smell honeysuckles er see a yaller moon.

LE

N.C. District: No. 3
Worker: Travis Jordan
Subject: Tempie Herdon Durham
Ex-Slave 103 Years Old
1312 Pine St., Durham, N.C.
Date Stamp: "AUG 23 1937"

TEMPIE HERNDON DURHAM

I was thirty-one years ole when de surrender come. Dat makes me sho nuff ole. Near 'bout a hundred an' three years done passed over dis here white head of mine. I'se been here, I mean I'se been here. 'Spects I'se de olest nigger in Durham. I'se been here so long dat I done forgot near 'bout as much as dese here new generation niggers knows or ever gwine know.

My white fo'ks lived in Chatham County. Dey was Marse George an' Mis' Betsy Herndon. Mis Betsy was a Snipes befo' she married Marse George. Dey had a big plantation an' raised cawn, wheat, cotton an' 'bacca. I don't know how many field niggers Marse George had, but he had a mess of dem, an' he had hosses too, an' cows, hogs an' sheeps. He raised sheeps an' sold de wool, an' dey used de wool at de big house too. Dey was a big weavin' room whare de blankets was wove, an' dey wove de cloth for de winter clothes too. Linda Hernton an' Milla Edwards was de head weavers, dey looked after de weavin' of de fancy blankets. Mis' Betsy was a good weaver too. She weave de same as de niggers. She say she love de clackin' soun' of de loom, an' de way de shuttles run in an' out carryin' a long tail of bright colored thread. Some days she set at de loom all de mawnin' peddlin' wid her feets an' her white han's flittin' over de bobbins.

De cardin' an' spinnin' room was full of niggers. I can hear dem spinnin' wheels now turnin' roun' an' sayin' hum-m-m-m, hum-m-m-m, an' hear de slaves singin' while dey spin. Mammy Rachel stayed in de dyein' room. Dey wuzn' nothin' she didn' know' bout dyein'. She knew every kind of root, bark, leaf an' berry dat made red, blue, green, or whatever color she wanted. Dey had a big shelter whare de dye pots set over de coals. Mammy Rachel would fill de pots wid water, den she put in de roots, bark an' stuff an' boil de juice out, den she strain it an'put in de salt an' vinegar to set de color. After de wool an' cotton done been carded an' spun to thread, Mammy take de hanks an' drap dem in de pot of bollin' dye. She stir dem' roun' an' lif' dem up an' down wid a stick, an' when she hang dem up on de line in de sun, dey was every color of de rainbow. When dey dripped dry dey was sent to de weavin' room whare dey was wove in blankets an' things.

When I growed up I married Exter Durham. He belonged to Marse Snipes Durham who had de plantation 'cross de county line in Orange County. We had a big weddin'. We was married on de front po'ch of de big house. Marse George killed a shoat an' Mis' Betsy had Georgianna, de cook, to bake a big weddin' cake all iced up white as snow wid a bride an' groom standin' in de middle holdin' han's. De table was set out in de yard under de trees, an' you ain't never seed de like of eats. All de niggers come to de feas' an' Marse George had a dram for everybody. Dat was some weddin'. I had on a white dress, white shoes an' long white gloves dat come to my elbow, an' Mis' Betsy done made me a weddin' veil out of a white net window curtain. When she played de weddin ma'ch on de piano, me an' Exter ma'ched down de walk an' up on de po'ch to de altar Mis' Betsy done fixed. Dat de pretties' altar I ever seed. Back 'gainst de rose vine dat was full or red roses, Mis' Betsy done put tables filled wid flowers an' white candles. She done spread down a bed sheet, a sho nuff linen sheet, for us to stan' on, an' dey was a white pillow to kneel down on. Exter done made me a weddin' ring. He made it out of a big red button wid his pocket knife. He done cut it so roun' an' polished it so smooth dat it looked like a red satin ribbon tide 'roun' my finger. Dat sho was a pretty ring. I wore it 'bout fifty years, den it got so thin dat I lost it one day in de wash tub when I was washin' clothes.

Uncle Edmond Kirby married us. He was de nigger preacher dat preached at de plantation church. After Uncle Edmond said de las' words over me an' Exter, Marse George got to have his little fun: He say, 'Come on, Exter, you an' Tempie got to jump over de broom stick backwards; you got to do dat to see which one gwine be boss of your househol'.' Everybody come stan' 'roun to watch. Marse George hold de broom 'bout a foot high off de floor. De one dat jump over it backwards an' never touch de handle, gwine boss de house, an' if bof of dem jump over widout touchin' it, dey won't gwine be no bossin', dey jus' gwine be 'genial. I jumped fus', an' you ought to seed me. I sailed right over dat broom stick same as a cricket, but when Exter jump he done had a big dram an' his feets was so big an' clumsy dat dey got all tangled up in dat broom an' he fell head long. Marse George he laugh an' laugh, an' tole Exter he gwine be bossed 'twell he skeered to speak less'n I tole him to speak. After de weddin' we went down to de cabin Mis' Betsy done all dressed up, but Exter couldn' stay no longer den dat night kaze he belonged to Marse Snipes Durham an' he had to back home. He lef' de nex day for his plantation, but he come back every Saturday night an' stay 'twell Sunday night. We had eleven chillun. Nine was bawn befo' surrender an' two after we was set free. So I had two chillun dat wuzn' bawn in bondage. I was worth a heap to Marse George kaze I had so manny chillun. De more chillun a slave had de more dey was worth. Lucy Carter was de only nigger on de plantation dat had more chillun den I had. She had twelve, but her chillun was sickly an' mine was muley strong an' healthy. Dey never was sick.

When de war come Marse George was too ole to go, but young Marse Bill went. He went an' took my brother Sim wid him. Marse Bill took Sim along to look after his hoss an' everything. Dey didn' neither one get shot, but Mis' Betsy was skeered near 'bout to death all de time, skeered dey was gwine be brung home shot all to pieces like some of de sojers was.

De Yankees wuzn' so bad. De mos' dey wanted was sumpin' to eat. Dey was all de time hungry, de fus' thing dey ax for when dey came was sumpin' to put in dey stomach. An' chicken! I ain' never seed even a preacher eat chicken like dem Yankees. I believes to my soul dey ain' never seed no chicken 'twell dey come down here.

An' hot biscuit too. I seed a passel of dem eat up a whole sack of flour one night for supper. Georgianna sif' flour 'twell she look white an' dusty as a miller. Dem sojers didn' turn down no ham neither. Dat de onlies' thing dey took from Marse George. Dey went in de smoke house an' toted off de hams an' shoulders. Marse George say he come off mighty light if dat all dey want, 'sides he got plenty of shoats anyhow.

We had all de eats we wanted while de war was shootin' dem guns, kaze Marse George was home an' he kep' de niggers workin'. We had chickens, gooses, meat, peas, flour, meal, potatoes an' things like dat all de time, an' milk an' butter too, but we didn' have no sugar an' coffee. We used groun' pa'ched cawn for coffee an' cane 'lasses for sweetnin'. Dat wuzn' so bad wid a heap of thick cream. Anyhow, we had enough to eat to 'vide wid de neighbors dat didn' have none when surrender come.

I was glad when de war stopped kaze den me an' Exter could be together all de time 'stead of Saturday an' Sunday. After we was free we lived right on at Marse George's plantation a long time. We rented de lan' for a fo'th of what we made, den after while be bought a farm. We paid three hundred dollars we done saved. We had a hoss, a steer, a cow an' two pigs, 'sides some chickens an' fo' geese. Mis' Betsy went up in de attic an' give us a bed an' bed tick; she give us enough goose feathers to make two pillows, den she give us a table an' some chairs. She give us some dishes too. Marse George give Exter a bushel of seed cawn an some seed wheat, den he tole him to go down to de barn an' get a bag of cotton seed. We got all dis den we hitched up de wagon an' th'owed in de passel of chillun an' moved to our new farm, an' de chillun was put to work in de fiel'; dey growed up in de fiel' kaze dey was put to work time dey could walk good.

Freedom is all right, but de niggers was better off befo' surrender, kaze den dey was looked after an' dey didn' get in no trouble fightin' an' killin' like dey do dese days. If a nigger cut up an' got sassy in slavery times, his Ole Marse give him a good whippin' an' he went way back an' set down an' 'haved hese'f. If he was sick, Marse an' Mistis looked after him, an' if he needed store medicine, it was bought an' give to him; he didn' have to pay nothin'. Dey didn' even have to think' bout clothes nor nothin' like dat, dey was wove an' made an' give to dem. Maybe everybody's Marse an' Mistis wuzn' good as Marse George an' Mis' Betsy, but dey was de same as a mammy an' pappy to us niggers.

N.C. District:	No. 2
Worker:	Mary A. Hicks
No. Words:	466
Subject:	EX-SLAVE STORY
Story Teller:	George Eatman
Editor:	Daisy Bailey Waitt
Date Stamp:	"JUN 1 1937"

GEORGE EATMAN

I belonged ter Mr. Gus Eatman who lived at de ole Templeton place on de Durham highway back as fer as I can 'member. I doan r'member my mammy an' pappy case dey wuz sold 'fore I knowed anything. I raised myself an' I reckon dat I done a fair job uv it. De marster an' missus wuz good to dere twenty-five slaves an' we ain't neber got no bad whuppin's.

I doan 'member much playin' an' such like, but I de 'members dat I wuz de handy boy 'round de house.

De Confederate soldiers camp at Ephesus Church one night, an' de nex' day de marster sent me ter de mill on Crabtree. Yo' 'members where ole Company mill is, I reckon? Well, as I rode de mule down de hill, out comes Wheeler's Calvalry, which am as mean as de Yankees, an' dey ax me lots uv questions. Atter awhile dey rides on an' leaves me 'lone.

While I am at de mill one uv Wheeler's men takes my mule an' my co'n, an' I takes de ole saddle an' starts ter walkin' back home. All de way, most, I walks in de woods, case Wheeler's men am still passin'.

When I gits ter de Morgan place I hyars de cannons a-boomin', ahh—h I ain't neber hyar sich a noise, an' when I gits so dat I can see dar dey goes, as thick as de hairs on a man's haid. I circles round an' gits behin' dem an' goes inter de back uv de-house. Well, dar stan's a Yankee, an' he axes Missus Mary fer de smokehouse key. She gibes it ter him an' dey gits all uv de meat.

One big can uv grease am all dat wuz saved, an' dat wuz burried in de broom straw down in de fiel'.

Dey camps roun' dar dat night an' dey shoots ever chicken, pig, an' calf dey sees. De nex' day de marster goes ter Raleigh, an' gits a gyard, but dey has done stole all our stuff an' we am liven' mostly on parched co'n.

De only patterollers I knowed wuz Kenyan Jones an' Billy Pump an' dey wuz called po' white trash. Dey owned blood houn's, an' chased de niggers an' whupped dem shamful, I hyars. I neber seed but one Ku Klux an' he wuz sceered o' dem.

Atter de war we stayed on five or six years case we ain't had no place else ter go.

We ain't liked Abraham Lincoln, case he wuz a fool ter think dat we could live widout de white folkses, an' Jeff Davis wuz tryin' ter keep us, case he wuz greedy an' he wanted ter be de boss dog in politics.

N.C. District: No. 32
Worker: Daisy Whaley
Subject: Ex-slave Story.
Interviewed: Doc Edwards
Ex-slave. 84 Yrs
Staggville, N.C.
Date Stamp: "AUG 6 1937"
HW: Capital A—circled

DOC EDWARDS

I was bawn at Staggville, N.C., in 1853. I belonged to Marse Paul Cameron. My pappy was Murphy McCullers. Mammy's name was Judy. Dat would make me a McCullers, but I was always knowed as Doc Edwards an' dat is what I am called to dis day.

I growed up to be de houseman an' I cooked for Marse Benehan,—Marse Paul's son. Marse Benehan was good to me. My health failed from doing so much work in de house an' so I would go for a couple of hours each day an' work in de fiel' to be out doors an' get well again.

Marse Paul had so many niggers dat he never counted dem. When we opened de gate for him or met him in de road he would say, "Who is you? Whare you belong?" We would say, "We belong to Marse Paul." "Alright, run along" he'd say den, an' he would trow us a nickel or so.

We had big work shops whare we made all de tools, an' even de shovels was made at home. Dey was made out of wood, so was de rakes, pitchforks an' some of de hoes. Our nails was made in de blacksmith shop by han' an' de picks an' grubbin' hoes, too.

We had a han' thrashing machine. It was roun' like a stove pipe, only bigger. We fed de wheat to it an' shook it' til de wheat was loose from de straw an' when it come out at de other end it fell on a big cloth, bigger den de sheets. We had big curtains all roun' de cloth on de floor, like a tent, so de wheat wouldn' get scattered. Den we took de pitchfork an' lifted de straw up an' down so de wheat would go on de cloth. Den we moved de straw when de wheat was all loose Den we fanned de wheat wid big pieces of cloth to get de dust an' dirt outen it, so it could be taken to de mill an' groun' when it was wanted.

When de fall come we had a regular place to do different work. We had han' looms an' wove our cotton an' yarn an' made de cloth what was to make de clothes for us to wear.

We had a shop whare our shoes was made. De cobbler would make our shoes wid wooden soles. After de soles was cut out dey would be taken down to de blacksmiyh an' he would put a thin rim of iron aroun' de soles to keep dem from splitting. Dese soles was made from maple an' ash wood.

We didn' have any horses to haul wid. We used oxen an' ox-carts. De horse and mules was used to do de plowin'.

When de Yankees come dey didn' do so much harm,

only dey tole us we was free niggers. But I always feel like I belong to Marse Paul, an' i still live at Staggville on de ole plantation. I has a little garden an' does what I can to earn a little somethin'. De law done fixed it so now dat I will get a little pension, an' I'll stay right on in dat little house 'til de good Lawd calls me home, den I will see Marse Paul once more.

only dey tole us we was free niggers. But I always feel like I belong to Marse Paul, an' I still live at Staggeville on de ole plantation. I has a little garden an' does what I can to earn a little somethin'. De law done fixed it so now dat I will get a little pension, an' I'll stay right on in dat little house till de good Lawd calls me home, den I will see Marse Paul once mo'.

N.C. District:	No. 11
Worker:	Mrs. W. N. Harriss
No. Words:	658
Subject:	John Evans
	Born in Slavery
Editor:	Mrs. W. N. Harriss
Date Stamp:	"SEP—1937"

JOHN EVANS

I was born August 15th, 1859. I am 78 years old. Dat comes out right, don't it? My mother's name was Hattie Newbury. I don't never remember seein' my Pa. We lived on Middle Sound an' dat's where I was born. I knows de room, 'twas upstairs, an' when I knowed it, underneath, downstairs dat is, was bags of seed an' horse feed, harness an' things, but it was slave quarters when I come heah.

Me an' my mother stayed right on with Mis' Newberry after freedom, an' never knowed no diffunce. They was jus' like sisters an' I never knowed nothin' but takin' keer of Mistus Newberry. She taught me my letters an' the Bible, an' was mighty perticler 'bout my manners. An' I'm tellin' you my manners is brought me a heap more money than my readin'—or de Bible. I'm gwine tell you how dat is, but fust I want to say the most I learned on Middle Sound was' bout fishin' an' huntin'. An' dawgs.

My! But there sho' was birds an' possums on de Sound in dem days. Pa'tridges all over de place. Why, even me an' my Mammy et pa'tridges fer bre'kfust. Think of dat now! But when I growed up my job was fishin'. I made enough sellin' fish to the summer folks all along Wrightsville and Greenville Sounds to keep me all winter.

My Mammy cooked fer Mis' Newberry. After a while they both died. I never did'nt git married.

I don't know nothin' 'bout all the mean things I hear tell about slaves an' sich. We was just one fam'ly an' had all we needed. We never paid no 'tention to freedom or not freedom. I remember eve'ybody had work to do in slavery an' dey gone right on doin' it sence. An' nobody don't git nowheres settin' down holdin' their han's. It do'n make so much diffunce anyhow what you does jes so's you does it.

One time when I was carryin' in my fish to "Airlie" Mr. Pem Jones heard me laff, an' after I opened dis here mouf of mine an' laffed fer him I didn't have to bother 'bout fish no mo'. Lordy, dose rich folks he used to bring down fum New Yo'k is paid me as much as sixty dollars a week to laff fer 'em. One of 'em was named Mr. Fish. Now you know dat tickled *me*. I could jes laff an' laff 'bout dat. Mr. Pem give me fine clo'es an' a tall silk hat. I'd eat a big dinner in de kitchen an' den go in' mongst de quality an' laff fer' em an' make my noise like a wood saw in my th'oat. Dey was crazy 'bout dat. An' then's when I began to be thankful 'bout my manners. I's noticed if you has nice manners wid eve'ybody people gwine to be nice to you.

Well, (with a long sigh) I don't pick up no sich money

nowadays; but my manners gives me many a chance to laff, an' I never don't go hungry.

John has been a well known character for fifty years among the summer residents along the sounds and on Wrightsville Beach. He was a fisherman and huckster in his palmy days, but now John's vigor is on the wane, and he has little left with which to gain a livelihood except his unusually contagious laugh, and a truly remarkable flow of words. "Old John" could give Walter Winchel a handicap of twenty words a minute and then beat him at his own game. His mouth is enormous and his voice deep and resonant. He can make a noise like a wood saw which he maintains for 2 or 3 minutes without apparent effort, the sound buzzing on and on from some mysterious depths of his being with amazing perfection of imitation.

Any day during the baseball season John may be seen sandwiched between his announcement boards, a large bell in one hand, crying the ball game of the day. "Old John" to the youngsters; but finding many a quarter dropped in his hand by the older men with memories of gay hours and hearty laughter.

[illegible]

[illegible]

[illegible]

N.C. District: No. 3
Worker: Daisy Whaley
Subject: EX-SLAVE
Story Teller: Lindsay Faucette
Ex-Slave
Church Street,
Durham, N.C.
Date Stamp: "JUL 2 1937"

LINDSEY FAUCETTE

Yes, Mis', I wuz bawn in 1851, de 16th of November, on de Occoneechee Plantation, owned by Marse John Norwood an' his good wife, Mis' Annie. An' when I say 'good' I mean jus dat, for no better people ever lived den my Marse John an' Mis' Annie.

One thing dat made our Marse an' Mistis so good wuz de way dey brought up us niggers. We wuz called to de big house an' taught de Bible an' dey wuz Bible readin's every day. We wuz taught to be good men an' women an' to be hones'. Marse never sold any of us niggers. But when his boys and girls got married he would give dem some of us to take with dem.

Marse never allowed us to be whipped. One time we had a white overseer an' he whipped a fiel' han' called Sam Norwood, til de blood come. He beat him so bad dat de other niggers had to take him down to de river an' wash de blood off. When Marse come an' foun' dat out he sent dat white man off an' wouldn' let him stay on de plantation over night. He jus' wouldn' have him roun' de place no longer. He made Uncle Whitted de overseer kase he wuz one of de oldest slaves he had an' a good nigger.

When any of us niggers got sick Mis' Annie would come down to de cabin to see us. She brung de best wine, good chicken an' chicken soup an' everything else she had at de big house dat she thought we would like, an' she done everything she could to get us well again.

Marse John never worked us after dark. We worked in de day an' had de nights to play games an' have singin's. We never cooked on a Sunday. Everything we ett on dat day was cooked on Saturday. Dey wuzn' lighted in de cook stoves or fire places in de big house or cabins neither. Everybody rested on Sunday. De tables wuz set an' de food put on to eat, but nobody cut any wood an' dey wuzn' no other work don' on dat day. Mammy Beckie wuz my gran'mammy an' she toted de keys to de pantry an' smoke house, an' her word went wid Marse John an' Mis' Annie.

Marse John wuz a great lawyer an' when he went to Pittsboro an' other places to practice, if he wuz to stay all night, Mis' Annie had my mammy sleep right in bed wid her, so she wouldn' be 'fraid.

Marse an Mistis had three sons an' three daughters,— De oldest son wuz not able to go to war. He had studied so hard dat it had 'fected his mind, so he stayed at home. De secon' son, named Albert, went to war an' wuz brought back dead with a bullet hole through his head. Dat liked to have killed Marse John an' Mis' Annie. Dey wuz three girls, named, Mis' Maggie, Mis' Ella Bella and Mis' Rebena.

I wuz de cow-tender. I took care of de cows an' de calves. I would have to hold de calf up to de mother cow 'til de milk would come down an' den I would have to hold it away 'til somebody done de milkin'. I tended de horses, too, an' anything else dat I wuz told to do.

When de war started an' de Yankees come, dey didn' do much harm to our place. Marse had all de silver an' money an' other things of value hid under a big rock be de river an' de Yankees never did fine anything dat we hid.

Our own sojers did more harm on our plantation den de Yankees. Dey camped in de woods an' never did have nuff to eat an' took what dey wanted. An' lice! I ain't never seed de like. It took fifteen years for us to get shed of de lice dat de sojers lef' behind. You jus' couldn' get dem out of your clothes les' you burned dem up. Dey wuz hard to get shed of.

After de war wuz over Marse John let Pappy have eighteen acres of land for de use of two of his boys for a year. My pappy made a good crop of corn, wheat an' other food on dis land. Dey wuz a time when you couldn' find a crust of bread or piece of meat in my mammy's pantry for us to eat, an' when she did get a little meat or bread she would divide it between us chillun, so each would have a share an' go without herself an' never conplained.

When pappy wuz makin' his crop some of de others would ask him why he didn' take up some of his crop and get somethin' to eat. He would answer an' say dat when he left dat place he intended to take his crop with him an' he did. He took plenty of corn, wheat, potatoes an' other food, a cow, her calf, mule an' hogs an' he moved to a farm dat he bought.

Later on in years my pappy an mammy come here in Durham an' bought a home. I worked for dem' til I wuz thirty-two years old an' give dem what money I earned. I worked for as little as twenty-five cents a day. Den I got a dray an' hauled for fifteen cents a load from de Durham depo' to West Durham for fifteen years. Little did I think at dat time dat I would ever have big trucks an' a payroll of $6,000.00 a year. De good Lawd has blest me all de way, an' all I have is His'n, even to my own breath.

Den one day I went back home to see my old Marse an' I foun' him sittin' in a big chair on de po'ch an' his health wuzn' so good. He sed, "Lindsey, why don' you stop runnin' roun' wid de girls an' stop you cou't 'n? You never will get nowhere makin' all de girls love you an' den you walk away an' make up with some other girl. Go get yourself a good girl an' get married an' raise a family an' be somebody." An' I did. I quit all de girls an' I foun' a fine girl and we wuz married. I sho got a good wife; I got one of de best women dat could be foun' an' we lived together for over forty-five years. Den she died six years ago now, an' I sho miss her for she wuz a real help-mate all through dese years. We raised five chillun an' educated dem to be school teachers an' other trades.

I have tried to live de way I wuz raised to. My wife never worked a day away from home all de years we wuz married. It wuz my raisin an' my strong faith in my Lawd an' Marster dat helped me to get along as well as I have, an' I bless Him every day for de strength He has given me to bring up my family as well as I have. Der is only one way to live an' dat is de right way. Educate your chillun, if you can, but be sho you give dem de proper moral training at home. De right way to raise your chillun is to larn dem to have manners and proper respect for their parents, be good citizens an' God fearin' men an' women. When you have done dat you will not be ashamed of dem in your old age. I bless my Maker dat I have lived so clos' to Him as I have all dese years an' when de time comes to go to Him I will have no regrets an' no fears.

N.C. District: No. 2
Worker: T. Pat Matthews
No. Words: 567
Subject: A SLAVE STORY
Story Teller: Ora M. Flagg
Editor: Daisy Bailey Waitt

ORA M. FLAGG

My name is Ora M. Flagg. I wus born in Raleigh near the Professional Building, in the year 1860, October 16. My mother wus named Jane Busbee. Her marster wus Quent Busbee, a lawyer. Her missus wus Julia Busbee. She wus a Taylor before she married Mr. Busbee. Now I tell you, I can't tell you exactly, but the old heads died. The old heads were the Scurlocks who lived in Chatham County. I heard their names but I don't remember them. Their children when they died drawed for the slaves and my mother wus brought to Raleigh when she wus eight years old. She came from the Scurlocks to the Busbees. The Taylors were relatives of the Scurlocks, and were allowed to draw, and Julia Taylor drawed my mother. It wus fixed so the slaves on this estate could not be sold, but could be drawed for by the family and relatives. She got along just middlin' after her missus died. When her missus died, mother said she had to look after herself. Mr. Busbee would not allow anyone to whip mother. He married Miss Lizzie Bledsoe the second time.

I wus only a child and, of course, I thought as I could get a little something to eat everything wus all right, but we had few comforts. We had prayer meeting and we went to the white people's church. I heard mother say that they had to be very careful what they said in their worship. Lots of time dey put us children to bed and went off.

About the time of the surrender, I heard a lot about the patterollers, but I did not know what they were. Children wus not as wise then as they are now. They didn't know as much about things.

Yes sir, I remember the Yankees coming to Raleigh, we had been taken out to Moses Bledsoe's place on Holleman's Road to protect Mr. Bledsoe's things. They said if they put the things out there, and put a family of Negroes there the Yankees would not bother the things. So they stored a lot of stuff there, and put my mother an' a slave man by the name o' Tom Gillmore there. Two Negro families were there. We children watched the Yankees march by.

The Yankees went through everything, and when mother wouldn't tell them where the silver wus hid they threw her things in the well. Mother cried, an' when the Yankee officers heard of it they sent a guard there to protect us. The colored man, Tom Gillmore, wus so scared, he and his family moved out at night leaving my mother alone with her family. The Yankees ate the preserves and all the meat and other things. They destroyed a lot they could not eat.

Mother and me stayed on with marster after the surrender, and stayed on his place till he died. After that we moved to Peck's Place, called Peck's Place because the property wus sold by Louis Peck. It wus also called the 'Save-rent' section, then in later years Oberlin Road.

I think slavery wus a bad thing, while it had its good points in building good strong men. In some cases where marsters were bad it wus a bad thing.

Abraham Lincoln wus our friend, he set us free. I don't know much about Booker T. Washington. Mr Roosevelt is all right. Jim Young seemed to be all right. Jeff Davis didn't bother me. I guess he wus all right.

EH

N.C. District:	No. 2
Worker:	Mary Hicks
No. Words:	361
Subject:	Ex-Slave Story
Story Teller:	Analiza Foster.
Editor:	Daisy Bailey Waitt

ANALIZA FOSTER

I wuz borned in Person County ter Tom Line an' Harriet Cash. My mammy belonged ter a Mr. Cash an' pappy belonged ter Miss Betsy Woods. Both of dese owners wuz mean ter dere slaves an' dey ain't carin' much if'en dey kills one, case dey's got plenty. Dar wuz one woman dat I hyard mammy tell of bein' beat clean ter death.

De 'oman wuz pregnant an' she fainted in de fiel' at de plow. De driver said dat she wuz puttin' on, an' dat she ort ter be beat. De master said dat she can be beat but don't ter hurt de baby. De driver says dat he won't, den he digs a hole in de sand an' he puts de 'oman in de hole, which am nigh 'bout ter her arm pits, den he kivers her up an' straps her han's over her haid.

He takes de long bull whup an' he cuts long gashes all over her shoulders an' raised arms, den he walks off an' leabes her dar fer a hour in de hot sun. De flies an' de gnats dey worry her, an' de sun hurts too an' she cries a little, den de driver comes out wid a pan full of vinegar, salt an' red pepper an' he washes de gashes. De 'oman faints an' he digs her up, but in a few minutes she am stone dead.

Dat's de wust case dat I'se eber hyard of but I reckon dar wuz plenty more of dem.

Ter show yo' de value of slaves I'll tell yo' 'bout my gran'ma. She wuz sold on de block four times, an' eber time she brung a thousand dollars. She wuz valuable case she wuz strong an' could plow day by day, den too she could have twenty chilluns an' wuck right on.

De Yankees come through our country an' dey makes de slaves draw water fer de horses all night. Course dey stold eber'thing dey got dere han's on but dat wuz what ole Abraham Lincoln tol' dem ter do.

MH:EH

N.C. District:	No. 2
Worker:	T. Pat Matthews
No. Words:	570
Subject:	A SLAVE STORY
Story Teller:	Georginna Foster
Editor:	George L. Andrews
Date Stamp:	"AUG 23 1937"

GEORGIANNA FOSTER

I wus born in 1861. I jes' can 'member de Yankees comin' through, but I 'members dere wus a lot of 'em wearin' blue clothes. I wus born at Kerney Upchurch's plantation twelve miles from Raleigh. He wus my marster an' Missus Enny wus his wife. My father wus named Axiom Wilder and my mother wus Mancy Wilder. De most I know 'bout slavery dey tole it to me. I 'members I run when de Yankees come close to me. I wus 'fraid of 'em.

We lived in a little log houses at marsters. De food wus short an' things in general wus bad, so mother tole me. She said dey wus a whole lot meaner den dey had any business bein'. Dey allowed de patterollers to snoop around an' whup de slaves, mother said dey stripped some of de slaves naked an' whupped 'em. She said women had to work all day in de fields an' come home an' do de house work at night while de white folks hardly done a han's turn of work.

Marse Kerney had a sluice of chilluns. I can't think of 'em all, but I 'members Calvin, James, Allen, Emily, Helen, an' I jest can't think of de rest of de chilluns names.

Mother said dey gathered slaves together like dey did horses an' sold 'em on de block. Mother said dey carried some to Rolesville in Wake County an' sold 'em. Dey sold Henry Temples an' Lucinda Upchurch from marster's plantation, but dey carried 'em to Raleigh to sell 'em.

We wore homemade clothes an' shoes wid wooden bottoms. Dey would not allow us to sing an' pray but dey turned pots down at de door an' sung an' prayed enyhow an' de Lord heard dere prayers. Dat dey did sing an' pray.

Mother said dey whupped a slave if dey caught him wid a book in his hand. You wus not 'lowed no books. Larnin' among de slaves wus a forbidden thing. Dey wus not allowed to cook anything for demselves at de cabins no time 'cept night. Dere wus a cook who cooked fur all durin' de day. Sometimes de field han's had to work 'round de place at night after comin' in from de fields. Mother said livin' at marster's wus hard an' when dey set us free we left as quick as we could an' went to Mr. Bob Perry's plantation an' stayed there many years. He wus a good man an' give us all a chance. Mother wus free born at Upchurch's but when de war ended, she had been bound to Wilder by her mother, an' had married my father who wus a slave belongin' to Bob Wilder. Dey did not like de fare at Marster Upchurch's or Marster Wilder's, so when dey wus set free dey lef' an' went to Mrs. Perry's place.

Dey had overseers on both plantations in slavery time but some of de niggers would run away before dey would take a whuppin'. Fred Perry run away to keep from bein' sold. He come back do' an' tole his marster to do what he wanted to wid him. His marster told him to go to work an' he stayed dere till he wus set free. God heard his prayer 'cause he said he axed God not to let him be sold.

Mother an' father said Abraham Lincoln come through there on his way to Jeff Davis. Jeff Davis wus de Southern President. Lincoln say, 'Turn dem slaves loose, Jeff Davis,' an' Jeff Davis said nuthin'. Den he come de second time an' say, 'Is you gwine to turn dem slaves loose?' an' Jeff Davis wouldn't do it. Den Lincoln come a third time an' had a cannon shootin' man wid him an' he axed, 'Is you gwine to set dem slaves free Jeff Davis?' An' Jeff Davis he say, 'Abraham Lincoln, you knows I is not goin' to give up my property, an' den Lincoln said, 'I jest as well go back an' git up my crowd den.' Dey talked down in South Carolina an' when Jeff Davis 'fused to set us free, Lincoln went home to the North and got up his crowd, one hundred an' forty thousand men, dey said, an' de war begun. Dey fighted an' fighted an' de Yankees whupped. Dey set us free an' dey say dat dey hung Jeff Davis on a ole apple tree.

EH HW

N.C. District:	No. 2
Worker:	T. Pat Matthews
No. Words:	815
Subject:	FRANK FREEMAN
Story Teller:	Frank Freeman
Editor:	Daisy Bailey Waitt

FRANK FREEMAN

I was born near Rolesville in Wake County Christmas Eve, 24 of December 1857. I am 76 years old. My name is Frank Freeman and my wife's name is Mary Freeman. She is 78 years old. We live at 216 Tuppers Lane, Raleigh, Wake County, North Carolina. I belonged to ole man Jim Wiggins jus' this side o' Roseville, fourteen miles from Raleigh. The great house is standin' there now, and a family by the name o' Gill, a colored man's family, lives there. The place is owned by ole man Jim Wiggins's grandson, whose name is O. B. Wiggins. My wife belonged to the Terrells before the surrender. I married after the war. I was forty years ole when I was married.

Old man Jim Wiggins was good to his niggers, and when the slave children were taken off by his children they treated us good. Missus dressed mother up in her clothes and let her go to church. We had good, well cooked food, good clothes, and good places to sleep. Some of the chimneys which were once attached to the slave houses are standing on the plantation. The home plantation in Wake County was 3000 acres.

Marster also owned three and a quarter plantations in Franklin County. He kept about ten men at home and would not let his slave boys work until they were 18 years old, except tend to horses and do light jobs around the house. He had slaves on all his plantations but they were under colored overseers who were slaves themselves. Marster had three boys and five girls, eight children of his own.

One of the girls was Siddie Wiggins. When she married Alfred Holland, and they went to Smithfield to live she took me with her, when I was two years old. She thought so much o' me mother was willing to let me go. Mother loved Miss Siddie, and it was agreeable in the family. I stayed right on with her after the surrender three years until 1868. My father decided to take me home then and went after me.

They never taught us books of any kind. I was about 8 years old when I began to study books. When I was 21 Christmas Eve 1880, father told me I was my own man and that was all he had to give me.

I had decided many years before to save all my nickles. I kept them in a bag. I did not drink, chew, smoke or use tobacco in any way during this time. When he told me I was free I counted up my money and found I had $47.75. I had never up to this tasted liquor or tobacco. I don't know anything about it yet. I have never used it. With that money I entered Shaw University. I worked eight hours a week in order to help pay my way.

Later I went into public service, teaching four months a year in the public schools. My salary was $25.00 per month. I kept going to school at Shaw until I could get a first grade teacher's certificate. I never graduated. I taught in the public schools for 43 years. I would be teaching now, but I have high blood pressure.

I was at Master Hollands at Smithfield when the Yankees came through. They went into my Marster's store and began breaking up things and taking what they wanted. They were dressed in blue and I did not know who they were. I asked and someone told me they were the Yankees.

My father was named Burton, and my mother was named Queen Anne. Father was a Freeman and mother was a Wiggins.

There were no churches on the plantation. My father told me a story about his young master, Joe Freeman and my father's brother Soloman. Marster got Soloman to help whip him. My father went in to see young Missus and told her about it, and let her know he was going away. He had got the cradle blade and said he would kill either of them if they bothered him. Father had so much Indian blood in him that he would fight. He ran away and stayed four years and passed for a free nigger. He stayed in the Bancomb Settlement in Johnson County. When he came home before the war ended, Old Marster said, 'Soloman why didn't you stay?' father said, 'I have been off long enough'. Marster said 'Go to work', and there was no more to it. Father helped build the breastworks in the Eastern part of the State down at Ft. Fisher. He worked on the forts at New Bern too.

I think Abraham Lincoln worked hard for our freedom. He was a great man. I think Mr. Roosevelt is a good man and is doing all he can for the good of all.

LE

N.C. District: No. 2
Worker: T. Pat Matthews
No. Words: 976
Subject: ADDY GILL
Story Teller: Addy Gill
Editor: G. L. Andrews
Date Stamp: "SEP 10 1937"

ADDY GILL

I am seventy four years of age. I wus born a slave Jan. 6, 1863 on a plantation near Millburnie, Wake County, owned by Major Wilder, who hired my father's time. His wife wus named Sarah Wilder. I don't know anything 'bout slavery 'cept what wus tole me by father and mother but I do know that if it had not been for what de southern white folks done for us niggers we'd have perished to death. De north turned us out wid out anything to make a livin' wid.

My father wus David Gill and, my mother wus Emily Gill. My father wus a blacksmith an he moved from place to place where dey hired his time. Dats why I wus born on Major Wilders place. Marster Gill who owned us hired father to Major Wilder and mother moved wid him. For a longtime atter de war, nine years, we stayed on wid Major Wilder, de place we wus at when dey set us free.

Mr. Wilder had a large plantation and owned a large

number of slaves before de surrender. I only 'members fourteen of de ones I know belonged to him. Mr. Wilder wus a mighty good man. We had plenty to eat an plenty work to do. Dere wus seven in the Major's family. Three boys, two girls, he an his wife. His boys wus named Sam, Will and Crockett. De girls wus named Florence and Flora. Dey are all dead, every one of 'em. De whole set. I don't know nary one of 'em dats livin. If dey wus livin I could go to 'em an' git a meal any time. Yes Sir! any time, day or night.

I farmed for a long time for myself atter I wus free from my father at 21 years of age. Den 'bout twelve years ago I come to Raleigh and got a job as butler at St. Augustine Episcopal College for Colored. I worked dere eight years, wus taken sick while workin dere an has been unable to work much since. Dat wus four years ago. Since den sometimes I ain't able to git up outen my cheer when I is settin down. I tells you, mister, when a nigger leaves de farm an comes to town to live he sho is takin a mighty big chance wid de wolf. He is just a riskin parishin, dats what he is a doin.

I married forty five years ago this past November. I wus married on de second Thursday night in November to Millie Ruffin of Wake County, North Carolina. We had leben chilluns, six boys an five gals. Four of the boys an one of de gals is livin now. Some of my chilluns went north but dey didn't stay dere but two months. De one dat went north wus Sam, dat wus de oldest one. He took a notion to marry so he went up to Pennsylvania and worked. Just as soon as he got enough money to marry on he come back an got married. He never went back north no more.

Mother belonged to Sam Krenshaw before she wus

bought by Marster Gill. Her missus when she was a girl growin up wus Mrs. Louise Krenshaw. De missus done de whuppin on Mr. Krenshaw's plantation an she wus mighty rough at times. She whupped mother an cut her back to pieces so bad dat de scars wus on her when she died. Father died in Raleigh an mother died out on Miss Annie Ball's farm 'bout seven miles from Raleigh. Mother an father wus livin there when mother died. Father den come to Raleigh an died here.

I caint read an write but all my chilluns can read and write. Mother and father could not read or write. I haint had no chance. I had no larnin. I had to depend on white folks I farmed wid to look atter my business. Some of em cheated me out of what I made. I am tellin you de truth 'bout some of de landlords, dey got mighty nigh all I made. Mr. Richard Taylor who owned a farm near Raleigh whur I stayed two years wus one of em. He charged de same thing three times an I had it to pay. I stayed two years an made nothin'. Dis is de truth from my heart, from here to glory. I members payin' fur a middlin of meat twice. Some of de white folks looked out fur me an prospered. Mr. Dave Faulk wus one of 'em. I stayed wid him six years and I prospered. Mr. John Bushnell wus a man who took up no time wid niggers. I rented from him a long time.

He furnished a nigger cash to run his crap on. De nigger made de crap sold it an carried him his part. He figgered 'bout what he should have an de nigger paid in cash. He wus a mighty good man to his nigger tenants. I never owned a farm, I never owned horses or mules to farm with. I worked de landlords stock and farmed his land on shares. Farmin' has been my happiest life and I wushes I wus able to farm agin cause I am happiest when on de farm.

I had a quiet home weddin' an I wus married by a white magistrate. I got up one night an' wus married at 1 o'clock.

Atter de weddin she went back home wid me. We have had our ups and downs in life. Sometimes de livin' has been mighty hard, but dere has never been a time since I been free when I could not git a handout from de white folks back yard.

LE

N.C. District: No. 2
Worker: T. Pat Matthews
No. Words: 2,118
Subject: A SLAVE STORY
Story Teller: Robert Glenn
Editor: George L. Andrews
Date Stamp: "SEP 10 1937"

ROBERT GLENN

I was a slave before and during the Civil War. I am 87 years old. I was born Sept. 16, 1850. I was born in Orange County, North Carolina near Hillsboro. At that time Durham was just a platform at the station and no house there whatever. The platform was lighted with a contraption shaped like a basket and burning coal that gave off a blaze. There were holes in this metal basket for the cinders to fall through.

I belonged to a man named Bob Hall, he was a widower. He had three sons, Thomas, Nelson, and Lambert. He died when I was eight years old and I was put on the block and sold in Nelson Hall's yard by the son of Bob Hall. I saw my brother and sister sold on this same plantation. My mother belonged to the Halls, and father belonged to the Glenns. They sold me away from my father and mother and I was carried to the state of Kentucky. I was bought by a Negro speculator by the name of Henry long who lived not far from Hurdles Mill in Person County. I was not allowed to tell my mother and father goodbye. I was bought and sold three times in one day.

My father's time was hired out and as he knew a trade he had by working overtime saved up a considerable amount of money. After the speculator, Henry Long, bought me, mother went to father and pled with him to buy me from him and let the white folks hire me out. No slave could own a slave. Father got the consent and help of his owners to buy me and they asked Long to put me on the block again. Long did so and named his price but when he learned who had bid me off he backed down. Later in the day he put me on the block and named another price much higher than the price formerly set. He was asked by the white folks to name his price for his bargain and he did so. I was again put on the auction block and father bought me in, putting up the cash. Long then flew into a rage and cursed my father saying, 'you damn black son of a bitch, you think you are white do you? Now just to show you are black, I will not let you have your son at any price.' Father knew it was all off, mother was frantic but there was nothing they could do about it. They had to stand and see the speculator put me on his horse behind him and ride away without allowing either of them to tell me goodbye. I figure I was sold three times in one day, as the price asked was offered in each instance. Mother was told under threat of a whupping not to make any outcry when I was carried away. He took me to his home, but on the way he stopped for refreshments, at a plantation, and while he was eating and drinking, he put me into a room where two white women were spinning flax. I was given a seat across the room from where they were working. After I had sat there awhile wondering where I was going and thinking about mother and home, I went to one of the women and asked, 'Missus when will I see my mother again?' She replied, I don't know child, go and sit down. I went back to my seat and as I did so both the women stopped spinning for a moment, looked at each other, and one of them remarked. "Almighty God, this slavery business is a horrible thing. Chances are this boy will never see his mother again." This remark nearly killed me, as I began to fully realize my situation. Long, the Negro trader, soon came back, put me on his horse and finished the trip to his home. He kept me at his home awhile and then traded me to a man named William Moore who lived in Person County. Moore at this time was planning to move to Kentucky which he soon did, taking me with him. My mother found out by the "Grapevine telegraph" that I was going to be carried to Kentucky. She got permission and came to see me before they carried me off. When she started home I was allowed to go part of the way with her but they sent two Negro girls with us to insure my return. We were allowed to talk privately, but while we were doing so, the two girls stood a short distance away and watched as the marster told them when they left that if I escaped they would be whipped every day until I was caught. When the time of parting came and I had to turn back, I burst out crying loud. I was so weak from sorrow I could not walk, and the two girls who were with me took me by each arm and led me along half carrying me.

This man Moore carried me and several other slaves to Kentucky. We traveled by train by way of Nashville, Tenn. My thoughts are not familiar with the happenings of this trip but I remember that we walked a long distance at one place on the trip from one depot to another.

We finally reached Kentucky and Moore stopped at his brother's plantation until he could buy one, then we moved on it. My marster was named William Moore and my missus was named Martha Whitfield Moore. It was a big plantation and he hired a lot of help and had white tenants besides the land he worked with slaves. There were only six slaves used as regular field hands during his first year in Kentucky.

The food was generally common. Hog meat and cornbread most all the time. Slaves got biscuits only on Sunday morning. Our clothes were poor and I worked barefooted most of the time, winter and summer. No books, papers or anything concerning education was allowed the slaves by his rules and the customs of these times.

Marster Moore had four children among whom was one boy about my age. The girls were named Atona, Beulah, and Minnie, and the boy was named Crosby. He was mighty brilliant. We played together. He was the only white boy there, and he took a great liking to me, and we loved each devotedly. Once in an undertone he asked me how would I like to have an education. I was overjoyed at the suggestion and he at once began to teach me secretly. I studied hard and he soon had me so I could read and write well. I continued studying and he continued teaching me. He furnished me books and slipped all the papers he could get to me and I was the best educated Negro in the community without anyone except the slaves knowing what was going on.

All the slaves on marster's plantation lived the first year we spent in Kentucky in a one room house with one fireplace. There was a dozen or more who all lived in this one room house. Marster built himself a large house having seven rooms. He worked his slaves himself and never had any overseers. We worked from sun to sun in the fields and then worked at the house after getting in from the fields as long as we could see. I have never seen a patteroller but when I left the plantation in slavery time I got a pass. I have never seen a jail for slaves but I have seen slaves whipped and I was whipped myself. I was whipped particularly about a saddle I left out in the night after using it during the day. My flesh was cut up so bad that the scars are on me to this day.

We were not allowed to have prayer meetings, but we went to the white folks church to services sometimes. There were no looms, mills, or shops on the plantation at Marster Moore's. I kept the name of Glenn through all the years as Marster Moore did not change his slaves names to his family name. My mother was named Martha Glenn and father was named Bob Glenn.

I was in the field when I first heard of the Civil War. The woman who looked after Henry Hall and myself (both slaves) told me she heard marster say old Abraham Lincoln was trying to free the niggers. Marster finally pulled me up and went and joined the Confederate Army. Kentucky split and part joined the North and part the South. The war news kept slipping through of success for first one side then the other. Sometimes marster would come home, spend a few days and then go again to the war. It seemed he influenced a lot of men to join the southern army, among them was a man named Enoch Moorehead. Moorehead was killed in a few days after he joined the southern army.

Marster Moore fell out with a lot of his associates

in the army and some of them who were from the same community became his bitter enemies. Tom Foushee was one of them. Marster became so alarmed over the threats on his life made by Foushee and others that he was afraid to stay in his own home at night, and he built a little camp one and one half miles from his home and he and missus spent their nights there on his visits home. Foushee finally came to the great house one night heavily armed, came right on into the house and inquired for marster. We told him marster was away. Foushee lay down on the floor and waited a long time for him. Marster was at the little camp but we would not tell where he was.

Foushee left after spending most of the night at marster's. As he went out into the yard, when leaving, marster's bull dog grawled at him and he shot him dead.

Marster went to Henderson, Kentucky, the County seat of Henderson County, and surrendered to the Federal Army and took the Oath of Allegiance. Up to that time I had seen a few Yankees. They stopped now and then at marster's and got their breakfast. They always asked about buttermilk, they seemed to be very fond of it. They were also fond of ham, but we had the ham meat buried in the ground, this was about the close of the war. A big army of Yankees came through a few months later and soon we heard of the surrender. A few days after this marster told me to catch two horses that we had to go to Dickenson which was the County seat of Webster County. On the way to Dickenson he said to me, 'Bob, did you know you are free and Lincoln has freed you? You are as free as I am.' We went to the Freedmen's Bureau and went into the office. A Yankee officer looked me over and asked marster my name, and informed me I was free, and asked me whether or not I wanted to keep living with Moore. I did not know what to do, so I told him yes. A fixed price of seventy-five dollars and board was then set as the salary I should receive per year for my work. The Yankees told me to let him know if I was not paid as agreed.

I went back home and stayed a year. During the year I hunted a lot at night and thoroughly enjoyed being free. I took my freedom by degrees and remained obedient and respectful, but still wondering and thinking of what the future held for me. After I retired at night I made plan after plan and built aircastles as to what I would do. At this time I formed a great attachment for the white man, Mr. Atlas Chandler, with whom I hunted. He bought my part of the game we caught and favored me in other ways. Mr. Chandler had a friend, Mr. Dewitt Yarborough, who was an adventurer, and trader, and half brother to my ex-marster, Mr. Moore, with whom I was then staying. He is responsible for me taking myself into my own hands and getting out of feeling I was still under obligations to ask my marster or missus when I desired to leave the premises. Mr. Yarborough's son was off at school at a place called Kiloh, Kentucky, and he wanted to carry a horse to him and also take along some other animals for trading purposes. He offered me a new pair of pants to make the trip for him and I accepted the job. I delivered the horse to his son and started for home. On the way back I ran into Uncle Squire Yarborough who once belonged to Dewitt Yarborough. He persuaded me to go home with him and go with him to a wedding in Union County, Kentucky. The wedding was twenty miles away and we walked the entire distance. It was a double wedding, two couples were married. Georgianna Hawkins was married to George Ross and Steve Carter married a woman whose name I do not remember. This was in the winter during the Christmas Holidays and I stayed in the community until about the first of January, then I went back home. I had been thinking for several days before I went back home as to just what I must tell Mr. Moore and as to how he felt about the matter, and what I would get when I got home. In my dilema I almost forgot I was free.

I got home at night and my mind and heart was full but I was surprised at the way he treated me. He acted kind and asked me if I was going to stay with him next year. I was pleased. I told him, yes sir! and then I lay down and went to sleep. He had a boss man on his plantation then and next morning he called me, but I just couldn't wake. I seemed to be in a trance or something, I had recently lost so much sleep. He called me the second time and still I did not get up. Then he came in and spanked my head. I jumped up and went to work feeding the stock and splitting wood for the day's cooking and fires. I then went in and ate my breakfast. Mr. Moore told me to hitch a team of horses to a wagon and go to a neighbors five miles away for a load of hogs. I refused to do so. They called me into the house and asked me what I was going to do about it. I said I do not know. As I said that I stepped out of the door and left. I went straight to the county seat and hired to Dr. George Rasby in Webster County for one hundred dollars per year. I stayed there one year. I got uneasy in Kentucky. The whites treated the blacks awful bad so I decided to go to Illinois as I thought a Negro might have a better chance there, it being a northern state. I was kindly treated and soon began to save money, but all through the years there was a thought that haunted me in my dreams and in my waking hours, and this thought was of my mother, whom I had not seen or heard of in many years. Finally one cold morning in early December I made a vow that I was going to North Carolina and see my mother if she was still living. I had plenty of money for the trip. I wrote the postmaster in Roxboro, North Carolina, asking him to inform my mother I was still living, and telling him the circumstances, mailing a letter at the same time telling her I was still alive but saying nothing of my intended visit to her. I left Illinois bound for North Carolina on December 15th and in a few days I was at my mother's home. I tried to fool them. There were two men with me and they called me by a ficticious name, but when I shook my mother's hand I held it a little too long and she suspicioned something still she held herself until she was more sure. When she got a chance she came to me and said ain't you my child? Tell me ain't you my child whom I left on the road near Mr. Moore's before the war? I broke down and began to cry. Mother nor father did not know me, but mother suspicioned I was her child. Father had a few days previously remarked that he did not want to die without seeing his son once more. I could not find language to express my feeling. I did not know before I came home whether my parents were dead or alive. This Christmas I spent in the county and state of my birth and childhood; with mother, father and freedom was the happiest period of my entire life, because those who were torn apart in bondage and sorrow several years previous were now united in freedom and happiness.

EH

N.C. District:	No. 3
Worker:	Travis Jordan
Subject:	SARAH ANNE GREEN
	Ex-Slave, 78 Years
	Durham County

SARAH ANNE GREEN

My mammy an' pappy wuz Anderson an' Hannah Watson. We fus' belonged to Marse Billy an' Mis Roby Watson, but when Marse Billy's daughter, Mis' Susie ma'ied young Marse Billy Headen, Ole Marse give her me, an' my mammy an' my pappy for er weddin' gif'. So, I growed up as Sarah Anne Headen.

My pappy had blue eyes. Dey wuz jus' like Marse Billy's eyes, kaze Ole Marse wuz pappy's marster an' his pappy too. Ole Marse wuz called Hickory Billy, dey called him dat kaze he chewed hickory bark. He wouldn' touch 'bacca, but he kept er twis' of dis bark in his pocket mos' all de time. He would make us chillun go down whare de niggers wuz splittin' rails an' peel dis bark off de logs befo' dey wuz split. De stuff he chewed come off de log right under de bark. After dey'd skin de logs we'd peel off dis hickory 'bacca in long strips an' make it up in twis's for Ole Marse. It wuz yellah an' tas' sweet an' sappy, an' he'd chew an' spit, an' chew an' spit. Mis' Roby wouldn' 'low no chewin' in de house, but Ole Marse sho done some spittin' outside. He could stan' in de barn door an' spit clear up in de lof'.

Ole Marse an' Mis Roby lived on er big plantation near Goldston an' dey had 'bout three hundred slaves. Hannah, my mammy, wuz de head seamstress. She had to 'ten' to de makin' of all de slaves clothes. De niggers had good clothes. De cloth wuz home woven in de weavin' room. Ten niggers didn' do nothin' but weave, but every slave had one Sunday dress a year made out of store bought cloth. Ole Marse seed to dat. Ole Marse made de niggers go to chu'ch too. He had er meetin' house on plantation an' every Sunday we wuz ma'ched to meetin'. Dey wuz preachin' every other Sunday an' Sunday School every Sunday. Marse Billy an' Mis' Roby teached de Sunday School, but dey didn' teach us to read an' write, no suh, dey sho didn'. If dey'd see us wid er book dey'd whip us. Dey said niggers didn' need no knowledge; dat dey mus' do what dey wuz tole to do. Marse Billy wuz er doctor too. He doctored de slaves when dey got sick, an' if dey got bad off he sen' for er sho nuff doctor an' paid de bills.

Every Chris'mas Marse Billy give de niggers er big time. He called dem up to de big house an' give dem er bag of candy, niggertoes, an' sugar plums, den he say: 'Who wants er egg nog, boys?' All dem dat wants er dram hol' up dey han's.' Yo' never seed such holdin' up of han's. I would hol' up mine too, an' Ole Marse would look at me an say, 'Go 'way from hear, Sarah Anne, yo' too little to be callin' for nog.' But he fill up de glass jus' de same an' put in er extra spoon of sugar an' give it to me. Dat sho wuz good nog. 'Twuz all foamy wid whipped cream an' rich wid eggs. Marse Billy an' Mis' Roby served it demselves from dey Sunday cut glass nog bowl, an' it kept Estella an' Rosette busy fillin' it up. Marse Billy wuz er good man.

When de war come on Marse Billy was too ole to go, but young Marse Billy an' Marse Gaston went. Dey wuz Ole Marse's two boys. Young Marse Billy Headen, Mis' Susie's husban' went too.

De day Ole Marse heard dat de Yankees wuz comin' he took all de meat 'cept two or three pieces out of de smoke house, den he got de silver an' things an' toted dem to de wood pile. He dug er hole an' buried dem, den he covered de place wid chips, but wid dat he wuzn' satisfied, so he made pappy bring er load of wood an' throw it on top of it, so when de Yankees come dey didn' fin' it.

When de Yankees come up in de yard Marse Billy took Mis' Roby an' locked her up in dey room, den he walk 'roun' an' watched de Yankees, but dey toted off what dey wanted. I wuzn' skeered of de Yankees; I thought dey wuz pretty mens in dey blue coats an' brass buttons. I followed dem all 'roun' beggin' for dey coat buttons. I ain't never seed nothin' as pretty as dem buttons. When dey lef' I followed dem way down de road still beggin', 'twell one of dem Yankees pull off er button an' give it to me. 'Hear, Nigger,' he say, 'take dis button. I's givin' it to you kaze yo's got blue eyes. I ain't never seed blue eyes in er black face befo'.' I had blue eyes like pappy an' Marse Billy, an' I kept dat Yankee button 'twell I wuz ma'ied, den I los' it.

De wus' thing I know dat happened, in de war wuz when Mis' Roby foun' de Yankee sojer in de ladies back house.

Down at de back of de garden behin' de row of lilac bushes wuz de two back houses, one for de mens an' one for de ladies. Mis' Roby went down to dis house one day, an' when she opened de door, dare lay er Yankee sojer on de floor. His head wuz tied up wid er bloody rag an' he look like he wuz dead.

Mammy say she seed Mis' Roby when she come out. She looked skeered but she didn' scream nor nothin'. When she seed mammy she motioned to her. She tole her 'bout de Yankee. 'He's jus' er boy, Hannah,' she say, 'he ain't no older den Marse Gaston, an' he's hurt. We got to do somethin' an' we can't tell nobody.' Den she sen' mammy to de house for er pan of hot water, de scissors an' er ole sheet. Mis' Roby cut off de bloody ran an' wash dat sojer boy's head den she tied up de cut places. Den she went to de house an' made mammy slip him er big milk toddy. 'Bout dat time she seed some ho'seman comin' down de road. When dey got closer she seed dey wuz 'Federate sojers. Dey rode up in de yard an' Marse Billy went out to meet dem. Dey tole him dat dey wuz lookin' for er Yankee prisoner dat done got away from dey camp.

After Ole Marse tole dem dat he ain't seed no Yankee sojer, dey tole him dat dey got to search de place kaze dat wuz orders.

When Mis Roby heard dem say dat she turned an' went through de house to do back yard. She walk 'roun' 'mong de flowers, but all de time she watchin' dem 'Federates search de barns, stables, an' everywhare. But, when dey start to de lilac bushes, Mis' Roby lif' her head an' walk right down de paf to de ladies back house, an' right befo' all dem mens, wid dem lookin' at her, she opened de door an' walk in. She sholy did.

Dat night when 'twuz dark Mis' Roby wrap' up er passel of food an' er bottle of brandy an' give it to dat sojer Yankee boy. She tole him dey wuz ho'ses in de paster an' dat de Yankee camp wuz over near Laurinburg or somewhare like dat.

Nobody ain't seed dat boy since, but somehow dat ho'se come back an' in his mane wuz er piece of paper. Marse Billy foun' it an' brung it to Mis' Roby an' ax her what it meant.

Mis' Roby took it an' 'twuz er letter dat sojer boy done wrote tellin' her dat he wuz safe an' thankin' her for what she done for him.

Mis' Roby tole Marse Billy she couldn' help savin' dat Yankee, he too much of er boy.

Marse Billy he look at Mis' Roby, den he say: 'Roby, honey, yo's braver den any sojer I ever seed.'

N.C. District:	No. 2
Worker:	T. Pat Matthews
No. Words:	624
Subject:	DORCAS GRIFFETH
Person Interviewed:	Dorcas Griffeth
Editor:	Daisy Bailey Waitt
Date Stamp:	"JUN 26 1937"

DORCAS GRIFFETH

You know me every time you sees me don't you? Who tole you I wus Dorcas Griffith? I seed you up town de other day. Yes, yes, I is old. I is 80 years old. I remember all about dem Yankees. The first biscuit I ever et dey give it to me. I wus big enough to nus de babies when de Yankees came through. Dey carried biscuits on dere horses, I wus jist thinkin' of my young missus de other day. I belonged to Doctor Clark in Chatham County near Pittsboro. My father wus named Billy Dismith, and my mother wus named Peggy Council. She belonged to the Councils. Father, belonged to the Dismiths and I belonged to the Clarks. Missus wus named Winnie. Dey had tolerable fine food for de white folks, but I did not get any of it. De food dey give us wus mighty nigh nuthin'. Our clothes wus bad and our sleepin' places wus not nuthin' at all. We had a hard time. We had a hard time then and we are havin' a hard time now. We have a house to live in now, and de chinches eat us up almos, and we have nuthin' to live on now, jist a little from charity. I fares mighty bad. Dey gives me a half peck of meal and a pound o' meat, a little oat meal, and canned grape juice, a half pound o' coffee and no sugar or lard and no flour. Dey gives us dat for a week's eatin'.

De Yankees called de niggers who wus plowin' de mules when dey came through an' made 'em bring 'em to 'em an' dey carried de mules on wid em. De niggers called de Yankees Blue Jackets.

I had two brothers, both older dan me. George de oldest and Jack. Let me see I had four sisters 1, 2, 3, 4; one wus named Annie, one named Rosa, Annie, and Francis and myself Dorcas. All de games I played wus de wurk in de field wid a hoe. Dere wus no playgrounds like we has now. No, no, if you got your work done you done enough. If I could see how to write like you I could do a lot o' work but I can't see. I kin write. I got a good education acording to readin', spellin, and writin'. I kin say de 2nd chapter of Matthey by heart, the 27 chapter of Ezelial by heart, or most of Ezekial by heart.

I learned it since I got free. I went to school in Raleigh to de Washington School. Dey wouldn't let us have books when I wus a slave. I wus afraid ter be caught wid a book. De patterollers scared us so bad in slavery time and beat so many uv de slaves dat we lef' de plantation jus' as soon as we wus free. Dat's de reason father lef' de plantation so quick. I also remember de Ku Klux. I wus afraid o' dem, and I did not think much of 'em. I saw slaves whupped till de blood run down dere backs. Once dey whupped some on de plantation and den put salt on de places and pepper on 'em. I didn't think nuthin in de world o' slavery. I think de it wus wrong. I didn't think a thing o' slavery.

All my people are dead, and I am unable to work. I haven't been able to work in six years. I thought Abraham Lincoln wus a good man. He had a good name.

I don't know much about Mr. Roosevelt but I hopes he will help me, cause I need it mighty bad.

All my people are dead, and I am unable to work. I haven't been able to work in six years. I'm [illegible]. Abraham Lincoln was a good man. He had a [illegible] [illegible].

I don't know much about Mr. Roosevelt, but I hope he will help me, cause I need it mighty bad.

Subject:	Sarah Gudger
Person Interviewed:	Sarah Gudger

TR: Added Header Page

SARAH GUDGER

Investigation of the almost incredible claim of Aunt Sarah Gudger, ex-slave living in Asheville, that she was born on Sept. 15, 1816, discloses some factual information corroborating her statements.

Aunt Sarah's father, Smart Gudger, belonged to and took his family name from Joe Gudger, who lived near Oteen, about six miles east of Asheville in the Swannanoa valley, prior to the War Between the States. Family records show that Joe Gudger married a Miss McRae in 1817, and that while in a despondent mood he ended his own life by hanging, as vividly recounted by the former slave.

John Hemphill, member of the family served by Aunt Sarah until "freedom," is recalled as being "a few y'ars younge' as me," and indeed his birth is recorded for 1822. Alexander Hemphill, mentioned by Aunt Sarah as having left to join the Confederate army when about 25 years of age, is authentic and his approximate age in 1861 tallies with that recalled by the ex-slave. When Alexander went off to the war Aunt Sarah was "gettin' t' be an ol' woman."

Aunt Sarah lives with distant cousins in a two-story frame house, comfortably furnished, at 8 Dalton street in South Asheville (the Negro section lying north of Kenilworth). A distant male relative, 72 years of age, said he has known Aunt Sarah all his life and that she was an old woman when he was a small boy. Small in stature, about five feet tall, Aunt Sarah is rathered rounded in face and body. Her milk-chocolate face is surmounted by short, sparse hair, almost milk white. She is somewhat deaf but understands questions asked her, responding with animation. She walks with one crutch, being lame in the right leg. On events of the long ago her mind is quite clear. Recalling the Confederate "sojers, marchin', marchin'" to the drums, she beat a tempo on the floor with her crutch. As she described how the hands of slaves were tied before they were whipped for infractions she crossed her wrists.

Owen Gudger, Asheville postmaster (1913-21), member of the Buncombe County Historical Association, now engaged in the real estate business, says he has been acquainted with Aunt Sarah all his life; that he has, on several occasions, talked to her about her age and early associations, and that her responses concerning members of the Gudger and Hemphill families coincide with known facts of the two families.

Interviewed by a member of the Federal Writers' Project, Aunt Sarah seemed eager to talk, and needed but little prompting.

(born September 15, 1816)
Interview with Mrs. Marjorie Jones, May 5, 1937

SARAH GUDGER

I wah bo'n 'bout two mile fum Ole Fo't on de Ole Mo'ganton Road. I sho' has had a ha'd life. Jes wok, an' wok, an' wok. I nebbah know nothin' but wok. Mah boss he wah Ole Man Andy Hemphill. He had a la'ge plantation in de valley. Plenty ob ebbathin'. All kine ob stock: hawgs, cows, mules, an' hosses. When Marse Andy die I go lib wif he son, William Hemphill.

I nebbah fo'git when Marse Andy die. He wah a good ole man, and de Missie she wah good, too. She usta read de Bible t' us chillun afoah she pass away.

Mah pappy, he lib wif Joe Gudgah (Gudger). He ole an' feeble, I 'membahs. He 'pend on mah pappy t' see aftah ebbathin' foah him. He allus trust mah pappy. One mo'nin' he follah pappy to de field. Pappy he stop hes wok and ole Marse Joe, he say: "Well, Smart (pappy, he name Smart), I's tard, wurried, an' trubble'. All dese yeahs I wok foah mah chillun. Dey nevah do de right thing. Dey wurries me, Smart. I tell yo', Smart, I's a good mind t' put mahself away. I's good mind t' drown mahself right heah. I tebble wurried, Smart."

Pappy he take hole Ole Marse Joe an' lead him t' de house. "Now Marse Joe, I wudden talk sich talk effen I's yo'. Yo' ben good t' yo' fambly. Jest yo' content yo'self an' rest."

But a few days aftah dat, Ole Marse Joe wah found ahangin' in de ba'n by de bridle. Ole Marse had put heself away.

No'm, I nebbah knowed whut it wah t' rest. I jes wok all de time f'om mawnin' till late at night. I had t' do ebbathin' dey wah t' do on de outside. Wok in de field, chop wood, hoe cawn, till sometime I feels lak mah back sholy break. I done ebbathin' 'cept split rails. Yo' know, dey split rails back in dem days. Well, I nevah did split no rails.

Ole Marse strop us good effen we did anythin' he didn' lak. Sometime he get hes dandah up an' den we dassent look roun' at him. Else he tie yo' hands afoah yo' body an' whup yo', jes lak yo' a mule. Lawdy, honey, I's tuk a thousand lashins in mah day. Sometimes mah poah ole body be soah foah a week.

Ole Boss he send us niggahs out in any kine ob weathah, rain o' snow, it nebbah mattah. We had t' go t' de mountings, cut wood an' drag it down t' de house. Many de time we come in wif ouh cloes stuck t' ouh poah ole cold bodies, but 'twarn't no use t' try t' git 'em dry. Ef de Ole Boss o' de Ole Missie see us dey yell: "Git on out ob heah yo' black thin', an' git yo' wok outen de way!" An' Lawdy, honey, we knowed t' git, else we git de lash. Dey did'n cah how ole o' how young yo' wah, yo' nebbah too big t' git de lash.

De rich white folks nebbah did no wok; dey had da'kies t' do it foah dem. In de summah we had t' wok outdoo's, in de wintah in de house. I had t' ceard an' spin till ten o'clock. Nebbah git much rest, had t' git up at foah de nex' mawnin' an' sta't agin. Didn' get much t' eat, nuthah, jes a lil' cawn bread an' 'lasses. Lawdy, honey, yo' caint know whut a time I had. All cold n' hungry. No'm, I aint tellin' no lies. It de gospel truf. It sho is.

I 'membah well how I use t' lie 'wake till all de folks wah sleepin', den creep outen de do' and walk barfoot in de snow, 'bout two mile t' mah ole Auntie's house. I knowed when I git dar she fix hot cawn pone wif slice o' meat an' some milk foah me t' eat. Auntie wah good t' us da'kies.

I nebbah sleep on a bedstead till aftah freedom, no'm till aftah freedom. Jes' an ole pile o' rags in de conah. Ha'dly 'nuf t' keep us from freezin'. Law, chile, nobuddy knows how mean da'kies wah treated. Wy, dey wah bettah t' de animals den t' us'ns. Mah fust Ole Marse wah a good ole man, but de las'n, he wah rapid—- he sho wah rapid. Wy, chile, times aint no mo' lak dey usta be den de day an' night am lak. In mah day an' time all de folks woked. Effen dey had no niggahs dey woked demselves. Effen de chillun wah too small tuh hoe, dey pull weeds. Now de big bottom ob de Swannano (Swannanoa) dat usta grow hunners bushels ob grain am jest a playgroun'. I lak t' see de chillun in de field. Wy, now dey fight yo' lak wilecat effen it ebben talked 'bout. Dat's de reason times so ha'd. No fahmin'. Wy, I c'n 'membah Ole Missie she say: "Dis gene'ation'll pass away an' a new gene'ation'll cum 'long." Dat's jes' it—ebbah gene'ation gits weakah an' weakah. Den dey talk 'bout goin' back t' ole times. Dat time done gone, dey nebbah meet dat time agin.

Wahn't none o' de slaves offen ouh plantation ebbah

sold, but de ones on de othah plantation ob Marse William wah. Oh, dat wah a tebble time! All de slaves be in de field, plowin', hoein', singin' in de boilin' sun. Ole Marse he cum t'ru de field wif a man call de specalater. Day walk round jes' lookin', jes'lookin', All de da'kies know whut dis mean. Dey didn' dare look up, jes' wok right on. Den de specalater he see who he want. He talk to Ole Marse, den dey slaps de han'cuffs on him an' tak him away to de cotton country. Oh, dem wah awful times! When de specalater wah ready to go wif de slaves, effen dey wha enny whu didn' wanta go, he thrash em, den tie em 'hind de waggin an' mek em run till dey fall on de groun', den he thrash em till dey say dey go 'thout no trubble. Sometime some of dem run 'way an cum back t' de plantation, den it wah hardah on dem den befoah. When de da'kies wen' t' dinnah de ole niggah mammy she say whar am sich an' sich. None ob de othahs wanna tell huh. But when she see dem look down to de groun' she jes' say: "De specalater, de specalater." Den de teahs roll down huh cheeks, cause mebbe it huh son o' husban' an' she know she nebbah see 'em agin. Mebbe dey leaves babies t' home, mebbe jes' pappy an' mammy. Oh, mah Lawdy, mah ole Boss wah mean, but he nebbah sen' us to de cotton country.

Dey wah ve'y few skules back in day day an time, ve'y few. We da'kies didn' dah look at no book, not ebben t' pick it up. Ole Missie, dat is, mah firs' Ole Missie, she wah a good ole woman. She read to de niggahs and t' de white chillun. She cum fum cross de watah. She wahn't lak de sma't white folks livin' heah now. When she come ovah heah she brung darky boy wif huh. He wah huh pussonal su'vant. Co'se, dey got diffent names foah dem now, but in dat day dey calls 'em ginney niggahs. She wah good ole woman, not lak othah white folks. Niggahs lak Ole Missie.

When de da'kies git sick, dey wah put in a lil' ole house close t' de big house, an' one of the othah da'kies waited on 'em. Dey wah ve'y few doctahs den. Ony three in de whole section. When dey wanted med'cine dey went t' de woods an' gathahed hoahhound, slipperelm foah poltices an' all kinds ba'k foah teas. All dis yarbs bring yo' round. Dey wah ve'y few lawyers den too, but lawsy me, yo' cain't turn round fer dem now.

I 'membahs when mah ole mammy die. She live on Rims (Reems) Crick with othah Hemphills. She sick long time. One day white man cum t' see me. He say: "Sarah, did yo' know yo' manmy wah daid?" "No," I say, "but I wants t' see mah mothah afoah dey puts huh away."

I went t' de house and say t' Ole Missie: "Mah mothah she die tofay. I wants t' see mah mothah afoah dey puts huh away," but she look at me mean an' say: "Git on outen heah, an' git back to yo' wok afoah I wallup yo' good." So I went back t' mah wok, with the tears streamin' down mah face, jest awringin' mah hands, I wanted t' see mah manmy so. 'Bout two weeks latah, Ole Missie she git tebble sick, she jes' lingah 'long foah long time, but she nebbah gits up no mo'. Wa'nt long afoah dey puts huh away too, jes' lak mah mammy.

I 'membahs de time when mah mammy wah alive, I wah a small chile, afoah dey tuk huh t' Rims Crick. All us chilluns wah playin' in de ya'd one night. Jes' arunnin' an' aplayin' lak chillun will. All a sudden mammy cum to de do' all a'sited. "Cum in heah dis minnit," she say. "Jes look up at what is ahappenin'", and bless yo' life, honey, de sta's wah fallin' jes' lak rain.[7] Mammy wah tebble skeered, but we chillun wa'nt afeard, no, we wa'nt afeard. But mammy she say evah time a sta' fall, somebuddy gonna die. Look lak lotta folks gonna die f'om de looks ob dem sta's. Ebbathin' wah jes' as bright as day. Yo' cudda pick a pin up. Yo' know de sta's don' shine as bright as dey did back den. I wondah wy dey don'. Dey jes' don' shine as bright. Wa'nt long afoah dey took mah mammy away, and I wah lef' alone.

On de plantation wah an ole woman whut de boss bought f'om a drovah up in Virginny. De boss he bought huh f'om one ob de specalaters. She laff an' tell us: "Some ob dese days yo'all gwine be free, jes' lak de white folks," but we all laff at huh. No, we jes' slaves, we allus hafta wok and nevah be free. Den when freedom cum, she say: "I tole yo'all, now yo' got no larnin', yo' got no nothin', got no home; whut yo' gwine do? Didn' I tell yo'?"

I wah gittin along smartly in yeahs when de wah cum. Ah 'membah jes' lak yestiddy jes' afoah de wah. Marse William wah atalkin' t' hes brothah. I wah standin' off a piece. Marse's brothah, he say: "William, how ole Aunt Sarah now?" Marse William look at me an' he say: "She gittin' nigh onta fifty." Dat wah jes' a lil while afoah de wah.

Dat wah awful time. Us da'kies didn' know whut it wah all bout. Ony one of de boys f'om de plantation go. He Alexander, he 'bout twenty-five den. Many de time we git word de Yankees comin'. We take ouh food an' stock an' hide it till we sho' dey's gone. We wan't bothahed much. One day, I nebbah fo'git, we look out an' see sojers ma'chin'; look lak de whole valley full ob dem. I thought: "Poah helpless crittahs, jes' goin' away t' git kilt." De drums wah beatin' an' de fifes aplayin'. Dey wah de foot comp'ny. Oh, glory, it wah a sight. Sometime dey cum home on furlough. Sometime dey git kilt afoah dey gits th'ough. Alexander, he cum home a few time afoah freedom.

When de wah was ovah, Marse William he say: "Did yo'all know yo'all's free, Yo' free now." I chuckle, 'membahin' whut ole woman tell us 'bout freedom, an' no larnin. Lotta men want me t' go t' foreign land, but I tell 'em I go live wif mah pappy, long as he live. I stay wif de white folks 'bout twelve months, den I stay wif mah pappy, long as he live.

I had two brothahs, dey went t' Califonny, nebbah seed 'em no mo', no' mah sistah, nuther. I cain't 'membah sech a lot 'bout it all. I jes' knows I'se bo'n and bred heah in dese pa'ts, nebbah been outten it. I'se well; nebbah take no doctah med'cine. Jes' ben sick once; dat aftah freedom.

[7] (One of the most spectacular meteoric showers on record, visible all over North America, occurred in 1833.)

N.C. District:	No. 2
Worker:	T. Pat Matthews
No. Words:	734
Subject:	THOMAS HALL
Person Interviewed:	Thomas Hall
Editor:	G. L. Andrews
Date Stamp:	"SEP 10 1937"

THOMAS HALL

My name is Thomas Hall and I was born in Orange County, N. C. on a plantation belonging to Jim Woods whose wife, our missus, was named Polly. I am eighty one years of age as I was born Feb. 14, 1856. My father Daniel Hall and my mother Becke Hall and me all belonged to the same man but it was often the case that this wus not true as one man, perhaps a Johnson, would own a husband and a Smith own the wife, each slave goin' by the name of the slave owners, family. In such cases the children went by the name of the family to which the mother belonged.

Gettin married an' having a family was a joke in the days of slavery, as the main thing in allowing any form of matrimony among the slaves was to raise more slaves in the same sense and for the same purpose as stock raisers raise horses and mules, that is for work. A woman who could produce fast was in great demand and brought a good price on the auction block in Richmond, Va., Charleston, S. C., and other places.

The food in many cases that was given the slaves was not given them for their pleasure or by a cheerful giver, but for the simple and practical reason that children would not grow into a large healthy slave unless they were well fed and clothed; and given good warm places in which to live.

Conditions and rules were bad and the punishments were severe and barbarous. Some marsters acted like savages. In some instances slaves were burned at the stake. Families were torn apart by selling. Mothers were sold from their children. Children were sold from their mothers, and the father was not considered in anyway as a family part. These conditions were here before the Civil War and the conditions in a changed sense have been here ever since. The whites have always held the slaves in part slavery and are still practicing the same things on them in a different manner. Whites lynch, burn, and persecute the Negro race in America yet; and there is little they are doing to help them in anyway.

Lincoln got the praise for freeing us, but did he do it? He give us freedom without giving us any chance to live to ourselves and we still had to depend on the southern white man for work, food and clothing, and he held us through our necessity and want in a state of servitude but little better than slavery. Lincoln done but little for the Negro race and from living standpoint nothing. White folks are not going to do nothing for Negroes except keep them down.

Harriet Beecher Stowe, the writer of Uncle Tom's

Cabin, did that for her own good. She had her own interests at heart and I don't like her, Lincoln, or none of the crowd. The Yankees helped free us, so they say, but they let us be put back in slavery again.

When I think of slavery it makes me mad. I do not believe in giving you my story 'cause with all the promises that have been made the Negro is still in a bad way in the United States, no matter in what part he lives it's all the same. Now you may be all right; there are a few white men who are but the pressure is such from your white friends that you will be compelled to talk against us and give us the cold shoulder when you are around them, even if your heart is right towards us.

You are going around to get a story of slavery conditions and the persecusions of Negroes before the civil war and the economic conditions concerning them since that war. You should have known before this late day all about that. Are you going to help us? No! you are only helping yourself. You say that my story may be put into a book, that you are from the Federal Writer's Project. Well, the Negro will not get anything out of it, no matter where you are from. Harriet Beecher Stowe wrote Uncle Tom's Cabin. I didn't like her book and I hate her. No matter where you are from I don't want you to write my story cause the white folks have been and are now and always will be against the negro.

LE

N.C. District:	No. 3
Worker:	Travis Jordan
Subject:	Hector Hamilton
	Ex-slave 90 Years.
Date Stamp:	"JUN 30 1937"

HECTER HAMILTON

Dey wuz two General Lee's, in de 'Federate War. One los' his fight, but de other won his.

One of dese Generals wuz a white man dat rode a white hoss, an' de other wuz a mean fightin' gander dat I named General Lee, though I didn' know den dat he wuz goin' to live up to his name. But when de time come dat long neck gander out fit de whole 'Federate army.

My white fo'ks lived in Virginia. Dey wuz Marse Peter an' Mis' Laura Hamilton. Dey lived on de big Hamilton plantation dat wuz so big dat wid all de niggers dey had dey couldn' 'ten' half of it. Dis lan' done been handed down to Marse Peter from more den six gran'pappys. Dey wuz cotton an' 'bacca fields a mile wide; de wheat fields as far as yo' could see wuz like a big sheet of green water, an' it took half hour to plow one row of cawn, but dey wuz plenty of slaves to do de work. Mistah Sidney Effort, Marse Peter's overseer, rode all over de fields every day, cussin' an' crackin' his long blacksnake whip. He drove dem niggers like dey wuz cattle, but Marse Peter wouldn' 'low no beatin' of his niggers.

Marse Peter had acres an' acres of woods dat wuz his huntin' 'zerve. Dey wuz every kind of bird an' animal in dem woods in shootin' season. Dey wuz snipes, pheasants, patridges, squirrels, rabbits, deers, an' foxes; dey wuz even bears, an' dey wuz wolfs too dat would come an' catch de sheeps at night.

Dey wuz always a crowd at Easy Acres huntin' ridin' dancin' an' havin' a good time. Marse Peter's stables wuz full of hunters an' saddlers for mens an' ladies. De ladies in dem days rode side saddles. Mis' Laura's saddle wuz all studded wid sho nuff gol' tacks. De fringe wuz tipped wid gol', an' de buckles on de bridle wuz solid gol'. When de ladies went to ride dey wore long skirts of red, blue, an' green velvet, an' dey had plumes on dey hats dat blew in de win'. Dey wouldn' be caught wearin' britches an' ridin' straddle like de womens do dese days. In dem times de women wuz ladies.

Marse Peter kept de bes' sideboa'd in Princess Anne County. His cut glass decanters cos' near 'bout as much as Mis' Laura's diamon' ear rings I's goin' tell yo' 'bout. De decanters wuz all set out on de sideboard wid de glasses, an' de wine an' brandy wuz so ole dat one good size dram would make yo' willin' to go to de jail house for sixty days. Some of dat wine an' likker done been in dat cellar ever since Ole Marse Caleb Hamilton's time, an' de done built Easy Acres befo' Mistah George Washington done cut down his pappy's cherry tree. Dat likker done been down in dat cellar so long dat yo' had to scrape de dus' off wid a knife.

I wuz Marse Peter's main sideboa'd man. When he had shootin' company I didn' do nothin' but shake drams. De mens would come in from de huntin' field col' an' tired, an' Marse Peter would say: 'Hustle up, Hecter, fix us a dram of so an' so.' Dat mean dat I wuz to mix de special dram dat I done learned from my gran'pappy. So, I pours in a little of dis an' a little of dat, den I shakes it 'twell it foams, den I fills de glasses an' draps in de ice an' de mint. Time de mens drink dat so an' so dey done forgot dey's tired; dey 'lax, an' when de ladies come down de stairs all dredd up, dey thinks dey's angels walkin' in gol' shoes. Dem wuz good times befo' de war an' befo' Marse Peter got shot. From de day Marse Peter rode his big grey hoss off to fight, we never seed him no more. Mis' Laura never even know if dey buried him or not.

After de mens all went to de war dey won't no use for no more drams, so Mis' Laura took me away from de sideboa'd an' made me a watchman. Dat is, I wuz set to watch de commissary to see dat de niggers wuzn' give no more den dey share of eats, den I looked after de chickens an' things, kaze de patter-rollers wuz all 'roun' de country an' dey'd steal everythin' from chickens to sweet taters an cawn, den dey'd sell it to de Yankees. Dat's when I named dat ole mean fightin' gander General Lee.

Everywhare I went 'roun' de place dat gander wuz right at my heels. He wuz de bigges' gander I ever seed. He weighed near 'bout forty pounds, an' his wings from tip to tip wuz 'bout two yards. He wuz smart too. I teached him to drive de cows an' sheeps, an' I sic'd him on de dogs when dey got 'streperous. I'd say, Sic him, General Lee, an' dat gander would cha'ge. He wuz a better fighter den de dogs kaze he fit wid his wings, his bill, an wid his feets. I seed him skeer a bull near 'bout to death one day. Dat bull got mad an' jump de fence an' run all de niggers in de cabins, so I called General Lee an' sic'd him on dat bull. Dat bird give one squawk an' lit on dat bull's back, an' yo' never seed such carryin's on. De bull reared an' snorted an' kicked, but dat gander held on. He whipped dat bull wid his wings 'twell he wuz glad to go back in de lot an' 'have hese'f. After dat all I had to do to dat bull wuz show him General Lee an' he'd quiet down.

Now I's goin' to tell yo' 'bout Mis' Laura's diamon' ear rings.

De fus' Yankees dat come to de house wuz gentlemens, 'cept dey made us niggers cook dey supper an' shine dey muddy boots, den dey stole everythin' dey foun' to tote away, but de nex ones dat come wuz mean. Dey got made kaze de fus' Yankees done got de pickin's of what Mis' Laura hadn' hid. Dey cut open de feather beds lookin' for silver; dey ripped open de chair cushings lookin' for money, dey even tore up de carpets, but dey didn' fin' nothin' kaze all de valuables done been buried. Even mos' of de wine done been hid, 'twuz' all buried in de ole graves down in de family grave yard wid de tombstones at de head an' foots. No Yankee ain't goin' be diggin' in no grave for nothin'.

Dey wuz one Yankee in dis las' bunch dat wuz big an' bustin'. He strut bigoty wid his chist stuck out. He walk 'roun' stickin' his sword in de chair cushions, de pictures on de walls an' things like dat. He got powerful mad kaze he couldn' fin' nothin', den he look out de window an' seed Mis' Laura. She wuz standin' on de po'ch an' de sun wuz shinin' on de diamon' ear rings in her ears. Dey wuz de ear rings dat belonged to Marse Peter's great-great-gran'mammy. When de sojer seed dem diamon's his eyes 'gun to shine. He went out on de po'ch an' went up to Mis' Laura. 'Gim me dem ear rings,' he say jus' like dat.

Mis' Laura flung her han's up to her ears an' run out in de yard. De sojer followed her, an' all de other sojers come too. Dat big Yankee tole Mis' Laura again to give him de ear rings, but she shook her head. I wuz standin' 'side de house near 'bout bustin' wid madness when dat Yankee reach up an' snatch Mis' Laura's hands down an' hold dem in his, den he laugh, an' all de other sojers 'gun to laugh too jus' like dey thought 'twuz funny. 'Bout dat time Ole General Lee done smell a fight. He come waddlin' 'roun' de house, his tail feathers bristled out an' tawkin' to he'sef. I point to dem sojers an say, "Sic him, General Lee, sic him."

Dat gander ain't waste no time. He let out his wings an' cha'ged dem Yankees an' dey scatter like flies. Den he lit on dat big sojer's back an' 'gun to beat him wid his wings. Dat man let out a yell an' drap Mis' Laura's hands; he try to shake dat goose, but General bit into his neck an' held on like a leech. When de other sojers come up an' try to pull him off, dat gander let out a wing an' near about slap dem down. I ain't never seed such fightin! Every time I holler, Sic him, General Lee start 'nother 'tack.

'Bout dat time dem Yankees took a runnin' nothin. Dey forgot de ear rings an' lit out down de road, but dat gander beat dat bigoty yellin' sojer clear down to de branch befo' he turned him loose, den he jump in de water an' wash hese'f off. Yes, suh, dat wuz sho some fightin' goose; he near 'bout out fit de sho nuff Marse General Lee.

N.C. District:	No. 2
Worker:	T. Pat Matthews
No. Words:	942
Subject:	GEORGE W. HARRIS
Story Teller:	George W. Harris
Editor:	Daisy Bailey Waitt

GEORGE W. HARRIS

Hey, don't go 'roun' dat post gitting it 'tween you and me, it's bad luck. Don't you know it's bad luck? Don't want no more bad luck den what I'se already got. My name is George Harris. I wuz born November 25, 82 years ago. I have been living in the City of Raleigh onto 52 years. I belonged to John Andrews. He died about de time I wuz born. His wife Betsy wuz my missus and his son John wuz my marster.

Deir plantation wuz in Jones County. Dere were about er dozen slaves on de plantation. We had plenty o' food in slavery days during my boyhood days, plenty of good sound food. We didn't have 'xactly plenty o' clothes, and our places ter sleep needed things, we were in need often in these things. We were treated kindly, and no one abused us. We had as good owners as there were in Jones County; they looked out for us. They let us have patches to tend and gave us what we made. We did not have much money. We had no church on the plantation, but there wuz one on Marster's brother's plantation next ter his plantation.

We had suppers an' socials, generally gatherings for eatin', socials jist to git together an' eat. We had a lot o' game ter eat, such as possums, coons, rabbits and birds.

De plantation wuz fenced in wid rails about 10 ft. in length split from pine trees. De cattle, hogs an' hosses run out on de free range. The hosses ran on free range when de crap wuz laid by. There wuz an ole mare dat led de hosses. She led 'em an' when she come home at night dey followed her.

De first work I done wuz drappin' tater sprouts, drappin' corn, thinnin' out corn and roundin' up corn an' mindin' the crows out of de field. Dey did not teach us to read an' write, but my father could read, and he read de hymn book and Testament to us sometimes. I do not remember ever goin' to church durin' slavery days.

I have never seen a slave whipped and none ever ran away to the North from our plantation.

When I wuz a boy we chillun played marbles, prison base, blind fold and tag, hide an' seek. Dey gave us Christmas holidays, an' 4th of July, an' lay-by time. Dey also called dis time "crap hillin' time." Most o' de time when we got sick our mother doctored us with herbs which she had in de garden. When we had side plurisy, what dey calls pneumonia now, dey sent fer a doctor. Doctor Hines treated us.

We lived near Trenton. When de Yankees took New Bern, our marster had us out in de woods in Jones County mindin' hosses an' takin' care o' things he had hid there.

We got afraid and ran away to New Bern in Craven County. We all went in a gang and walked. De Yankees took us at Deep Gully ten miles dis side o' New Bern an' carried us inside de lines. Dey asked us questions and put us all in jail. Dey put my father ter cookin' at de jail and give us boys work 'roun' de yard. Dey put de others at work at de horse stables and houses.

De smallpox and yaller fever caught us dere and killed us by de hundreds. Thirteen doctors died dere in one day. Jist 'fore Gen. Lee surrendered dey carried us to Petersburg, Va., and I waited on Major Emory and de others worked fer de Yankees. When de surrender came we went back home to Craven County, next to Jones County, and went to farmin'. Sumpin' to eat could not hardly be found. De second year atter de war we went back to old marster's plantation. He wuz glad ter see us, we all et dinner wid him. We looked over de place. I looked over de little log cabin where I wuz born. Some of de boys who had been slaves, farmed wid old marster, but I worked at my trade. I wuz a brick moulder. Yes, a brick maker.

My mother was named Jennie Andrews and my father was Quash Harris. My father belonged to de Harris family on de nex' plantation in Jones County. Atter de surrender we all went in his name. We changed from Andrews to Harris. I do not recollect my grandmother and grandfather. I can't recollect them.

Marster told us directly after dey declared war dat he expected we would all soon be free. De majority of de slaves did not want to be free. Dey were stirred up. Dey didn't want it to be. Dey didn't want no fightin'. Dey didn't know.

I married Mary Boylan first, of Johnston County, at Wilsons Mills, Jan. 4, 1878. Here is de family record. Ole marster made me copies after de war, and I copied dis. 'George Harris was married the year 1878, January the 4th. George Harris was born the year 1855 November the 25th.'

I had five brothers, but they are all dead, fur as I know: John Nathan, Louis, David, Jefferson, Donald and my name George. My sisters, Mary Ann, Sara, Lucy, Penny, Emaline, Lizzie, Nancy, Leah and one I can't remember. Dats all.

I thought Abraham Lincoln wuz a great man. I remember him well. I think he done de best he knowed how to settle de country. Mr. Roosevelt is a smart man. He is doing de best he can. I think he is goin' to help de country.

N.C. District: No. 2
Worker: Mary A. Hicks
No. Words: 660
Subject: AN EX-SLAVE STORY
Story Teller: Sarah Harris
Editor: Daisy Bailey Waitt
Date Stamp: "JUN 11 1937"
Good points

SARAH HARRIS

Sarah Harris is my name. I wuz borned April 1861, on the plantation of Master John William Walton. My father wuz name Frank Walton and my mother wuz name Flora Walton. My brothers wuz name Lang and Johnny. My sisters: Hannah, Mary, Ellen, Violet and Annie. My grandmother wuz name Ellen Walton. She wuz 104 years old when she died. My mother wuz 103 years old when she died; she has been dead 3 years. She died in October, 3 years this pas' October.

I 'member seeing the Yankees. I wuz not afraid of 'em, I thought dey were the prettiest blue mens I had ever seed. I can see how de chickens and guineas flew and run from 'em. De Yankees killed 'em and give part of 'em to the colored folks. Most of de white folks had run off and hid.

I can't read and write. I nebber had no chance.

De Yankees had their camps along the Fayetteville road.

Dey called us Dinah, Sam, and other names.

Dey later had de place dey call de bureau. When we left de white folks we had nothing to eat. De niggers wait there at de bureau and they give 'em hard tack, white potatoes, and saltpeter meat. Our white folks give us good things to eat, and I cried every day at 12 o'clock to go home. Yes, I wanted to go back to my white folks; they were good to us. I would say, 'papa le's go home, I want to go home. I don't like this sumptin' to eat.' He would say, 'Don't cry, honey, le's stay here, dey will sen' you to school.'

We had nothing to eat 'cept what de Yankees give us. But Mr. Bill Crawford give my father and mother work. Yes, he wuz a Southern man, one o' our white folks. Daddy wuz his butcher. My mother wuz his cook. We were turned out when dey freed us with no homes and nuthin'. Master said he wuz sorry he didn't give us niggers part of his lan'.

While I wuz big enough to work I worked for Porter Steadman. I got 25 cent a week and board. We had a good home then. I just shouted when I got dat 25 cent, and I just run. I couldn't run fas' anuff to git to my mother to give dat money to her. My father died, and my mother bought a home. She got her first money to buy de home by working for de man who give her work after de surrender. The first money she saved to put on de home wuz a dime. Some weeks she only saved 5 cents. Lan' sold fur $10 a acre den.

Just after de war de white and colored children played

together. Dey had a tent in our neighborhood. I wuz de cook for de white chilluns parties. We played together fer a long time after de war.

I married Silas Cooper of Norfolk Va. He worked in the Navy yard. I wuz married in Raleigh. I had a church wedding.

I think Abraham Lincoln wuz a great man. He would cure or kill. But I like my ole master. The Lord put it into Abraham Lincoln to do as he done. The Lord knowed he would be killed.

I think slavery wuz wrong. I have a horror of being a slave. You see all dis lan' aroun' here. It belongs to colored folks. Dey were cut off wid nothin', but dey is strugglin' an' dey are comin' on fast. De Bible say dat de bottom rail will be on top, and it is comin' to pass. Sometime de colored race will git up. De Bible say so.

I think Mr. Roosevelt is one of the greatest mans in de world. He wants to help everybody.

I doan think much of Mr. Jeff Davis. Dey used to sing songs uv hanging him to a apple tree. Dey say he libed a long time atter de war dressed like a 'oman, he wuz so skeered.

TPM:EH

N.C. District: No. 3
Worker: Daisy Whaley
Subject: Cy Hart
Ex-slave, 78 years.
Durham, N.C.
Date Stamp: "AUG 6 1937"

CY HART

Ephram Hart was my pappy and my mammy's name was Nellie. He belonged to Marse Ephram Hart. One day Marse Hart took some of his niggers to de slave market an' my pappy was took along too. When he was put on de block an' sold Marse Paul Cameron bought him. Den Marse Hart felt so sorry to think he done let my pappy be sold dat he tried to buy him back from Marse Paul, an' offered him more den Marse Paul paid for him. But Marse Paul said, "No, Suh. I done bought him an' I want det nigger myself an' I am goin' take him home wid me to Snow Hill farm."

Pappy married my mammy an' raised a family on Marse Paul's plantation. We had to be eight years ole before we 'gun to work. I tended de chickens an' turkeys an' sech. I helped tend de other stock too as I growed older, an' do anythin' else dat I was tole to do. When I got bigger I helped den wid de thrashin' de wheat an' I helped dem push de straw to de stack.

We had what wuz den called a 'groun' hog. It wuz a cylinder shaped contraption. We put de wheat straw an all in it an' knock de grain loose from de straw. Den we took de pitchforks an' tossed de straw up an' about, an' dat let de wheat go to de bottom on a big cloth. Den we fan de wheat, to get de dust an' dirt out, an' we had big curtains hung 'roun' de cloth whar de wheat lay, so de wheat wouldn' get all scattered, on de groun'. Dis wheat was sacked an' when wanted 'twus took to de mill an' groun' into flour. De flour wuz made into white bread an' de corn wuz groun' into meal an' grits.

When de war started der wuz some bad times. One day some of Wheeler's men come an' dey tried to take what dey wanted, but Marge Paul had de silver money another things hid. Dey wanted us niggers to tell dem whar everythin' wuz, but we said we didn' know nuthin'. Marse Paul wuz hid in de woods wid de horses an' some of de other stock.

Den Wheeler's men saw de Yankees comin' an' dey run away. De Yankees chased dem to de bridge an' dey done some fightin' an' one or two of Wheeler's men wuz killed an' de rest got away.

Den de captain of de Yankees come to Mammy's cabin an' axed her whar de meat house an' flour an' sech at. She tole him dat Pappy had de keys to go an' ax him. "Ax him nothin'", de captain said. He called some of his mens an' dey broke down de door to de meat house. Den dey trowed out plenty of dose hams an' dey tole Mammy to cook dem somethin' to eat and plenty of it. Mammy fried plenty of dat ham an' made lots of bread an' fixed dem coffee. How dey did eat! Dey wuz jus' as nice as dey could be to Mammy an' when dey wuz through, dey tole

Mammy dat she could have de rest, an' de captain gave her some money an' he tole her dat she wuz free, dat we didn' belong to Marse Paul no longer. Dey didn' do any harm to de place. Dey wuz jus' looking for somethin' to eat. Den dey left.

We didn' leave Marse Paul but stayed on an' lived wid him for many years. I lived wid Marse Paul 'til he died an' he done selected eight of us niggers to tote his coffin to de chapel, an' de buryin' groun'. He said, "I want dese niggers to carry my body to de chapel an' de grave when I die." We did. It wuz a lood I would have been glad had der been two or four more to help tote Marse Paul for he sho wuz heavy. After everythin' wuz ready we lifted him up an' toted him to de chapel an' we sat down on de floor, on each side of de coffin, while de preacher preached de funeral sermon. We didn' make any fuss while sittin' dere on de floor, but we sho wuz full of grief to see our dear ole Marse Paul lying dere dead.

N.C. District:	No. 2
Worker:	Mary A. Hicks
No. Words:	381
Subject:	THE BLACKSMITH
Person Interviewed:	Alonzo Haywood
Editor:	G. L. Andrews
Date Stamp:	"AUG—1937"

ALONZO HAYWOOD

On East Cabarrus Street is a blacksmith shop which is a survival of horse and buggy days, and the smiling blacksmith, a Negro, although he has hazel eyes, recounts the story of his father's life and his own.

My father was Willis Haywood and in slavery days he belonged to Mr. William R. Pool. Mr. Pool liked father because he was quick and obedient so he determined to give him a trade.

Wilson Morgan run the blacksmith shop at Falls of Neuse and it was him that taught my father the trade at Mr. Pool's insistence.

While father, a young blade, worked and lived at Falls of Neuse, he fell in love with my mother, Mirana Denson, who lived in Raleigh. He come to see her ever' chance he got and then they were married.

When the Yankees were crossing the Neuse Bridge at the falls, near the old paper mill, the bridge broke in. They were carrying the heavy artillery over and a great many men followed, in fact the line extended to Raleigh, because when the bridge fell word passed by word of mouth from man to man back to Raleigh.

Father said that the Yankees stopped in the shop to make some hoss shoes and nails and that the Yankees could do it faster than anybody he ever saw.

Father told me a story once 'bout de devil traveling and he got sore feet and was awful lame but he went in a blacksmith shop and the blacksmith shoed him.

The devil traveled longer and the shoes hurt his feet and made him lamer than ever so he went back and asked the blacksmith to take off de shoes.

The blacksmith took them off under the condition that wherever the devil saw a horse shoe over a door he would not enter. That's the reason that people hang up horseshoes over their door.

Mother died near twenty years ago and father died four years later. He had not cared to live since mother left him.

I've heard some of the young people laugh about slave love, but they should envy the love which kept mother and father so close together in life and even held them in death.

N.C. District:	No. 2
Worker:	Mary A. Hicks
No. Words:	547
Subject:	AUNT BARBARA'S LOVE STORY
Story Teller:	Barbara Haywood
Editor:	Geo. L. Andrews
Date Stamp:	"AUG 4 1937"

BARBARA HAYWOOD

Anything dat I tells you will near 'bout all be 'bout Frank Haywood, my husban'.

I wus borned on de John Walton place seben miles southeast of Raleigh. My father, Handy Sturdivant, belonged to somebody in Johnston County but mother an' her chilluns 'longed ter Marse John Walton.

Marse John had a corn shuckin' onct an' at dat corn shuckin' I fust saw Frank. I wus a little girl, cryin' an' bawlin' an' Frank, who wus a big boy said dat he neber wanted ter spank a youngin' so bad, an' I ain't liked him no better dan he did me.

He 'longed ter Mr. Yarborough, what runned de hotel in Raleigh, but he wus boun' out ter anybody what'ud hire him, an' I doan know whar he got his name.

I seed Frank a few times at de Holland's Methodist Church whar we went ter church wid our white folks.

You axes iffen our white folks wus good ter us, an' I sez ter yo' dat none of de white folks wus good ter none of de niggers. We done our weavin' at night an' we wurked hard. We had enough ter eat but we was whupped some.

Jest 'fore de war wus ober we wus sent ter Mr. William Turner's place down clost ter Smithfield an' dats whar we wus when de Yankees come.

One day I wus settin' on de porch restin' atter my days wurk wus done when I sees de hoss-lot full of men an' I sez ter Marse William, who am talkin' ter a soldier named Cole, 'De lot am full of men.'

Marse Cole looks up an' he 'lows, 'Hits dem damned Yankees,' an' wid dat he buckles on his sword an' he ain't been seen since.

De Yankees takes all de meat outen de smokehouse an' goes 'roun' ter de slave cabins an' takes de meat what de white folkses has put dar. Dat wus de fust hams dat has eber been in de nigger house. Anyhow de Yankees takes all de hams, but dey gibes us de shoulders.

Atter de war we moved ter Raleigh, on Davie Street an' I went ter school a little at Saint Paul's. Frank wus wurkin' at de City Market on Fayetteville Street an' I'd go seberal blocks out of my way mornin' an' night on my way ter school ter look at him. You see I has been in love with him fer a long time den.

Atter awhile Frank becomes a butcher an' he am makin' pretty good. I is thirteen so he comes ter see me an' fer a year we cou'ts. We wus settin' in de kitchen at de house on Davie Street when he axes me ter have him an' I has him.

I knows dat he tol' me dat he warn't worthy but dat he loved me an' dat he'd do anything he could ter please me, an' dat he'd always be good ter me.

When I wus fourteen I got married an' when I wus fifteen my oldes' daughter, Eleanor, wus borned. I had three atter her, an' Frank wus proud of dem as could be. We wus happy. We libed together fifty-four years an' we wus always happy, havin' a mighty little bit of argument. I hopes young lady, dat you'll be as lucky as I wus wid Frank.

N.C. District:	No. 2
Worker:	Mrs. Edith S. Hibbs
No. Words:	550
Subject:	Story of Isabell Henderson, Negro
Interviewed:	Isabell Henderson
	1121 Rankin St., Wilmington, N.C.
Editor:	Mrs. W. N. Harriss

ISABELL HENDERSON

I'll be 84 years old come August 9. My gran'-daughter can tell you what year it was I was born I don' 'member but we has it down in the Bible.

I lived near the "Clock Church" (Jewish Synagogue)[8], 4th and Market. We had a big place there. My gran'mother did the cookin'. My mother did the sewin'. I was jus five years old when the men went away. I guess to the war, I don' know. Some men came by and conscip' dem. I don' know where they went but I guess dey went to war. I was such a little girl I don't 'member much. But I does know my Missus was good to me. I used to play with her little boy. I was jes' one of the family. I played with the little boy around the house' cause I was never 'lowed to run the streets. They was good to me. They kept me in clothes, pretty clothes, and good things to eat. Yes'm we was slaves but we had good times.

Interviewer: "What did you eat?"

Isabell: "Oh I don't 'member 'special but I et jes what the family et."

Maybe my father was killed in the war maybe he run away I don' know, he jus' neber come back no mo'.

Yes'm I remember when the soldiers came along and freed us. They went through breakin' down peoples shops and everything.

My mother married again. She married Edward Robertson. He was good to me. Yes'm he was better to me than my father was. He was a preacher and a painter. My mother died. When my father, (step-father) went off to preach, me and my sister stayed in the house.

I stayed home all my life. I just wasn't 'llowed to run around like most girls. I never been out of Wilmington but one year in my life. That year I went to Augusta. No'm I don't likes to go away. I don't like the trains, nor the automobiles. But I rides in 'em (meaning the latter).

I remember when the 4th Street bridge was built. I was married over there in St. Stephen's Church, 5th and Red Cross. Yes M'am my auntie she gib me a big weddin'. I was 22 and my husband was 22 too not quite 23. Not a year older than I was. He was a cooper. Yes Ma'm I had a big weddin'. The church was all decorated with flowers. I had six attendants. Four big ones and two little ones. My husband he had the same number I did four big ones and two little ones. I had on a white dress. Carried flowers. Had carriages and everything. My husband was good to me. I didn't stay home with my father but about a month. We wanted to go to ourselves.

We went in our own home and stayed there until I got

a "sickness." (She looked shy) I didn't know what was the matter with me. My father told me I better come home. So I went home to my father and stayed there about two years.

I have had five children. Three are livin'. Two are dead.

I never worked until after he died. He left me with five little children to raise.

He was the only man I ever 'knowed' in all my life from girlhood up.

[8] The Synagogue has no clock on the exterior, but Isabell persisted with her name of "Clock Church."

N.C. District: No. 2
Worker: Mary A. Hicks
No. Words: 738
Subject: Ex-Slave Story
Story Teller: Essex Henry
Editor: Daisy Bailey Waitt
Date Stamp: "JUN 26 1937"

ESSEX HENRY

I wus borned five miles north of Raleigh on de Wendell Road, 83 years ago. My mammy wus Nancy an' my pappy wus Louis. I had one sister, Mary, an' one bruder, Louis.

We 'longed ter Mr. Jake Mordecai, an' we lived on his six hundert acres plantation 'bout a mile from Millbrook. Right atter de war he sold dis lan' ter Doctor Miller an' bought de Betsy Hinton tract at Milburnie. Mr. Jake had four or five hundert niggers hyar an' I doan know how many at de Edgecombe County place.

De wuck wus hard den, I knows case I'se seed my little mammy dig ditches wid de best of 'em. I'se seed her split 350 rails a day many's de time. Dat wus her po'tion you knows, an' de mens had ter split 500. I wus too little ter do much but min' de chickens outen de gyarden, an' so I fared better dan most of 'em. You see Miss Tempie 'ud see me out at de gate mornin's as dey wus eatin' breakfas' on de ferander, an' she'ud call me ter her an' give me butter toasted lightbread or biscuits. She'd give me a heap in dat way, an' do de rest of de slaves got hungry, I doan think dat I eber did. I know dat Miss Jenny Perry, on a neighborin' plantation, 'ud give my mammy food, fer us chilluns.

Mo'nin's we sometimes ain't had nothin' ter eat. At dinner time de cook at de big house cooked nuff turnip salet, beans, 'taters, er peas fer all de han's an' long wid a little piece of meat an' a little hunk of co'nbread de dinner wus sont ter de slaves out in de fiel' on a cart.

De slaves 'ud set roun' under de trees an' eat an' laugh an' talk till de oberseer, Bob Gravie, yells at 'em ter git back ter wuck. Iffen dey doan git back right den he starts ter frailin' lef' an' right.

Dar wus a few spirited slaves what won't be whupped an' my uncle wus one. He wus finally sold fer dis.

Hit wus different wid my gran'mother do'. De oberseer tried ter whup her an' he can't, so he hollers fer Mr. Jake. Mr. Jake comes an' he can't, so he hauls off an' kicks granny, mashin' her stomick in. He has her carried ter her cabin an' three days atterward she dies wid nothin' done fer her an' nobody wid her.

Mr. Jake orders de coffinmaker ter make de pine box, an' den he fergits hit. De slaves puts de coffin on de cyart hin' de two black hosses an' wid six or maybe seben hundert niggers follerin' dey goes ter de Simms' graveyard an' buries her. All de way ter de graveyard dey sings, 'Swing Low Sweet Chariot,' 'De Promised Lan', 'De Road ter Jordan,' an' 'Ole Time Religion.'

Hit's a good thing dat none of de white folkses ain't

went to de funerals case iffen dey had de niggers can't sing deir hymns. Does you know dat dey warn't no 'ligion 'lowed on dat plantation. Ole lady Betsy Holmes wus whupped time an' ag'in fer talkin' 'ligion er fer singin' hymns. We sometimes had prayermeetin' anyhow in de cabins but we'd turn down de big pot front o' de door ter ketch de noise.

Dey won't gib us no pass hardly, an' iffen we runs 'way de patterollers will git us. Dey did let us have some dances do' now an' den, but not offen. Dey let us go possum huntin' too case dat wus gittin' something ter eat widout Mr. Jake payin' fer hit.

Mr. Henry, Mr. Jake's bruder an' his Uncle Moses uster come a-visitin' ter de house fer de day. Mr. Henry wus little wid a short leg an' a long one, an' he had de wust temper dat eber wus in de worl'; an' he loved ter see slaves suffer, near 'bout much as he loved his brandy. We knowed when we seed him comin' dat dar wus gwine ter be a whuppin' frolic 'fore de day wus gone.

Dar wus three niggers, John Lane, Ananias Ruffin an' Dick Rogers what got de blame fer eber'thing what happens on de place. Fer instance Mr. Henry 'ud look in de hawg pen an' 'low dat hit 'peared dat he bruder's stock wus growin' less all de time. Den Mr. Jake sez dat dey done been stold.

'Why doan you punish dem thievin' niggers, Jake'?

Jake gits mad an' has dese three niggers brung out, deir shirts am pulled off an' dey am staked down on deir stomichs, an' de oberseer gits wored out, an' leavin' de niggers tied, dar in de sun, dey goes ter de house ter git some brandy.

Dey more dey drinks from de white crock de better humor dey gits in. Dey laughs an' talks an' atter awhile dey think o' de niggers, an' back dey goes an' beats 'em some more. Dis usually lasts all de day, case hit am fun ter dem.

Atter so long dey ketched Jack Ashe, a Free Issue, wid one of de pigs, an' dey whups him twixt drinks all de day, an' at night dey carried him ter de Raleigh jail. He wus convicted an' sent ter Bald Head Island ter wuck on de breastworks durin' de war an' he ain't neber come back.

Dar wus a man in Raleigh what had two blood houn's an' he made his livin' by ketchin' runaway niggers. His name wus Beaver an' he ain't missed but onct. Pat Norwood took a long grass sythe when he runned away, an' as de fust dog come he clipped off its tail, de second one he clipped off its ear an' dem dawgs ain't run him no more.

De war lasted a long time, an' hit wus a mess. Some of Marster Jake's slaves lef' him an' when de Yankees got ter Raleigh dey come an' tol' 'em 'bout de way Mr. Jake done. Well in a few days hyar comes de Yankees a-ridin', an' dey sez dat dey had tentions o' hangin' Mr. Jake on de big oak in de yard iffen he 'uv been dar, but he ain't. He an' his family had flewed de coop.

Dem Yankees went in de big house an' dey tored an' busted up all dey pleased, dey eben throwed de clothes all ober de yard.

Dey took two big barns o' corn an' haul hit off an'

down Devil's Jump on Morris Creek dey buried ever so much molasses an' all.

At Rattlesnake Spring de Yankees fin's whar Marster Jake's still had been, an' dar buried, dey fin's five barrels o' brandy.

Atter de war we stayed on as servants o' Doctor Miller fer seberal years. I 'members de only time dat I eber got drunk wus long den. De doctor an' his frien's wus splurgin', an' I went wid another nigger ter git de brandy from de cellar fer de guests. When I tasted hit, hit drunk so good, an' so much lak sweetin water dat I drunk de pitcher full. I wus drunk three days.

I married Milly, an' sixty years ago we moved ter town. We scuffled along till twenty-eight years ago we buyed dis shack. I hopes dat we can git de ole age pension, case we shore need hit.

N.C. District:	No. 2
Worker:	Mary A. Hicks
Subject:	Ex-Slave Story
Story Teller:	Milly Henry
Editor:	Daisy Bailey Waitt
Date Stamp:	"JUN 26 1937"

MILLY HENRY

I wus borned a slave ter Mr. Buck Boylan in Yazoo City, Mississippi. I doan know nothin' 'bout my family 'cept my gran'maw an' she died in Mississippi durin' de war.

Marster Buck owned three plantations dar, de Mosley place, Middle place, an' de Hill place. Me an' gran'maw lived at de Mosley place. One day Marster Buck comes in, an' we sees dat he am worried stiff; atter awhile he gangs us up, an' sez ter us:

De Yankees am a-comin' to take my slaves 'way from me an' I don't 'pose dat dey am gwine ter do dat. Fer dem reasons we leaves fer No'th Carolina day atter termorror an' I ain't gwine ter hyar no jaw 'bout hit.'

Dat day he goes over de slaves an' picks out 'roun' five hundret ter go. He picks me out, but my gran'maw he sez dat he will leave case she am so old an' feeble. I hates dat, but I don't say nothin' at all.

We leaves home in kivered wagons, wid a heap walkin' an' in 'bout three weeks, I reckon, we gits ter Raleigh. You should have been 'long on dat trip, honey; When we camps side of de road an' sleeps on de groun' an' cooks our rations at de camp fires. I think dat dat wus one spring 'fore de surrender wus de nex'.

Marster Buck carries us ter Boylan Avenue dar whar de bridge am now an' we camps fer a few days, but den he sen's us out ter de Crabtree plantation. He also buys a place sommers east o' Raleigh an' sen's some dar.

I misses my gran'maw fer awhile, but at last Uncle Green comes from Mississippi an' he sez dat gran'maw am daid, so I pretty quick stops worrin' over hit.

Marster' cides ter hire some o' us out, an' so I gits hired out ter Miss Mary Lee, who I wucks fer till she got so pore she can't feed me, den I is hired out ter Miss Sue Blake an' sent ter de Company Shop up above Durham.

Miss Mary wus good, but Miss Sue she whup me, so I runs away. I went barefooted an' bareheaded ter de train, an' I gits on. Atter awhile de conductor comes fer a ticket an' I ain't got none. He axes me whar I'se gwine an' I tells him home, so he brung me on ter Raleigh.

I went right home an' tol' Mr. Buck dat Miss Sue whupped me, an' dat I runned away. He said dat hit wus all right, an' he hired me out ter Mis' Lee Hamilton who lived dar on de Fayetteville Street.

She wus a widder an' run a boardin' house an' dar's whar I seed de first drunk man dat eber I seed. He put de back o' his knife ginst my neck an' said dat he wus gwine ter cut my throat. I tell you dat I is knowed a drunk eber since dat time.

I wus drawin' water at de well at de end of Fayetteville Street when de Yankees comed. I seed 'em ridin' up de street wid deir blue coats shinin' an' deir hosses steppin' high. I knowed dat I ought ter be skeered but I ain't, an' so I stands dar an' watches.

Suddenly as dey passes de bank out rides two mens frum Wheeler's calvary an' dey gits in de middle o' de street one of de hosses wheels back an' de man shot right at de Yankees, den he flewed frum dar.

Two of de Yankees retracts frum de army an' dey flies atter de Rebs. When de Rebs git ter de Capitol one o' dem flies down Morgan Street an' one goes out Hillsboro Street wid de Yankees hot in behin' him.

Dey ketched him out dar at de Hillsboro Bridge when his hoss what wus already tired, stumbles an' he falls an' hurts his leg.

Durin' dat time de big man wid de red hair what dey calls Kilpatrick brung his men up on de square an' sets under de trees an' a gang o' people comes up.

When dey brung de young good lookin' Reb up ter de redheaded Gen'l he sez 'What you name Reb?'

De boy sez, 'Robert Walsh, sir.

What for did you done go an' shoot at my army?

"Case I hates de Yankees an' I wush dat dey wus daid in a pile," de Reb sez, an' laughs.

"De Gen'l done got his dander up now, an' he yells," 'Carry de Reb sommers out'r sight o' de ladies an' hang him.'

De Reb laughs an' sez, 'kin' o' you sir,' an' he waves goodbye ter de crowd an' dey carried him off a laughin' fit ter kill.

Dey hanged him on a ole oak tree in de Lovejoy grove, whar de Governor's mansion am now standin' an' dey buried him under de tree.

Way atter de war dey moved his skileton ter Oakwood Cemetery an' put him up a monument. His grave wus kivered wid flowers, an' de young ladies cry.

He died brave do', an' he kep' laughin' till his neck broke. I wus dar an' seed hit, furdermore dar wus a gang of white ladies dar, so dey might as well a hanged him on de Capitol Square.

De Yankees wus good ter me, but hit shore wus hard ter git a job do', an' so I ain't fared as good as I did' fore de war.

Mr. Buck wus good ter us. Sometimes he'd lose his temper an' cuss, den he'd say right quick, 'God forgive me, I pray.' Dat man believed in 'ligion. When de oberseer, George Harris, 'ud start ter beat a slave dey larned ter yell fer Mr. Buck an' make lak dey wus gittin' kilt.

Mr. Buck'd come stompin' an' yellin' 'stop beatin' dat nigger.

Course dis ruint de slaves, case dey could talk lak dey pleased ter Mr. Harris, an' iffen dey could yell loud nuff dey ain't got no whuppin'.

Yessum, I'se glad slavery am over; we owns dis home an' some chickens, but we shore does need de ole age pension. I'se got two fine gran'sons, but let me tell you dey needs ter wuck harder, eat less, an' drink less.

On de count o' dem boys I wants de ABC Stores so's dey won't drink box lye.

EH

N.C. District:	No. 2
Worker:	T. Pat Matthews
No. Words:	737
Subject:	CHANEY HEWS
Person Interviewed:	Chaney Hews
Editor:	G. L. Andrews

CHANEY HEWS

My age, best of my recollection, is about eighty years. I was 'bout eight years ole when de Yankees come through. Chillun in dem days wus not paid much mind like dey is now. White chillun nor nigger chillun wus not spiled by tenshun.

I got enough to eat to live on an' dat wus 'bout all I keered 'bout. Des so I could git a little to eat and could play all de time. I stayed outen de way of de grown folks. No, chillun wus not noticed like dey is now.

I heard de grown folks talkin' 'bout de Yankees. De niggers called 'em blue jackets. Den one mornin', almost 'fore I knowed it, de yard wus full of 'em. Dey tried to ride de hosses in de house, dey caught de chickens, killed de shoats and took de horses an' anything else dey wanted. Dey give de nigger hardtack an' pickled meat. I 'members eating some of de meat, I didn't like.

We had reasonably good food, clothin', and warm log

houses wid stick an' dirt chimleys. De houses wus warm enough all de time in winter, and dey didn't leak in rainy weather neither.

Dere wus a lot of slaves an' marster an' missus wus good to father an' mother. When dey had a cornshuckin' we slaves had a good time, plenty to eat, whiskey for de grown folks and a rastlin' match after de corn wus shucked. A nigger dat shucked a red ear of corn got a extra drink of whiskey. Dat wus de custom in dem days.

No prayermeetings wus allowed on de plantation but we went to Salem to white folks church and also to white folks church at Cary.

Dey whupped mother 'cause she tried to learn to read, no books wus allowed. Mother said dat if de blue jackets had not come sooner or later I would have got de lash.

Mother belonged to Sam Atkins who owned a plantation about ten miles down de Ramkatte Road in Wake County. Father belonged to Turner Utley and father wus named Jacob Utley and mother wus named Lucy Utley. My maiden name wus Chaney Utley. Dey wurked from sun to sun on de plantation.

When de surrender come father an' mother come to town an' stayed about a year an' den went back to ole marster's plantation. Dey wus fed a long time on hardtack and pickled meat, by de Yankees, while in town. Dey stayed a long time wid ole marster when dey got back. Mother wus his cook. Rats got after mother in town an' she went back to marsters an' tole him 'bout it an' tole him she had come back home, dat she wus fraid to stay in town an' marster jes' laughted an' tole us all to come right in. He tole mother to go an' cook us all sumptin to eat an' she did. We wus all glad to git back home.

I wus too little to wurk much but I played a lot an' swept yards. We drank water outen gourds an' marster would tell me to bring him a gourd full of cool water when he wus settin' in his arm chair on de porch. I thought big of waitin' on marster, yes, dat I did.

Dere wus fourteen of us in family, father, mother an' twelve chilluns. Dere is three of us livin', two of de boys an' me.

Slavery wus a good thing from what I knows 'bout it. While I liked de Yankees wid dere purty clothes, I didn't like de way dey took marster's stuff an' I tole 'em so. Mother made me hush. Dey took chickens, meat, hogs an' horses.

We finally left ole marster's plantation an' moved Jes' a little way over on another plantation. Mother an' father died there.

I married Sam Hews in Wake County when I wus fifteen years old. I had no children. After we wus married we stayed on de farm a year or two den we moved to Raleigh. We have wurked for white folks ever since, an' I am still wurkin' for 'em now all I am able. I washes an' irons clothes. Sometimes I can't wash, I ain't able, but I does de bes' I can. De white folks is still good to me an' I likes' em.

LE

N.C. District:	No. 2
Worker:	T. Pat Matthews
No. Words:	1554
Subject:	Joe High
Person Interviewed:	Joe High
Editor:	Daisy Bailey Waitt
Date Stamp:	"JUN 1 1937"

JOE HIGH

Joe High interviewed May 18, 1937 has long been one of the best independent gardners in Raleigh, working variously by the hour or day.

My name is Joe High. I lives at 527 So. Haywood. St. Raleigh, N.C. Now dere is one thing I want to know, is dis thing goin' to cost me anything. Hold on a minute, and le' me see. I want to be square, and I must be square. Now le' me see, le' me see sumpin'. Sometimes folks come here and dey writes and writes; den dey asts me, is you goin' to pay dis now? What will it cost? Well, if it costs nothin' I'll gib you what I knows.

Let me git my Bible. I wants to be on de square, because I got to leave here some of dese days. Dis is a record from de slave books. I've been tryin' to git my direct age for 35 years. My cousin got my age. I wuz born April 10, 1857. My mother's name wuz Sarah High. Put down when she wuz born, Oct. 24, 1824. This is from the old slave books.

We both belonged to Green High, the young master. The old master, I nebber seed him; but I saw old missus, Mis' Laney High. The old master died before I wuz born. We lived two miles north uv Zebulon. You know where Zebulon is in Wake County? I had two brothers, one brother named Taylor High, 'nother named Ruffin High. My sister died mighty young. She come here wrong; she died. I' member seeing my uncle take her to the grave yard. I don't know whe're there's enny rec'ord o' her or not.

My work in slavery times wuz ridin' behin' my Missus, Clara Griffin, who wuz my old missus' sister's daughter. She came to be our missus. When she went visiting I rode behind her. I also looked atter de garden, kept chickens out uv de garden, and minded de table, fanned flies off de table. They were good to us. Dey whupped us sometime. I wuz not old enough to do no fiel' work.

One time I slep' late. It wuz in the fall uv the year. The other chilluns had lef' when I got up. I went out to look for 'em. When I crossed the tater patch I seen the ground cracked and I dug in to see what cracked it. I found a tater and kept diggin' till I dug it up. I carried it to the house. They had a white woman for a cook that year. I carried the tater and showed it to her. She took me and the tater and told me to come on. We went from the kitchen to the great house and she showed the tater to the old missus sayin', 'Look here missus, Joe has been stealin' taters. Here is the tater he stole'. Old missus said, 'Joe belongs to me, the tater belongs to me, take it back and cook it for him. When the cook cooked the tater she asked me for half uv it. I gave it to her. If I had known den lak I knows now, she wuz tryin' to git me to git a whoppin' I wouldn't 'er give her none uv dat tater.

There were some frame houses, an part log houses, we called 'em the darkey houses. The master's house wuz called 'the great house'. We had very good places to sleep and plenty to eat. I got plenty uv potlicker, peas, and pumpkins. All us little darkies et out uv one bowl. We used mussel shells, got on the branch, for spoons. Dey must not er had no spoons or sumpin. The pea fowls roosted on de great house evey night. I didn't know whut money nor matches wuz neither.

I 'member seein' Henry High, my first cousin, ketch a pike once, but I never done no fishin' or huntin'. I 'member seein' the grown folks start off possum huntin' at night, but I did not go.

I wore wooden bottom shoes and I wore only a shirt. I went in my shirt tail until I wuz a great big boy, many years atter slavery. There were 50 or more slaves on the plantation. Old women wove cloth on looms. We made syrup, cane syrup, with a cane mill. We carried our corn to Foster's Mill down on Little River to have it ground. It wuz called Little River den; I don't know whut it is called in dis day.

There wuz a block in de yard, where missus got up on her horse. There were two steps to it. Slaves were sold from this block. I 'member seein' them sold from this block. George High wuz one, but they got him back.

Dey did not teach us anything about books; dey did not teach us anything about readin' and writin'. I went to church at the Eppsby Church near Buffalo, not far from Wakefield. We sat in a corner to ourselves.

My brother Taylor ran away. Young master sent him word to come on back home; he won't goin' to whup him, and he come back. Yes, he come back.

We played the games uv marbles, blind fold, jumpin', and racin', and jumpin' the rope. The doctor looked atter us when we were sick, sometimes, but it wuz mostly done by old women. Dey got erbs and dey gib us wormfuge. Dey worked us out. I wuz not old enough to pay much attention to de doctor's name.

I 'members one day my young master, Green High, and me wuz standin' in de front yard when two men come down the avenue from de main road to the house. Dey wanted to know how fer it wuz to Green High's. Master told 'em it wuz about 2 miles away and gave 'em the direction. Dey were Yankees. Dey got on their horses and left. Dey didn't know dey wuz talking to Green High then. When dey left, master left. I didn't see him no more in a long time. Soon next day the yard wuz full uv Yankee soldiers. I 'members how de buttons on dere uniforms shined. Dey got corn, meat, chickens, and eveything they wanted. Day didn't burn the house.

Old man Bert Doub or Domb kept nigger hounds. When a nigger run away he would ketch him for de master. De master would send atter him and his dogs when a nigger run away. I 'member one overseer, a Negro, Hamp High and another Coff High. Nobody told me nothin' about being free and I knowed nothin' 'bout whut it meant.

I married Rosetta Hinton. She belonged to the Hintons

during slavery. She is dead; she's been dead fourteen years. We were married at her mother's home; the river plantation belonging to the Hintons. I wuz married by a preacher at this home. Atter the wedding we had good things to eat and we played games. All stayed there that night and next day we went back to whar I wuz workin' on de Gen. Cox's farm. I wuz workin' dere. We had 6 chillun. Two died at birth. All are dead except one in Durham named Tommie High and one in New York City. Tommie High works in a wheat mill. Eddie High is a cashermiser, (calciminer) works on walls.

I thought slavery wuz right. I felt that this wuz the way things had to go, the way they were fixed to go. I wuz satisfied. The white folks treated me all right. My young missus loved me and I loved her. She whupped me sometimes. I think just for fun sometimes, when I wuz ridin' behind her, she would tell me to put my arms around her and hold to her apron strings. One day she wuz sittin' on the side saddle; I wuz sittin' behind her. She wud try to git old Dave, the horse she wuz a ridin to walk; she would say, 'Ho Dave', den I wud kick de horse in de side and she wud keep walkin' on. She asked me, 'Joe, why does Dave not want to stop?'

I saw a lot of Yankees, I wuz afraid of 'em. They called us Johnnie, Susie, and tole us they wouldn't hurt us.

I think Abraham Lincoln is all right, I guess, the way he saw it. I think he was like I wuz as a boy from what I read, and understand; he wuz like me jest the way he saw things. I liked the rules, and ways o' my old master and missus, while the Yankees and Abraham Lincoln gave me more rest.

How did I learn to read? Atter de war I studies. I wonts ter read de hymms an' songs. I jis picks up de readin' myself.

It's quare to me, I cannot remember one word my mother ever said to me, not nary a word she said can I remember. I remember she brought me hot potlicker and bread down to the house of mornings when I wuz small; but I'se been tryin to 'member some words she spoke to me an' I cain't.

N.C. District:	No. 2
Worker:	T. Pat Matthews
No. Words:	936
Subject:	SUSAN HIGH
Story Teller:	Susan High
Editor:	Daisy Bailey Waitt

SUSAN HIGH

My name is Susan High. I wus born in June. I am 70 years old. My mother wus named Piety an' she belonged to de ole man Giles Underhill before de surrender. My father he wus George Merritt an' he belonged to Ben Merritt, Ivan Proctor's grandfather. Dey lived on a plantation near Eagle Rock, Wake County. Dey called de creek near by Mark's Creek.

My parents said dat dey had a mighty hard time, an' dat durin' slavery time, de rules wus mighty strict. De hours of work on de farm wus from sun to sun wid no time 'cept at Christmas and at lay-by time, 4th of July for anything but work. Dey were not 'lowed no edication, and very little time to go to church. Sometimes de went to de white folks church. Mother said dey whupped de slaves if dey broke de rules.

Dey said de overseers were worse den de slave owners. De overseers were ginerally white men hired by de marster. My father said dey had poor white men to overseer, and de slave owner would go on about his business and sometimes didn't know an' didn't eben care how mean de overseer wus to de slaves.

Dere wus a lot o' things to drink, dey said, cider, made from apples, whiskey, an' brandy. Dey said people didn't notice it lak dey do now, not many got drunk, cause dere wus plenty of it. Father said it wus ten cents a quart, dat is de whiskey made outen corn, and de brandy wus cheap too.

Dey said de clothes were wove, an' dat mos' chillun went barefooted, an' in dere shirt tails; great big boys, goin' after de cows, and feedin' de horses, an' doin' work around de house in deir shirt tails. Grown slaves got one pair o' shoes a year an' went barefooted de res' o' de time. Biscuit wus a thing dey seldom got.

Women cleared land by rollin' logs into piles and pilin' brush in de new grounds. Dey were 'lowed patches, but dey used what dey made to eat. Daddy said dey didn't have time to fish and hunt any. Dey were too tired for dat. Dey had to work so hard.

Daddy said he wus proud o' freedom, but wus afraid to own it. Dey prayed fer freedom secretly. When de Yankees come daddy saved a two horse wagon load of meat for marster by takin' it off in de swamp and hidin' it, an' den marster wouldn't give him nary bit uv it. After de surrender, dey turned him out wid a crowd o' little chillun wid out a thing. Dey give him nothin'. My mother saved her marster's life, Charles Underhill.

Well you see he wus takin' care uv a lot o' meat and whiskey for Dick Jordon, an' de Yankees come an' he treated 'em from whiskey he had in a bottle, an' tole 'em he had no more. Dey searched his home an' found it in a shed room, an' den dey said dey were goin' to kill him for tellin' 'em a lie. She herd 'em talkin' and she busted through de crowd and told 'em dat de stuff belonged to anudder man and dat her marster was not lyin', an' not to hurt 'im. De Yankees said, 'You have saved dis ole son of a bitch, we won't kill' em den.' Dey took all de meat, whiskey, an' everything dey wanted. Marster promised mother a cow, and calf, a sow, and pigs for what she had done for him an' to stay on an' finish de crop. When de fall o' de year come he did not give her de wrappin's o' her finger. Dat's what my mudder tole me. We wus teached to call 'em mammie and pappie. I is gwine to tell you just zackly like it is we were taught dese things. I wants to be pasidefily right in what I tell you.

We lef' dat place an' mammie an' pappie farmed wid Solomon Morgan a Free Issue for several years. De family had typhoid fever an' five were down with it at one time. But de Lawd will provide. Sich as dat makes me say people wont die till deir time comes. Dere is some mighty good white people in dis place in America, and also bad. If it hadn't been for 'em we colored folks would have ben in a mighty bad fix. We got our jobs and help from 'em to git us to de place we are at. Dr. Henry Montague doctored us and none died. It wusn't dere time to go. No, no, hit wasn't deir time to go. We then moved back to Marster's for a year, and then we moved to Rolesville in Wake County.

I married den and moved to Raleigh. I married Robert High. He is dead. He been dead 'bout 30 years. I don't know much ‘bout Abraham Lincoln I think he wus a fine man. Mr. Roosevelt’s ideas is fine if he can carry ‘em out.

AC

N.C. District:	No. 2
Worker:	T. Pat Matthews
No. Words:	878
Subject:	KITTY HILL
Person Interviewed:	Kitty Hill
Editor:	G. L. Andrews
Date Stamp:	"AUG 17 1937"

KITTY HILL

I tole you yisterday dat my age wus 76 years old, but my daughter come home, an' I axed her' bout it an' she say I is 77 years old. I don't know exactly the date but I wus born in April. I wus a little girl 'bout five years ole when de surrender come, but I don't' member anything much' bout de Yankees.

I wus born in Virginia, near Petersburg, an' mother said de Yankees had been hanging' round dere so long dat a soldier wus no sight to nobody.

'Bout de time de Yankees come I' member hearin' dem talk 'bout de surrender. Den a Jew man by the name of Isaac Long come to Petersburg, bought us an' brought us to Chatham County to a little country town, named Pittsboro. Ole man Isaac Long run a store an' kept a boarding house. We stayed on de lot. My mother cooked. We stayed there a long time atter de war. Father wus sent to Manassas Gap at the beginning of de war and I do not 'member ever seein' him.

My mother wus named Viney Jefferson an' my father wus named Thomas Jefferson. We 'longed to the Jeffersons there and we went by the name of Jefferson when we wus sold and brought to N.C. I do not 'member my grandparents on my mother's or father's side. Mother had one boy an' three girls. The boy wus named Robert, an' the girls were Kate, Rosa and Kitty. Marster Long bought mother an' all de chilluns, but mother never seed father anymore atter he wus sent off to de war.

I married Green Hill in Chatham County. I married him at Moncure about nine miles from Pittsboro. We lived at Moncure and mother moved there an' we lived together for a long time. When we left Moncure we come ter Raleigh. Mother had died long time 'fore we left Moncure, Chatham County. We moved ter Raleigh atter de World War.

Mother used ter tell we chilluns stories of patterollers ketchin' niggers an' whuppin' 'em an' of how some of de men outrun de patterollers an' got away. Dere wus a song dey used to sing, it went like dis. Yes sir, ha! ha! I wants ter tell you dat song, here it is:

'Somefolks say dat a nigger wont steal, I caught two in my corn field, one had a bushel, one had a peck, an' one had rosenears, strung 'round his neck. 'Run nigger run, Patteroller ketch you, run nigger run like you did de udder day.'

My mother said she wus treated good. Yes she said dey wus good ter her in Virginia. Mother said de slave men on de Jefferson plantation in Virginia would steal de hosses ter ride ter dances at night. One time a hoss dey stole an' rode ter a dance fell dead an' dey tried ter tote him home. Mother laughted a lot about dat. I heard my mother say dat de cavalry southern folks was bout de meanest in de war. She talked a lot about Wheeler's cavalry.

Dere wus a lot of stealin' an' takin' meat, silver, stock an' anything. Hosses, cows an' chickens jist didn't have no chance if a Yankee laid his eyes on 'em. A Yankee wus pisen to a yard full of fowls. Dey killed turkeys, chickens and geese. Now dats de truth. Mother said de Yankees skinned turkeys, chickens and geese 'fore dey cooked 'em. Sometimes dey would shoot a hog an' jist take de hams an' leave de rest dere to spile. Dey would kill a cow, cut off de quarters an' leave de rest ter rot.

Mother said no prayer meetings wus allowed de slaves in Virginia where she stayed. Dey turned pots down ter kill de noise an' held meetings at night. Dey had niggers ter watch an' give de alarm if dey saw de white folks comin'. Dey always looked out for patterollers. Dey were not allowed any edication an' mother could not read and write nuther.

I 'member de Ku Klux an' how dey beat people. One night a man got away from 'em near whar we lived in Chatham County. He lived out in de edge of de woods; and when dey knocked on de door he jumped out at a back window in his night clothes wid his pants in his hands an' outrun 'em. Dere wus rocks in de woods whar he run an' dat nigger jist tore his feet up. Dey went ter one nigger's house up dere an' de door' wus barred up. Dey got a ax an' cut a hole in de door. When de hole got big enough de nigger blammed down on 'em wid a gun an' shot one of dere eyes out. You know de Ku Klux went disguised an' when dey got ter your house dey would say in a fine voice, Ku Klux, Ku Klux, Ku Klux, Ku Klux.

Some people say dey are in slavery now an' dat de niggers never been in nothin' else; but de way some of it wus I believe it wus a bad thing. Some slaves fared all right though an' had a good time an' liked slavery.

LE

N.C. District:	No. 2
Worker:	T. Pat Matthews
No. Words:	997
Subject:	JERRY HINTON
Person Interviewed:	Jerry Hinton
Editor:	Daisy Bailey Waitt

JERRY HINTON

My full name is Jerry Hinton. I wus borned in February, 1855. I am not able ter work. I work all I can. I am trying ter do de best I can ter help myself. Yes, just tryin' ter do sumpin, ain't able ter work much. I am ruptured, an' old. My old house looks 'bout old as I do, it's 'bout to fall down, ain't able ter fix it up. It needs repairing. I ain't able ter make no repairs.

I wus born on a plantation in Wake County. My master wus Richard Seawell, an' Missus wus named Adelaide. His plantation wus on Neuse River. He had two plantations, but I wus a little boy, an' don't remember how many acres in de plantation or how many slaves. There wus a lot of 'em tho'. I would follow master 'round an' look up in his face so he would give me biscuit an' good things ter eat.

My mother, before marriage, wus named Silvia Seawell, an' father wus named Andrew Hinton. Atter they wus married mother went by the name of Hinton, my father's family name. I had—I don't know—mos' anything wus good ter me. Master brought me biscuit an' I thought that wus the greatest thing at all. Yes, I got purty good food. Our clothes wus not fine, but warm. I went barefooted mos' o' the time, an' in summer I went in my shirt tail.

Dey called de slave houses 'quarters', de house where de overseer lived wus de 'Overseer's House'. Master had a overseer to look atter his men; De overseer wus named Bridgers. De house where Master lived wus de 'Great House'.

Dey would not allow us any books. I cannot read an' write. I have seen de patterollers, but I neber saw' em whip nobody; but I saw' em lookin' fer somebody ter whup. I've neber seen a slave sold. I've neber seen a jail fer slaves or slaves in chains. I have seen master whup slaves though. I wus neber whupped. Dey wrung my ears an' pulled my nose to punish me.

Dere wus no churches on de plantation, but we had prayer meetin's in our homes. We went to de white folks church. My father used to take me by de hand an' carry me ter church. Daddy belonged ter de Iron Side Baptist Church. We called our fathers 'daddy' in slavery time. Dey would not let slaves call deir fathers 'father'. Dey called 'em 'daddy', an' white children called deir father, 'Pa'. I didn't work any in slavery time, 'cept feed pigs, an' do things fer my master; waited on him. I went 'round wid him a lot, an' I had rather see him come on de plantation any time dan to see my daddy. I do not remember any possums or other game being eaten at our house. I do not remember eber goin' a-fishin durin' slavery time.

Master had two boys ter go off ter de war. Dey carried ‘em off ter de war. I don’t know how many children dey had, but I remember two of ‘em goin’ off ter de war. Don’t know what became of ‘em.

I shore remember de Yankees. Yes sir, Ha! ha! I shore remember dem. Dem Yankees tore down an’ drug out ever’thing, dey come across. Dey killed hogs, an’ chickens. Dey took only part of a hog an’ lef’ de rest. Dey shot cows, an’ sometimes jest cut off de hind quarters an’ lef de rest. Dey knocked de heads out o’ de barrels o’ molasses. Dey took horses, cows an’ eber’thing, but they did not hurt any o’ de children. Dey wus folks dat would tear down things.

Atter de surrender my mother moved over on de plantation where my father stayed. We stayed dere a long time, an’ den we moved back to Richard Seawell’s, old master’s plantation, stayin’ dere a long time. Den we moved to Jessie Taylor’s place below Raleigh between Crabtree Creek an’ Neuse River. When we lef’ Taylor’s we moved ter Banner Dam northeast of Raleigh near Boone’s Pond. Mother an’ father both died dere. Atter leaving dere I come here. I have lived in Oberlin ebery since. Guess I’ll die here; if I can git de money to pay my taxes, I know I will die here.

I think slavery wus good because I wus treated all right. I think I am ‘bout as much a slave now as ever.

I don’t think any too much o’ Abraham Lincoln, Jeff Davis or any o’ dem men. Don’t know much ‘bout ‘em. Guess Mr. Roosevelt is all right. ‘Bout half the folks both black an’ white is slaves an’ don’t know it. When I wus a slave I had nothin’ on me, no responsibility on any of us, only to work. Didn't have no taxes to pay, neber had to think whur de next meal wus comin' from.

Dis country is in a bad fix. Looks like sumptin got to be done someway or people, a lot of 'em, are goin' to parish to death. Times are hard, an' dey is gettin' worse. Don't know how I am goin' to make it, if I don't git some help. We been prayin' fer rain. Crops are done injured, but maybe de Lawd will help us. Yes, I trust in de Lawd.

I been married twice. I married Henritta Nunn first, an' den Henritta Jones. I had three children by first marriage, an' none bi second marriage. My wife is over seventy years old. We have a hard time making enough to git a little sumptin to eat. I wus mighty glad to see you when you come up dis mornin', an' I hopes what I have told you will help some one to know how bad we need help. I feels de Lawd will open up de way. Yes sir, I do.

LE

N.C. District:	No. 2
Worker:	T. Pat Matthews
No. Words:	568
Subject:	MARTHA ADELINE HINTON
Person Interviewed:	Martha Adeline Hinton
Editor:	G. L. Andrews
Date Stamp:	**HW Date "8/31/37"**

MARTHA ADELINE HINTON

I wus born May 3, 1861 at Willis Thompson's plantation in Wake County about fifteen miles from Raleigh. He wus my marster an' his wife Muriel wus my missus. My father's name wus Jack Emery an' mother's name was Minerva Emery. My mother belonged to Willis Thompson and my father belonged to Ephriam Emery. Mother stayed with my marster's married daughter. She married Johnny K. Moore.

Marster had three children, all girls; dere names wus Margaret, Caroline and Nancy. There wus only one slave house dere 'cause dey only had one slave whur my mother stayed. Marster Thompson had five slaves on his plantation. He wus good to slaves but his wife wus rough. We had a resonably good place to sleep an' fair sumptin to eat. You sees I wus mighty young an' I members very little 'bout some things in slavery but from what my mother an father tole me since de war it wus just 'bout middlin' livin' at marster's. Slaves wore homemade clothes an' shoes. De shoes had wooden bottoms but most slave chilluns went barefooted winter an' summer till dey wus ole 'nough to go to work. De first pair of shoes I wore my daddy made 'em. I 'member it well. I will never furgit it, I wus so pleased wid 'em. All slave chillun I knows anything 'bout wore homemade clothes an' went barefooted most of the time an' bareheaded too.

I member de Yankees an' how dey had rods searchin' for money an' took things. I members a Yankee goin' to mother an' sayin' we was free. When he lef' missus come an' axed her what he say to her an' mother tole missus what he said an' missus says 'No he didn't tell you you is free, you jes axed him wus you free.' Father wus hired out to Frank Page of Gary. He wus cuttin cord wood for him, when he heard de Yankees wus coming he come home. When he got dere de Yankees had done been to de house an' gone.

Durin' slavery dey tried to sell daddy. De speculator wus dere an 'daddy suspicion sumpin. His marster tole him to go an' shuck some corn. Dey aimed to git him in de corn crib an' den tie him an' sell him but when he got to the crib he kept on goin'. He went to Mr. Henry Buffaloe's an' stayed two weeks den he went back home. Dere wus nuthin' else said 'bout sellin him. Dey wanted to sell him an buy a 'oman so dey could have a lot of slave chilluns cause de 'oman could multiply. Dey hired men out by the year to contractors to cut cord wood an' build railroads. Father wus hired out dat way. Ole man Rome Harp wus hired out day way. He belonged to John Harp.

Daddy said his marster never did hit him but one blow. Daddy said he wurked hard everyday, an' done as near right as he knowed how to do in everything. His marster got mad ah' hit him wid a long switch. Den daddy tole him he wus workin' bes' he could for him an' dat he wus not goin' to take a whuppin. His marster walked off an' dat wus de last of it, an' he never tried to whup him again.

N.C. District:	No. 2
Worker:	T. Pat Matthews
No. Words:	775
Subject:	ROBERT HINTON
Person Interviewed:	Robert Hinton
Editor:	Daisy Bailey Waitt

ROBERT HINTON

My name is Robert Hinton. I ain't able to work, ain't been able to do any work in five years. My wife, Mary Hinton, supports me by workin' with the WPA. She was cut off las' May. Since she has had no job, we have to live on what she makes with what little washin' she gets from de white folks; an' a little help from charity; dis ain't much. Dey give you for one week, one half peck meal, one pound meat, one pound powdered milk, one half pound o' coffee. Dis is what we git for one week.

I wus borned in 1856 on de Fayetteville Road three miles from Raleigh, south. I belonged to Lawrence Hinton. My missus wus named Jane Hinton. De Hintons had 'bout twenty slaves on de plantation out dere. Dey had four chillun, de boy Ransom an' three girls: Belle, Annie an' Miss Mary. All are dead but one, Miss Mary is livin' yit. My mother wus named Liza Hinton an' my father wus named Bob Hinton. My gran'mother wus named Mary Hinton an' gran'father Harry Hinton.

We had common food in slavery time, but it wus well fixed up, an' we were well clothed. We had a good place to sleep, yes sir, a good place to sleep. We worked from sunrise to sunset under overseers. Dey were good to us. I wus small at dat time. I picked up sticks in de yard an' done some work around de house, but when dey turned deir backs I would be playin' most o' de time. We played shootin' marbles, an' runnin', an' jumpin'. We called de big house de dwelling house an' de slave quarters de slave houses. Some of 'em were in marster's yard and some were outside. Dey give all de families patches and gardens, but dey did not sell anything.

We had prayer meetin' in our houses when we got ready, but dere were no churches for niggers on de plantation. We had dances and other socials durin' Christmas times. Dey give us de Christmas holidays.

No sir, dey did not whup me. I wus mighty young. Dey didn't work chillun much. I have seen 'em whup de grown ones do'. I never saw a slave sold and never saw any in chains. Dey run away from our plantation but dey come back again. William Brickell, Sidney Cook, Willis Hinton all run away. I don't know why dey all run away but some run away to keep from being whupped.

I have lived in North Carolina all my life, right here in Wake County. We used to set gums and catch rabbits, set traps and caught patridges and doves.

Yes sir, I went blindin'. I 'members gittin' a big light an' jumpin' 'round de bresh heaps, an' when a bird come out we frailed him down. We went gigging fish too. We found 'em lying on de bottom o' de creeks an' ponds at night, an' stuck de gig in 'em an' pulled 'em out.

De white folks, ole missus, teached us de catechism, but dey didn't want you to learn to read and write. I can read and write now; learned since de surrender. Sometimes we went to de white folks church. I don't know any songs.

When we got sick our boss man sent for a doctor, Dr. Burke Haywood, Dr. Johnson, or Dr. Hill.

I 'members when de North folks and de Southern folks wus fightin'. De Northern soldiers come in here on de Fayetteville Road. I saw 'em by de hundreds. Dey had colored folks soldiers in blue clothes too. In de mornin' white soldiers, in de evenin' colored soldiers; dats de way dey come to town.

I married first Almeta Harris. I had six children by her. Second, I married Mary Jones. She is my wife now. We had six children. My wife is now 65 years old and she has to support me. I am done give out too much to work any more.

Yes sir, that I have seen de patterollers, but my old boss didn't 'low 'em to whup his niggers. Marster give his men passes.

I know when de Ku Klux was here, but I don't know much about 'em.

I thought slavery wus a bad thing' cause all slaves did not fare alike. It wus all right for some, but bad for some, so it wus a bad thing.

I joined the church because I got religion and thought the church might help me keep it.

I think Abraham Lincoln wus a good man, but I likes Mr. Roosevelt; he is a good man, a good man.

AC

N.C. District:	No. 2
Worker:	T. Pat Matthews
No. Words:	922
Subject:	WILLIAM GEORGE HINTON
Person Interviewed:	William George Hinton
Editor:	G. L. Andrews
Date Stamp:	**HW Date: "8/31/37"**

WILLIAM GEORGE HINTON

I was born in Wake County in de year 1859. August 28th. I 'members seeing de Yankees, it seems like a dream. One come along ridin' a mule. Dey sed he wus a Yankee bummer, a man dat went out raging on peoples things. He found out whur the things wus located an' carried the rest there. The bummers stole for de army, chickens, hogs, an' anything they could take. Atter de bummer come along in a few minutes de whole place wus crowded wid Yankees. De blue coats wus everywhere I could look.

Marster didn't have but five slaves, an' when de Yankees come dere wus only me an' my oldest sister dere. All de white folks had left except missus and her chillun. Her baby wus only three weeks ole then.

A Yankee come to my oldest sister an' said, 'Whur is dem horses?' He pulled out a large pistol an' sed, 'Tell me whur dem horses is or I will take your damn sweet life.' Marster hid de horses an' sister didn't know, she stuck to it she didn't know an' de Yankees didn't shoot.

Dey come back, de whole crowd, de next day an' made marster bring in his horses. Bey took de horses an' bought some chickens an' paid for 'em, den dey killed an' took de rest. Ha! ha! dey shore done dat. Paid for some an' took de rest.

I seed de Yankees atter de surrender. Dey wus staying at de ole Soldiers Home on New Bern Avenue. One day mother carried me there to sell to 'em. One time she went there an' she had a rooster who wus a game. His eyes wus out from fighting another game rooster belonging to another person near our home, Mr. Emory Sewell. She carried de rooster in where dere wus a sick Yankee. De Yankee took him in his hands an' de rooster crowed. He give mother thirty-five cents for him. De Yankee said if he could crow an' his eyes out he wanted him. He said, he called dat spunk.

Dere wus a man who wus a slave dat belonged to Mr. Kerney Upchurch come along riding a mule. My oldest sister, de one de Yankees threatened, tole him de Yankees are up yonder. He said, 'Dad lim de Yankees.' He went on, when he got near de Yankees dey tole him to halt.' Instead of haltin' he sold out runnin' the mule fur de ole field. Der wus a gang of young fox hounds dere. When he lit out on de mule, dey thought he wus goin' huntin' so dey took out atter him, jest like dey wus atter a fox. Some of de Yankees shot at him, de others just almost died a laughin'.

We didn't git much to eat. Mother said it wus missus fault, she was so stingy.

We had homemade clothes an' wooden bottom shoes for de grown folks, but chillun did not wear shoes den, dey went barefooted.

All de slaves lived in one house built about one hundred yards from the great house, marsters house wus called the great house.

My father wus named Robin Hinton an' my mother wus named Dafney Hinton. My father belonged to Betsy Ransom Hinton an' mother belonged first to Reddin Cromb in Lenoir County an' then to James Thompson of Wake County. I wus borned after mother wus brought to Wake County. Marster had one boy named Beuregard, four girls, Caroline, Alice, Lena and Nellie. I do not remember my grandparents.

I saw a slave named Lucinda, sold to ole man Askew, a speculator, by Kerney Upchurch. I seed 'em carry her off.

One of de slave men who belonged to ole man Burl Temples wus sent to wurk for Mr. Temples' son who had married. His missus put him to totin' water before goin' to wurk in de mornin'. Three other slaves toted water also. He refused to tote water an' ran. She set de blood hounds atter him an' caught him near his home, which wus his ole marster's house. Ole marster's son come out, an' wouldn't let 'em whup him, an' they wouldn't make him go back.

Missus Harriet Temples wus a terrible 'oman, a slave jest couldn't suit her. De slave dat run away from young marster wus finally sent back. His marster give him a shoulder of meat before he left. He hung it in a tree. Missus tole him to put it in the smoke house. He refused, sayin' he would see it no more.

A slave by the name of Sallie Temples run away 'cause her missus, Mary Temples, wus so mean to her. She stuck hot irons to her. Made 'em drink milk an' things for punishment is what my mother an' father said. Sallie never did come back. Nobody never did know what become of her.

Soon as de war wus over father an' mother left dere marsters. Dey went to Mr. Tom Bridgers. We lived on de farm atter dis. Mother cooked, sister an' I worked on de farm. Sister plowed like a man. De first help my mammy got wus from de Yankees, it wus pickle meat an' hardtack. I wus wid her an' dey took me in an' give me some clothes. Mother drawed from 'em a long time. We have farmed most our lives. Sometimes we worked as hirelings and den as share croppers. I think slavery wus a bad thing.

N.C. District:	No. 2
Worker:	Mary A. Hicks
No. Words:	465
Subject:	Eustace Hodges
Story Teller:	Eustace Hodges
Editor:	Geo. L. Andrews
Date Stamp:	"AUG 6 1937"

EUSTACE HODGES

I doan know when I wus borned, ner where but at fust my mammy an' me 'longed ter a McGee here in Wake County. My mammy wurked in de fiel's den, ditchin' an' such, even plowin' while we 'longed ter McGee, but he sold us ter Mr. Rufus Jones. My daddy still 'longed ter him but at de close of de war he comed ter Mr. Jones' plantation an' he tuck de name of Jones 'long wid us.

Marse Rufus wus gooder dan Marse McGee, dey said. He give us more ter eat an' wear an' he ain't make us wurk so hard nother. We had our wurk ter do, of course, but mammy ain't had ter ditch ner plow no mo'. She wurked in de house den, an' none of de wimmen done men's wurk. Course she can't wurk so hard an' have 'leben chilluns too. She had a baby one day an' went ter wurk de nex' while she 'longed ter McGee, but at Marse Rufus' she stayed in de bed seberal days an' had a doctor.

Marse Rufus uster let us take Sadday evenin' off an'

go swimmin' er fishin' er go ter Raleigh. I 'members dat somebody in town had a fuss wid Marse Rufus 'bout lettin' his niggers run loose in town. Marse Rufus atter dat had a oberseer in town ter see 'bout his niggers.

I got a whuppin' once fer punchin' out a frog's eyes. Miss Sally giv' hit ter me long wid a lecture 'bout bein' kin' ter dumb brutes, but I ain't neber seed whar a frog am a brute yit.

Yes'um I heard a heap 'bout de Yankees but I ain't prepared fer dere takin' eben our bread. Miss Sally ain't prepared nother an' she tells' em whar ter go, den she goes ter bed sick. I wus sorry fer Miss Sally, dat I wus.

De day dat news of de surrender come Miss Sally cried some more an' she ain't wanted mammy ter go, so Marse Rufus said dat we can stay on. Dey said dat Mister McGee runned his niggers offen his place wid a bresh broom dat day.

Atter de war we stayed on Marse Rufus' place till 1898 when pa died. I had married a feller by de name of Charlie Hodges, what lived on a nearby plantation an' we wus livin' on Marse Rufus' place wid pa an' ma. We moved ter Raleigh den an' atter seberal years mammy moved hear too. You can fin' her on Cannon Street, but I'll tell you dat she's pretty puny now, since her stroke.

N.C. District:	No. 2
Worker:	Mrs. Edith S. Hibbs and Mrs. W. N. Harriss
No. Words:	795
Subject:	Alex Huggins' Story
Interviewed:	Alex Huggins
	920 Dawson St, Wilmington, N.C.
Editor:	Mrs W. N. Harriss

ALEX HUGGINS

I was born in New Bern on July 9, 1850. My father and mother belonged to Mr. L. B. Huggins. My father was a carpenter and ship builder an' the first things I remember was down on Myrtle Grove Sound, where Mr. Huggins had a place. I was a sort of bad boy an' liked to roam 'round. When I was about twelve years old I ran away. It was in 1863 when the war was goin' on.

Nobody was bein' mean to me. No, I was'nt bein' whipped. Don't you know all that story 'bout slaves bein' whipped is all Bunk, (with scornful emphasis). What pusson with any sense is goin' to take his horse or his cow an' beat it up. It's prope'ty. We was prope'ty. Val'able prope'ty. No, indeed, Mr. Luke give the bes' of attention to his colored people, an' Mis' Huggins was like a mother to my mother. Twa'nt anythin' wrong about home that made me run away. I'd heard so much talk 'bout freedom

I reckon I jus' wanted to try it, an' I thought I had to get away from home to have it.

Well, I coaxed two other boys to go with me, an' a grown man he got the boat an' we slipped off to the beach an' put out to sea. Yes'm, we sho' was after adventure. But, we did'n get very far out from sho', an' I saw the lan' get dimmer an' dimmer, when I got skeered, an' then I got seasick, an' we was havin' more kinds of adventure than we wanted, an' then we saw some ships. There was two of 'em, an' they took us on board.

They was the North Star an' the Eastern Star of the Aspinwal Line, a mail an' freighter runnin' between Aspinwal near the Isthmus of Panama and New York. We used to put in off Charleston.

Then, in 1864 I joined the Union Navy. Went on board our convoy, the Nereus. We convoyed to keep the Alabama, a Confederate privateer, away. The Commander of the Nereus asked me how's I like to be his cabin boy. So I was 2nd class cabin boy an' waited on the Captain. He was Five Stripe Commander J. C. Howell. He was Commander of the whole fleet off Fort Fisher. When the Captain wanted somethin' good to eat he used to send me ashore for provisions. He liked me. He was an old man. He didn't take much stock in fun, but he was a real man. I was young an' was'nt serious. I jus' wanted a good time. I don't know much about the war, but I do know two men of our boat was killed on shore while we was at Fort Fisher.

After the battle of Fort Fisher, we was on our way to Aspinwal. Layin' off one day at Navassa Island, the Mast Head reported a strange sail. 'Where away?' 'Just ahead'. 'She seems to be a three mast steamer!' 'Which way headed?' We decided it was the Alabama going to St. Nicholas Mole, West Indies.

Our Captain called the officers together an' held a meetin'. Says he: 'We'll go under one bell (slow). Lieutenant will go ashore an' get some information.' When we got there she had a coal schooner alongside taking on coal. Our Captain prepared to capture her when she came out. But she did'n come out 'til night. She dodged. Good thing too. She'd a knocked hells pete out o' us. She was close to the water and could have fought us so much better than we could her. We didn't want to fight 'cause we knowed enough to jest natu'ally be skeered. She was a one decker man o' war. We was a two decker with six guns on berth deck, an' five guns on spar deck. I never saw her after that, but I heard she was contacted by the Kearsage which sunk her off some island.

I stayed in the navy eighteen months. Was discharged at the Brooklyn Navy Yard. Admiral Porter was Admiral of the U. S. Navy at that time.

I stayed in New York five or six years, then I cane home to my mother. I was in the crude drug business in Wilmington for twenty years.

Yes'm I went to church and Sunday school when I was a child, when they could ketch me. Whilst I was in New York I went to church regular.

I married after awhile. My wife died about ten years ago. We had one son. I b'lieve he's in Baltimore, but I ain't heard from him in a long time. He don't keer nothin' about me. Of co'se I'm comfortable. I gits my pension, $75 a month. I give $10 of it to my nephew who's a cripple.

N.C. District:	No. 2
Worker:	T. Pat Matthews
No. Words:	645
Subject:	CHARLIE H. HUNTER
Person Interviewed:	Charlie H. Hunter
Editor:	Geo. L. Andrews
Date Stamp:	"AUG 4 1937"

CHARLIE H. HUNTER

My full name is Charlie H. Hunter. I wus borned an' reared in Wake County, N.C., born May, 1857. My mother wus Rosa Hunter an' my father wus named Jones. I never saw my father. We belonged to a family named Jones first, an' then we wus sold to a slave owner seven miles Northwest by the name Joe Hayes an' a terrible man he wus. He would get mad 'bout most anything, take my mother, chain her down to a log and whup her unmercifully while I, a little boy, could do nothing but stan' there an' cry, an' see her whupped. We had fairly good food an' common clothing. We had good sleeping places. My mother wus sold to a man named Smith. I married first Annie Hayes who lived sixteen months.

No prayer meetings wus allowed on de plantations an' no books of any kind. I can read an' write, learned in a school taught by Northern folks after the surrender, Mr. an' Mrs. Graves who taught in Raleigh in the rear of the

African Methodist Episcopal church. The school house wus owned by the church. We played no games in slavery times. I saw slaves sold on the block once in Raleigh.

I wus to be sold but the surrender stopped it. When the Yankees come they asked me where wus my marster. I told them I didn't know. Marster told me not to tell where he wus. He had gone off into the woods to hide his silver. In a few minutes the ground wus covered with Yankees. The Yankees stole my pen knife. I thought a lot of it. Knives wus scarce and hard to get. I cried about they taking it. They got my marster's carriage horses, two fine gray horses. His wife had lost a brother, who had been in the army but died at home. He wus buried in the yard. The Yankees thought the grave wus a place where valuables wus buried and they had to get a guard to keep them from diggin' him up. They would shoot hogs, cut the hams and shoulders off, stick them on their bayonetts, throw them over the'r shoulders an' go on.

We called our houses shanties in slavery time. I never saw any patterollers. I don't remember how many slaves on the plantation wus taken to Richmond an' sold. My mother looked after us when we wus sick. I had four brothers an' no sisters. They are all dead. I did house work an' errands in slavery time. I have seen one gang of Ku Klux. They wus under arrest at Raleigh in Governor Holden's time. I don't remember the overseer.

We moved to Raleigh at the surrender. Marster give us a old mule when we left him, an' I rode him into Raleigh. We rented a house on Wilmington Street, an' lived on hard tack the Yankees give us 'til we could git work.

Mother went to cooking for the white folks, but I

worked for Mr. Jeff Fisher. I held a job thirty-five years driving a laundry truck for L. R. Wyatt. The laundry wus on the corner of Jones an' Salisbury Street.

I married Cenoro Freeman. We lived together fifty-six years. She wus a good devoted wife. We wus married Dec. 9, 1878. She died in May 1934. Booker T. Washington wus a good man. I have seen him. Abraham Lincoln wus one of my best friends. He set me free. The Lawd is my best friend. I don't know much 'bout Jefferson Davis. Jim Young an' myself wus pals.

My object in joining the church wus to help myself an' others to live a decent life, a life for good to humanity an' for God.

N.C. District:	No. 2
Worker:	Mary A. Hicks
No. Words:	670
Subject:	EX-SLAVE STORY
Story Teller:	Elbert Hunter
Editor:	Daisy Bailey Waitt
Date Stamp:	"JUN 1 1937"

ELBERT HUNTER

I wuz borned eight miles from Raleigh on de plantation of Mr. Jacob Hunter in 1844. My parents were Stroud and Lucy an' my brothers wuz Tom, Jeems an' Henderson. I had three sisters who wuz named Caroline, Emiline an' Ann.

Massa Hunter wuz good to us, an' young Massa Knox wuz good too. My mammy wuz de cook an' my pappy wuz a field hand. Massa ain't 'lowed no patterollers on his place, but one time when he wuzn't ter home my mammy sent me an' Caroline ter de nex' door house fer something an' de patterollers got us. Dey carried us home an' 'bout de time dat dey wuz axin' questions young Massa Knox rid up.

He look dem over an' he sez, 'Git off dese premises dis minute, yo' dad-limb sorry rascals, if us needs yo' we'll call yo'. 'My pappy patterolls dis place hisself.'

Dey left den, an' we ain't been bothered wid 'em no more.

I toted water 'fore de war, minded de sheeps, cows and de geese; an' I ain't had many whuppin's neither. Dar wuz one thing dat massa ain't 'low an' dat wuz drinkin' 'mong his niggers.

Dar wuz a ole free issue named Denson who digged ditches fer massa an' he always brung long his demijohn wid his whiskey. One ebenin' Missus tells me an' Caroline ter go ter de low groun's an' git up de cows an' on de way we fin' ole man Denson's demijohn half full of whiskey. Caroline sez ter lets take er drink an' so we does, an' terreckly I gits wobbly in de knees.

Dis keeps on till I has ter lay down an' when I wakes up I am at home. Dey says dat Massa Jacob totes me, an' dat he fusses wid Denson fer leavin' de whiskey whar I can fin' it. He give me a talkin' to, an' I ain't neber drunk no more.

When we hyard dat de Yankees wuz comin' ole massa an' me takes de cattle an' hosses way down in de swamp an' we stays dar wid dem fer seberal days. One day I comes ter de house an' dar dey am, shootin' chickens an' pigs an' everthing. I'se seed dem cut de hams off'n a live pig or ox an' go off leavin' de animal groanin'. De massa had 'em kilt den, but it wuz awful.

Dat night dey went away but de nex' day a bigger drove come an' my mammy cooked fer 'em all day long. Dey killed an' stold ever'thing, an' at last ole massa went to Raleigh an' axed fer a gyard. Atter we got de gyard de fuss ceased. One of de officers what spent de night dar lost his pocket book an' in it wuz seven greenback dollars, de fust I eber seed.

We wuz glad ter be free even do' we had good white folks. De wuck hours wuz frum daybreak till dark, an' de wimmens had ter card an' spin so much eber night. We had our own chickens an' gyarden an' little ways of makin' money, but not so much fun.

We played cat, which wuz like base ball now, only different. De children played a heap but de grown folks wucked hard. De cruelest thing I eber seed wuz in Raleigh atter slavery time, an' dat wuz a nigger whuppin'.

De pillory wuz whar de co'rthouse am now an' de sheriff, Mr. Ray whupped dat nigger till he bled.

I neber seed a slave sale, an' I neber seed much whuppin's. I larned some long wid de white chilluns, 'specially how ter spell.

No mam, I doan know nothin' 'bout witches, but I seed a ghos'. Hit wuz near hyar, an' hit wuz a animal as big as a yearlin' wid de look of a dog. I can't tell you de color of it case I done left frum dar.

B. N.

www.ingramcontent.com/pod-product-compliance
Lightning Source LLC
Chambersburg PA
CBHW071646160426
43195CB00012B/1372